Parsing through Customs

Alan Dundes

Parsing through Customs

Essays by a Freudian Folklorist

The University of Wisconsin Press

Published 1987

The University of Wisconsin Press
114 North Murray Street
Madison, Wisconsin 53715

The University of Wisconsin Press, Ltd.
1 Gower Street
London WC1E 6HA, England

First printing

Printed in the United States of America

Library of Congress Cataloging-in-Publication Data
Dundes, Alan.
Parsing through customs.
Bibliography: pp. 197–210.
Includes index.
1. Psychoanalysis and folklore. I. Title.
GR42.D86 1987   398'.019   87-1675
ISBN 0-299-11260-8

Contents

Preface

There are no magic wands or vagina dentatas in real life. Folklorists, however, have persisted in treating folklore in solely literal and historical rather than symbolic and psychological terms. The emphasis has been on collection and classification, not on interpretation. Folklorists have sought to ask and answer the question "What?" but have essentially ignored the more difficult and challenging question "Why?" Description is surely a prerequisite for analysis, but it is no substitute for it.

The discipline of folkloristics, the scientific study of folklore, may be said to have begun at the end of the eighteenth century in Europe. J. G. Herder, the German philosopher and educator coined the term *Volkslied* (folksong) in 1773, and his idea that the folksongs of a people reflected the soul of that people was a direct inspiration to the brothers Grimm. The publication of the brothers' celebrated *Kinder und Hausmärchen* (vol. 1 in 1812 and vol. 2 in 1815), sparked an intellectual revolution throughout Europe, and the entire world for that matter; members of the academy left the sanctuary of the ivory tower to sit at the feet of the common man to record stories and songs in dialect.

The stunning success of the Grimm brothers' collection of folktales led scholars in other countries, also imbued with feelings of romanticism and nationalism, to prove that they too had a folklore patrimony worthy of preservation. So Jorgen Moe teamed up with Peter Christen Asbjornsen in the 1840s to jointly collect and publish a famous collection of Norwegian folktales. In much the same fashion, the great Russian folklorist Aleksandr Nikolaevich Afanasyev published *Narodnye russkie skazki* (Popular Russian Tales) from 1855 to 1864. Numerous collections of folktales from many countries published in the nineteenth century resulted from the initial impetus provided by the Grimm brothers.

These collectors recognized the fantastic content of the tales they collected, but they could make little headway in elucidating the content of folktales and other genres of folklore. In fact, some of the first theories proposed were almost as fantastic as the tales themselves, e.g., that primitive man was solely concerned with the rising and setting of the sun and that most myths reflected this concern. Folktales as secular, weakened versions of sacred myths, so the theory of solar mythology went, retained vestigial remains of articulations of these solar activities. A rival theory, lunar mythology, argued that it was the movements of the moon, not the sun, which preoccupied primitive man. (A Freudian could well suggest that these theories themselves with their obsession with the rising and setting of suns and moons are merely projections of phallic tumescence and detumescence displaced to "heavenly" *bodies.*) In retrospect, one might well regret that the field of psychology which might have facilitated the interpretation of folktale content, was not yet sufficiently developed when the tales were collected.

Psychoanalytic theory began with the writings of Sigmund Freud. He was much interested in folklore and encouraged many of his earliest disciples—Otto Rank, Karl Abraham, Carl Jung—to investigate myth and folktale, utilizing psychoanalytic techniques. So folkloristics, which emerged in the beginning of the nineteenth century—the word *folklore* was coined by an Englishman named William Thoms only in 1846—had to wait until the end of that century for psychoanalytic theory to be formulated before there was any real possibility of applying such theory to the materials of folklore.

Freud's *The Interpretation of Dreams* (1900), and his *Wit and Its Relation to the Unconscious* (1905) with its brilliant content analyses of traditional Jewish jokes, both pointed out the enormous potential of psychoanalytic theory as a tool for deciphering the symbolic content of myths, folktales, legends, and other forms of folklore such as custom and belief. But folklorists of the late nineteenth and early twentieth centuries paid no attention to Freud whatsoever. Freudian theory, if mentioned at all, was strictly an object of ridicule. Not even the stimulating monographs published by Freud's early followers (e.g., Otto Rank's *The Myth of the Birth of the Hero* [1909]; Karl Abraham's *Dreams and Myths* [1909]; the remarkable writings of Ernest Jones—especially his *Essays in Applied Psycho-Analysis,* vol. 2, *Essays in Folklore, Anthropology and Religion* [1951]—and Géza Róheim's *The Gates of the Dream* [1953]) seem to have had the slightest influence on the direction of folklore scholarship. If one examines any of the standard works available on the history or state of folkloristics, e.g., Giuseppe Cocchiara's *Storia del Folklore in Europa* (1952) (*The History of Folklore in Europe,* 1981), one finds no mention of Freud. He is not even listed in the index. *Trends in Nordic Tradition Research* (1983) reveals that Scandinavian folklorists who are among the leaders in folkloristics have made no attempt to utilize psychoanalytic concepts in their research.

As far as mainstream folkloristics is concerned, it is as though Freud never lived. While one can cite occasional exceptions, Brazilian folklorist Paulo de Carvalho-Neto's *Folklore y Psicoanalisis* (1956), (*Folklore and Psychoanalysis,* 1972), one looks in vain in the standard folklore periodicals, (for example, the *Journal of American Folklore,* published since 1888), for psychoanalytic studies of folklore. The same holds for the more than two hundred professional folklore periodicals published around the world. So while psychoanalysts have continued to be interested in folklore—see Bruno Bettelheim's *The Uses of Enchantment* (1976)—folklorists have continued to be *un*interested in psychoanalysis.

How can one account for this long-standing and consistent resistance on the part of folklorists to any serious consideration of psychoanalytic theory? One reason is the refusal to accept the fact that the greater part of folklore data is fantasy material. From my psychoanalytic perspective, it seems that some of my folklore colleagues will go to any lengths to deny the fantastic content of folklore and its close relationship to everyday psychological realities of child-parent and sibling antagonisms, to mention just two obvious examples from common fairy-tale projections. It is surely no accident that we find same-sex oppositions between hero/heroine and villain in fairy tales. Male heroes must oppose and conquer male giants, dragons, or serpents, while heroines must overcome wicked stepmothers or witches. And what of the widespread appearance of giants and giantesses in fairy tales? Where a die-hard historically oriented folklorist might postulate an earlier time when an actual tall or large people roamed the earth, a psychoanalytically oriented folklorist might realize that giants are nothing but infantile projections of parents. An infant does not necessarily see itself as small in comparison to adults, but in this infant's view adults, especially parents, are simply larger versions of the same kind of being that the infant is.

One of the most infuriating, exasperating, and unfortunately all too common reactions of colleagues and students to my Freudian analyses of folklore consists of the comment that these analyses are "reductionistic." But reductionism per se is neither good nor evil. No one criticizes Einstein for being reductionistic in having formulated the $e = mc^2$ equation. Most natural science can be "accused" of being reductionistic. The issue ought to be: is the formula proposed accurate or illuminating? Does it yield insight where perhaps understanding was absent before the formula was articulated? Dismissing Freudian analysis a priori on the alleged grounds of reductionism is simply a modern-dress form of name calling, which is no substitute for honest debate and criticism. Many folklorists who are wont to call Freudian analyses of folklore reductionistic themselves translate the content of folktales into abstract tale-type or motif numbers, or to structural slots or binary oppositions such as "nature versus culture," the epitome of reductionistic thinking.

In the present volume, I have brought together seven of my essays which are all concerned with the application of psychoanalytic theory to folklore, my major intellectual goal as a folklorist. The essays included appeared originally in a variety of journals, as noted in the acknowlegments. One disadvantage of publishing essays in diverse periodicals is that not even those few readers who are favorably disposed to psychoanalytic readings of folklore can easily locate all of the essays. Bringing these essays together under one cover will at the very least make it possible for those interested to read these psychoanalytic studies of folklore.

The initial essay is in part a historical survey of the field of inquiry. The second essay offers a new interpretation of the potlatch ritual of the Northwest Coast American Indians. For nearly one hundred years, instructors in introductory anthropology classes have sought to explain why the physical destruction of property and wealth should be the primary means of achieving social status, a puzzle that conventional economic theory has been thus far unable to unravel. If, and I use the conditional advisedly, I am right in my analysis of potlatch with respect to its symbolic import, then for nearly one century the standard anthropological explanations of this ritual have been inadequate, or, to put it bluntly, wrong.

The third and fourth essays, written with the help of coauthors, use psychoanalytic theory to explicate the dynamics and nuances of verbal dueling traditions among Turkish and Spanish-American young men. These traditions are very much alive in contemporary Turkey, Spain, and Latin America, and I believe the analyses of the respective traditions sheds light on Turkish and Hispanic folk conceptualizations of masculinity.

The fifth essay is also concerned with male-female relationships, in this case, with couvade, a widespread custom in which men go through the motions of simulating female parturition. Some elements from the Book of Genesis, specifically the tradition of the Sabbath as the day of rest and the creation of Eve from Adam's rib, are reexamined as instances of couvade behavior.

The final two essays address one of the most critical problems in the psychoanalytic study of folklore, namely, the question of the validation of so-called Freudian symbolism. Is Freudian theory simply a matter of faith or are there empirical, nonsubjective, replicable methods by which the symbolic content of folklore can be scientifically ascertained? The final essay not only seeks to address this issue but also returns to an extension of the theme of verbal dueling considered earlier in the volume.

In commenting upon the seven essays as a whole, I would like to think that they succeed in exploring two facets of the interrelationship of psychoanalytic theory and folklore. The first and most obvious is drawing upon psychoanalytic theory to explain a hitherto enigmatic piece of data. This was my aim in the essay on potlatch. The second is to try to show how folklore can be used to illuminate issues and concepts in psychoanalytic theory, topics such as symbolism and projection, for example. I believe Freud himself was well aware of how important folklore was with respect to documenting the validity of portions of psychoanalytic theory. It is unfortunate that later generations of analysts have failed to appreciate the richness of folklore with respect to its critical bearing on the endless debate over the validity of psychoanalytic reasoning.

It has become increasingly fashionable to "revise" Freudian theory to the point where, frankly, it becomes difficult to recognize or salvage much of the original Freud. Advocates of ego psychology, for instance, may argue that this is the way of the future, but they err in failing to realize that folklore represents primary-process material. The content of folklore, I would maintain, is largely unconscious. Hence it represents id, not ego, for the most part. From this perspective, ego psychology cannot possibly illuminate much of the content of folklore.

Although psychoanalysts have at least continued to be interested in folklore, they tend to be somewhat narrowly focused. When a psychoanalyst thinks about folklore, it is typically a question of a classical tale (usually Oedipus), a story from the Bible (the Old Testament), or a Grimm tale. The world is full of folklore, even though it is largely ignored by Western-oriented psychoanalysts. I would hope that these essays might encourage ethnocentric psychoanalysts to look beyond the conventional Grimm tales (which are literary, rewritten, and bowdlerized derivatives from authentic tales) and the Bible to other genres of folklore and to non-Western data.

Most psychoanalysts are not scholars, and it may be unfair to ask them to learn more about folkloristics. It is perhaps more reasonable to ask folklorists to learn more about psychoanalytic theory. The history of folkloristics thus far would not tend to make one optimistic about this possibility. Folklorists, like other scholars, are uncomfortable with the idea that life is not always governed by reason and that there may be unconscious forces at work controlling their thought and behavior. If the study of folk-lore is truly the study of human fantasy, then there may well be compelling reasons why folklorists do not want to know what folklore *means,* or why they are so fascinated by a particular magic motif, or why they have chosen to devote their lives to the dreamlike world of ballad and folktale. Yet some open-minded students who read these essays may see some of the exciting po-tential of combining psychoanalytic theory and folklore data.

One of the goals of social science is, or ought to be, to make the unconscious conscious. If one accepts the premise that much of the content of folklore is unconscious, then it should be per-fectly obvious that psychoanalytic theory is a legitimate and nec-essary tool for the study of folklore.

Acknowledgments

"The Psychoanalytic Study of Folklore" appeared in *Annals of Scholarship* 3, no. 3 (1985): 1–42, and is reprinted by permission of the editor of that journal. An earlier version of this paper was originally presented at a special meeting of the Southern California Psychoanalytic Society on 24 September 1983, honoring Dr. Samuel Eisenstein.

"Heads or Tails: A Psychoanalytic Study of Potlatch" first appeared in the *Journal of Psychological Anthropology* 2 (1979): 395–424, and is reprinted with the permission of the Association for Psychohistory, Inc.

"The Strategy of Turkish Boys' Verbal Dueling Rhymes" first appeared in the *Journal of American Folklore* 83 (1970): 325–349, and is reprinted by permission of the American Folklore Society.

"The *Piropo* and the Dual Image of Women in the Spanish-Speaking World" originally appeared in the *Journal of Latin American Lore,* 10:1 (1984), 111–133, and is reprinted with the permission of The Regents of the University of California for the Latin American Center, University of California, Los Angeles.

"Couvade in Genesis" first appeared in Issachar Ben-Ami and Joseph Dan, eds., *Studies in Aggadah and Jewish Folklore,* Folklore Research Center Studies (Jerusalem: The Magnes Press, 1983), pp. 35–53 and is reprinted by permission of the Folklore Research Center at the Hebrew University of Jerusalem.

"The Symbolic Equivalence of Allomotifs in the Rabbit-Herd

(AT 570)," appeared originally in *Arv: Scandinavian Yearbook of Folklore,* vol. 36 (1980)[1982], 91–98, and is reprinted by permission of the editor of *Arv.*

"The American Game of 'Smear the Queer' and the Homosexual Component of Male Competitive Sport and Warfare," appeared first in the *Journal of Psychoanalytic Anthropology* 8 (1985): 115–129.

I wish to thank the above-mentioned publishers and societies for their kindness in allowing me to reprint the essays in this volume.

Parsing through Customs

1 The Psychoanalytic Study of Folklore

The principal raison d'être for psychoanalysis is medical in nature. Through usually extended periods of therapy, the mental health of neurotic and sometimes psychotic individuals can be improved. Psychoanalysis has produced a subset of the category of psychiatrists. Some psychiatrists are psychoanalytic in orientation, but many are not. If one can believe a standard piece of folklore, psychiatry, including psychoanalytic psychiatry, has provided a good living for a number of its practitioners. "Neurotics build castles in the air; psychotics live in them; and psychiatrists collect the rent."

Aside from the undoubted therapeutic contributions of psychoanalytic theory which even critics admit are considerable, it is also true that psychoanalytic theory has been applied to the subject matter studied by various academic disciplines. For example, one can find psychoanalytically informed investigations of anthropology, art, history, literature, philosophy, religion, etc. One need only consult the multivolume bibliographic *Index of Psychoanalytic Writings* (1950–) to gain some idea of the enormity of the scholarship in these areas. Essays in psychoanalytic literary criticism or in psychohistory, to mention but two fields, number in the hundreds. My concern in the present essay is to consider the applications of psychoanalytic theory in the field of folklore. I shall also suggest that psychoanalytic theory may be usefully employed to illuminate popular culture as well as folklore.

3

The word *folklore* was coined in 1846 but the field is much older than that. Herder, who believed that the soul of a people was expressed in that people's folksongs, had proposed the term *Volkslied* (folksong) as early as 1773, and the Grimm brothers, much influenced by Herder's ideology, published their famous *Kinder und Hausmärchen* in 1812 and 1815. It was in the nineteenth century that currents of nationalism and romanticism combined, mostly in Europe, to encourage selected individuals to collect the oral traditions (folktales, legends, folksongs, proverbs, riddles, charms, children's games, etc.) from peasant informants. It was believed that these traditions were survivals from earlier ages and that they were dying out. Hence there was some urgency to record and preserve the old customs, beliefs, ballads, and the like before they disappeared forever.

As more and more folklorists in different countries began to collect the oral traditions of their regions, a form of the comparative method began to be practiced. It soon became obvious that the "same" folktale or legend existed among different, even apparently unrelated peoples. The Grimms were comparative in outlook and imbued as they were with Herder's notion of folklore expressing the folk-soul of a people, they had initially hoped to show how their collected materials reflected something quintessentially Teutonic. However, their comparative inquiries demonstrated that their Hessian (German) texts had cognates among French, Italian, Scandinavian, and Near Eastern peoples. Jacob Grimm, for example, was amazed to discover that one of the folktales collected was the story of the cyclops which was nearly identical to the Polyphemus episode contained in Homer's *Odyssey*. In his essay on the subject, he concluded that Homer must have heard an oral tale of his own era and simply incorporated it in his celebrated epic.

The two traits of folklore which most troubled folklorists were (1) the multiple existence of folklore, and (2) its apparent irrationality. How could the same item of folklore exist in diverse cultures? There were two basic theoretical positions. One theory assumed monogenesis (one birth), that is, that the item of folklore must have originated in one particular place. After monogenesis, diffusion occurred, which explained how the item moved from its presumed point of origin to the other areas. The competing theory was polygenesis (many births), which was typically based on the assumption of some form of psychic unity. For example, according to unilinear (one line) evolutionary theory in nineteenth-century anthropology, it was believed that *all* peoples progressed in an unvarying three-stage sequence: savagery, barbarism, and civilization. Since the folk was defined as the illiterate in a literate society, that is peasants or barbarians living in or near civilized peoples (like those intellectuals in England, France, etc., constructing these deplorable ethnocentric and racist schemes), it was assumed that savages moving towards civilization passed through a folk stage. Whole genres of folklore were believed to have evolved along similar lines. Supposedly, myths found among savages or primitives degenerated into folktales among the peasant or folk. According to this devolutionary premise, as the peasant became civilized, as the illiterate became literate, as the rural became urban, he lost what little folklore he had retained. This is why it was a matter of some urgency to collect these remaining vestigial fragments from peasants in order to have some record, albeit partial, from prehistoric savage times.

The methodology employed in nineteenth-century folkloristics was like the methodology of so many academic disciplines of that time. It was primarily concerned with the historical reconstruction of the past. In order to understand a piece of folklore, deemed to be a relic or mental fossil from an era in the far distant past, it was necessary to reconstruct the presumed original, complete form of that item of folklore. Fortunately, since there were still savage peoples roaming the earth (e.g., Australian aborigines, North and South American Indians, black Africans, etc.), one could still collect these "original" full forms from which it was assumed that all peasant cultures had derived. Remember that with unilinear evolutionary theory, all peoples were thought to have passed through the same, identical stages. In this light, present-day savages were perceived as being equivalent to the ancestors of the civilized English, French, and other Europeans. Even some old-fashioned twentieth-century folklorists are mostly interested in attempting to reconstruct the presumed original fuller version of an item of folklore, though to be sure most have abandoned the overly rigid unilinear evolutionary schema.

The evolutionary framework in late nineteenth-century folkloristics explained both the multiple existence of folklore and its apparent irrationality. If all peoples passed through exactly the same stages, then it was perfectly clear why different peoples—even if not historically related or in contact with one another—would come up with the same myths, tales, customs, and the like. Moreover, what appeared on the surface to be irrational elements in myths or customs could be explained by examining the fuller forms of those myths or customs still to be found among savage peoples where such elements were rational enough (according to the logic and reasoning of such peoples).

It in this context that one can understand the view of Adolf Bastian, a German ethnologist, who believed in independent invention rather than diffusion as an explanation for apparently parallel phenomena among different peoples. He argued that the psychic unity of mankind everywhere produced similar *Elementargedanken* (elementary ideas). Also relevant are the ideas of French philosopher Lucien Lévy-Bruhl, whose books *Les fonctions mentales dans les sociétés inférieures* (Paris, 1910)—note the title!—and *La mentalité primitive* (Paris, 1922) essentially tried to define the so-called primitive mind which he claimed was incapable of the rationality of civilized peoples. Lévy-Bruhl is famous, or, rather, infamous, for introducing the term "pre-logical" mentality for primitive peoples, a term which he sought to repudiate in his posthumously published notebooks (1975: 49), claiming instead that "The logical structure of the mind is the same in all known human societies."

Such notions of monolithic unilinear evolutionary theory and primitive mentality which was irrational rather than rational are no longer held by professional anthropologists and folklorists, but they are important because they constituted part of the zeitgeist in which psychoanalytic theory developed. It should already be clear that some of the underlying assumptions and basic premises of psychoanalytic theory share a good deal with the above-mentioned folkloristic theories. Neurotic symptoms found among adult individuals were understood to be a kind of survival from the past, in this case, infancy rather than savagery. The methodology employed to explain the apparent irrationality of these neurotic survivals was basically a form of historical reconstruction of the past. Just as a knowledge of the original, fuller form of a custom as practiced among savages could theoretically explain the logic of a quaint folk belief found among peasants, so a knowledge of the original, fuller form of an event which occurred in infancy could explain the logic of an idiosyncratic belief or practice carried on compulsively by an adult patient.

The parallels between folkloristic and psychoanalytic theory and method were noted by early psychoanalysts. One must keep in mind also the nineteenth-century equation of child = savage. Just as savagery evolved into civilization so children evolved into adults. Sigmund Freud, in accepting Austrian folklorist Friedrich S. Krauss's invitation to write a preface to the German translation of John G. Bourke's pioneering study *Scatalogic Rites of All Nations,* observed in 1913, "Folklore has adopted a quite different method of research, and yet it has reached the same results as psychoanalysis. It shows us how incompletely the repression of coprophilic inclinations has been carried out among various peoples at various times and how closely at other cultural levels the treatment of excretory substances approximates to that practised by children" (1913a: 337). (All works by Freud cited in this chapter are from the *Complete Psychological Works: Standard Edition*.) Freud was presumably referring to Bourke's suggestion —Bourke's work was first published in 1891—that whereas savage peoples openly practiced excrementitious rites, e.g., the eating of pure excrement, civilized peoples retained only burlesque survivals of such practices, e.g., playing with the *boudin* or blood pudding in European feast-of-fools celebrations. This corresponded in Freud's mind with the way in which infantile play with excrement survives in some adults in the form of telling "dirty" jokes. (See *Jokes and Their Relation to the Unconscious* [1905]: 97–98.)

One must not blame Freud for accepting the anthropological theory of his own day as dogma. But at the same time, one should be aware of that theory's serious deficiencies. That Freud did accept unilinear evolutionary theory and that he did consider folklore as survivals from days of primitive savagery is made abundantly clear by his opening remarks in *Totem and Taboo*:

> Prehistoric man, in the various stages of his development, is known to us through the inanimate monuments and implements which he has left behind, through the information about his art, religion and his attitude towards life which has come to us either directly or by way of tradition handed down in legends, myths and fairy tales, and through the relics of his mode of thought which survive in our own manners and customs. But apart from this, in a certain sense, he is still our contemporary. There are men still living who, as we believe, stand very near to primitive man, far nearer than we do, and whom we therefore regard as his direct heirs and representatives. Such is our view of those whom we describe as savages or half-savages; and their mental life must have a peculiar interest for us if we are right in seeing in it a well-preserved picture of an early stage of our own development.

> If that supposition is correct, a comparison between the psychology of primitive peoples, as it is taught by social anthropology, and the psychology of neurotics, as it has been revealed by psycho-analysis, will be bound to show numerous points of agreement and will throw new light upon familiar facts in both sciences. (1913d:1)

Karl Abraham in his *Dreams and Myths: A Study in Race Psychology*, first published in 1909, also remarked on the parallelism. "The race, in prehistoric times, makes its wishes into structures of phantasy, which as myths reach over into the historical ages. In the same way the individual in his 'prehistoric' period makes structures of phantasy out of his wishes which persist as dreams in the 'historical' period. So is the myth a retained fragment from the infantile psychic life of the race and the dream is the myth of the individual" (1913: 72). Freud had encapsulated this view in his 1908 paper "Creative Writers and Day-Dreaming" when he said, "...but it is extremely probable that myths, for instance, are distorted vestiges of the wishful phantasies of whole nations, the *secular dreams* of youthful humanity" (1908: 152).

But it was not just parallelism per se which excited early psychoanalysts. Rather it was an extension of the Haeckelian formula of ontogeny's recapitulation of phylogeny which made folklore so intriguing. Ernest Jones makes this clear in his articulation of the parallels between folklore and psychoanalytic theory in a paper entitled "Psycho-Analysis and Folklore" which was delivered at the English Folk-Lore Society's Jubilee Congress in 1928. Jones states that "there is a far-reaching parallelism between the survivals of primitive life from the racial past and survivals from the individual past. The practical value of this generalization is that the study of survivals in folklore can be usefully supplemented by the study of survivals in living individuals, where they are far more accessible to direct investigation... we have before us in the individual the whole evolution of beliefs, and customs or rituals based on them, which is parallel to what in the field of folklore has run a course of perhaps thousands of years" (1930: 224–226). Silberer in his 1910 essay "Phantasie und Mythos," which was essentially a review commentary on the early works of Abraham, Ricklin, and Rank, specifically drew attention to the would-be application of the law of Ernst Haeckel to mythology (1910: 563). The Haeckelian formula was sometimes explicitly invoked. For example, in a paper entitled "The Psychology of Mythology" by Clarence O. Cheney, M.D., Superintendent of the Hudson River State Hospital in Poughkeepsie, New York, which was published in the first volume of the *Psychiatric Quarterly* in 1927, we find the following contention:

> Our attitude is that the myth or mythology in general is the product of the longings, cravings and wishes of mankind existing under varying conditions, and that they are analogous to the longings, cravings or wishes of children, to the dreams of adults, and to the delusional ideas of persons with mental disorder.

> Ontogeny repeats phylogeny, the anatomical or physical development of the individual goes through stages similar to those passed through by man in his racial development.

> The mental development of the individual repeats the stages of the mental development of the race. The myths were the manifestations essentially of a primitive mind. The dreams and imaginings of children are similar productions... (Cheney 1927: 199)

Although the validity of the Haeckelian principle of recapitulation continues to be debated in biology (cf. Gould: 1977), its influence upon the early psychoanalytic study of folklore cannot be denied. A form of the Haeckelian principle was espoused by both Jung and Freud, to the detriment of both analytical psychology and psychoanalysis in my view.

Jung's position is perhaps better known. Carl Jung believed in the existence of a 'collective unconscious' which he claimed was common to all mankind, an intellectual position strikingly similar to the psychic unity claims made by various nineteenth-century theorists. From this instinctive and precultural stratum, according to Jung, come 'archetypes' which appear in dreams and in myth, among other manifestations. In his essay "The Psychology of the Child Archetype," Jung spells out his position, and it is relevant here because myth is one major genre of folklore. Jung differentiates between what he terms "fantasies (including dreams) of a personal character, which go back unquestionably to personal experiences, things forgotten or repressed" on the one hand and

> fantasies (including dreams) of an impersonal character, which cannot be reduced to experiences in the individual's past, and thus cannot be explained as something individually acquired. These fantasy-images undoubtedly have their closest analogues in mythological types. We must therefore assume that they correspond to certain *collective* (and not personal) structural elements of the human psyche in general, and, like the morphological elements of the human body, are *inherited*. Although tradition and transmission by migration certainly play a part, there are, as we have said, very many cases that cannot be accounted for in this

way and drive us to the hypothesis of 'autochthonous re-vival.' (Jung 1963: 74)

Products of this second category, says Jung, "resemble the types of structures to be met with in myth and fairytale so much that we must regard them as related." Archetypes in myths, for Jung, "hark back to a prehistoric world whose spiritual preconceptions and general conditions we can still observe today among existing primitives...Primitive mentality differs from the civilized chiefly in that the conscious mind is far less developed in scope and intensity. Functions such as thinking, willing, etc. are not yet differentiated...and in the case of thinking, for instance, this shows itself in the circumstance that the primitive does not think *consciously*, but that thoughts *appear*. The primitive cannot assert that he thinks; it is rather that 'Something thinks in him.'" (Jung 1963: 72).

Jung has this to say about primitive mentality and myths: "The primitive mentality does not *invent* myths, it *experiences* them. Myths are original revelations of the preconscious psyche, involuntary statements about unconscious psychic happenings, and anything but allegories of physical processes"—this latter remark being a snide criticism of psychoanalysis (Jung 1963: 73). Jung's theories of myth are a perfect exemplification of ethnocentric, racist nineteenth-century evolutionary theory. His mystical and antirational approach is very different from the psychoanalytic approach to myth. Says Jung, "*Contents of an archetypal character are manifestations of processes in the collective unconscious*. Hence they do not refer to anything that is, or has been conscious, but to something *essentially unconscious*. In the last analysis, therefore, *it is impossible to say what they refer to*." (Italics added.) So archetypes are basically unknowable, according to Jung. Jung's approach to myth and folktale is remarkably similar to the anthroposophical theory championed by Rudolf Steiner. Steiner's 1908 lecture "The Interpretation of Fairy Tales," and the numerous books on fairy tales inspired by it also speak of mystical archetypes which early man, untainted by civilization, could still experience and understand directly, such archetypes being strongly tinged with Christian overtones. But

Jung's views are, of course, analytical psychology, not psychoanalysis. Yet one can find traces of a similar notion of a collective or unified racial unconscious in early Freud as well. In terms of the Haeckelian model, the dreams of an individual supposedly recapitulate events from the phylogenetic past.

Let us consider briefly a portion of Freud's twenty-third lecture of his *Introductory Lectures on Psycho-Analysis*. He is trying to explain the multiple existence of certain fantasies, e.g., seduction by an adult, observation of parental intercourse (the primal scene), the threat of castration. In Freud's own words,

> Whence comes the need for these phantasies and the material for them? There can be no doubt that their sources lie in the instincts; but it has still to be explained why the same phantasies with the same content are created on every occasion. I am prepared with an answer which I know will seem daring to you. I believe that these *primal phantasies*, as I should like to call them, and no doubt a few others as well, are a phylogenetic endowment. In them the individual reaches beyond his own experience into primaeval experience at points where his own experience has been too rudimentary. It seems to me quite possible that all the things that are told to us to-day in analysis as phantasy—the seduction of children, the inflaming of sexual excitement by observing parental intercourse, the threat of castration (or rather castration itself)—were once real occurrences in the primaeval times of the human family, and that children in their phantasies are simply filling in the gaps in individual truth with prehistoric truth. (1916: 370-371)

This is an unequivocal statement. If an individual lacks a symbol or fantasy in his or her own life, that symbol or fantasy will be provided through the ontogenetic recapitulation of phylogeny.

Freud argued along similar lines at the conclusion of his controversial study of incest, *Totem and Taboo*. As is well known, Freud claimed that the origin of the incest taboo and the Oedipus complex was a prehistoric event in which the sons in a kind of primal horde banded together to kill their father. In sum, he attempted to make psychology into history. At the end of *Totem and Taboo*, Freud reveals that he is well aware of the theoretical problem involved. He knows that neurotics feel guilt, not for actual deeds committed, but merely for impulses and feelings. In other words, it is enough for a son to think of killing his father to cause guilt. If it is "always *psychical* realities and never *factual* ones" which "lie behind the sense of guilt of neurotics," then perhaps, Freud muses, the primal horde brothers did not actually kill their father. "Accordingly the mere hostile *impulse* against the father, the mere existence of a wishful *phantasy* of killing and devouring him, would have been enough to produce the moral reaction that created totemism and taboo" (1913d: 159–160). Freud continues, "In this way we should avoid the necessity for deriving the origin of our cultural legacy, of which we justly feel so proud, from a hideous crime, revolting to all our feelings." But in the very last words of the book, Freud decides that there is an important difference between primitives and neurotics. Whereas the neurotic is inhibited in his actions, primitive man is not. So "that is why, without laying claim to any finality of judgment, I think that in the case before us it may safely be assumed that 'in the beginning was the Deed'" (1913d: 161). Freud in this way attempts—in my opinion unwisely—to translate psychology into history, and a phylogenetic event is presumed to be the originating impulse for the incest wishes felt by present-day individuals.

Freud's Haeckelian bias has been pointed out by a number of scholars (Ritvo 1965; Heyman 1977; Gould 1977; Sulloway 1983; Wallace 1983), and there are numerous passages in Freud's writings reflecting this theoretical stance. It is a shock, for example, to compare Jung's distinction between personal and impersonal or collective fantasy-images with the following statement from Freud's *Introductory Lectures* on dream-work:

> The prehistory into which the dream-work leads us back is of two kinds—on the one hand, into the individual's prehistory, his childhood, and on the other, in so far as each individual recapitulates in an abbreviated form the entire development of the human race, into phylogenetic prehis-

tory too. Shall we succeed in distinguishing which portion
of the latent mental processes is derived from the individual prehistoric period and which portion from the phylogenetic one? It is not, I believe impossible that we shall. It
seems to me, for instance, that symbolic connections,
which the individual has never acquired by learning, may
justly claim to be regarded as a phylogenetic heritage.
(1916: 199)

Fortunately, one can discard the Haeckelian framework from
Freudian theory and still retain most of the valuable concepts
and insights made possible by the application of psychoanalytic
theory to folkloristic data. Freudian notions of repression, regression, condensation, displacement, projection, symbolism,
etc., may still be valid even if ontogeny does not recapitulate phylogeny in terms of cultural features. I may add parenthetically
that I find the supposed phylogenetic origin of symbols equally
implausible chez Freud as chez Jung.

In considering the relationship or interrelationship between
folklore and psychoanalysis, one might legitimately ask whether
it is psychoanalytic theory which illuminates the content of folklore or rather folklore which illuminates psychoanalytic theory.
Does a psychoanalyst use one of his patient's free associations to
explain the latent content of a Grimm tale? Or does he use folkloristic data to explain the behavior of a difficult patient? The
answer is pretty clearly that the relationship between folklore
and psychoanalysis is mutually beneficial. It is unquestionably a
reciprocal relationship.

Freud himself in his various writings on folklore demonstrates
the two-way interplay of psychoanalysis and folklore. In his 1913
paper "The Occurrence in Dreams of Material from Fairy Tales"
(1913b: 279–287), Freud recognized that fairy tales have a great
influence "in the mental life of our children" and that they are
responsible for some of the content of patients' dreams. He demonstrates this by analyzing a case history of a young woman
whose dream contained elements of the tale of Rumpelstiltskin,
which is tale-type 500 in the standard international Aarne-
Thompson folktale typological system. Although Freud's pri-

mary objective is a therapeutic one in terms of helping his patient, he ends his discussion of this case with these words, "If we
carefully observe from clear instances the way in which dreamers
use fairy tales and the point at which they bring them in, we may
perhaps also succeed in picking up hints which will help in interpreting remaining obscurities in the fairy tales themselves"
(1913b: 283). In the second of his two case histories, he interprets
both "Little Red Riding Hood" (AT tale-type 333) and "The
Wolf and the Seven Little Goats" (AT tale-type 123), which modern folklorists might well argue are cognate tale-types, in order to
explain a male patient's dream. There is no doubt that Freud was
intrigued equally by the challenge of helping a patient *and* by ex-
plicating the latent content of fairy tales. In another essay written in 1913, "The Theme of the Three Caskets" (1913c: 289–301),
Freud makes no mention of specific patients, but rather he is
solely concerned with analyzing the content of the folkloristic
motif which Shakespeare borrowed for a scene in *The Merchant
of Venice* (cf. Motif H511.1, Three Caskets, in Stith Thompson's
Motif-Index of Folk-Literature, as well as Aarne-Thompson tale-
type 890, A Pound of Flesh.)

It is not difficult to find other instances in Freud's writings of
his drawing upon folklore to support a particular theoretical
point in psychoanalytic theory as well as drawing upon psychoanalytic theory to explain a particular item of folklore. In the
remarkable tenth lecture of his *Introductory Lectures on Psycho-
Analysis*, a lecture entitled "Symbolism in Dreams," Freud's debt
to folklore is made explicit. After surveying a host of "Freudian"
interpretations of symbols, Freud asks the question how do we
"in fact come to know the meaning of these dream-symbols,
upon which the dreamer himself gives us insufficient informa-
tion or none at all?" His response is an important commentary
on the critical utility of folklore. "My reply is that we learn it
from very different sources—from fairy tales and myths, from
buffoonery and jokes, from folklore (that is, from knowledge
about popular manners and customs, sayings and songs) and
from poetic and colloquial linguistic usage. In all these directions
we come upon the same symbolism, and in some of them we can
understand it without further instruction. If we go into these

sources in detail, we shall find so many parallels to dream-symbolism that we cannot fail to be convinced of our interpretations" (1916: 158–159). Someone not familiar with the discipline of folklore might not immediately realize that the "very different sources" mentioned by Freud *all* belong to folklore. Fairy tales, myths, jokes, manners, customs, sayings, colloquial language are all forms of folklore. In the same lecture, Freud even went so far as to suggest that a far better collection of symbolic interpretations might be made "not by amateurs like us, but by real professionals in mythology, anthropology, philology and folklore" (1916: 165). It is sad to report that most of such experts have utterly rejected Freudian theory and have failed to make use of the vast array of available data with respect to elucidating the nature of symbols.

It is of interest that Freud modestly referred to himself as an amateur or dilettante in folklore. It was true, but at the same time one can honestly say that Freud ultimately made more of a contribution to the study of folklore than most of the so-called experts in the field to whom he deferred. Freud's recognition that he and his early followers were only amateurs in the field of folklore was made explicit in a letter of 28 October, 1909, which he wrote to Professor D. E. Oppenheim, a specialist in classical mythology. In that letter Freud said

> I have long been haunted by the idea that our studies on the content of the neuroses might be destined to solve the riddle of the formation of myths, and that the nucleus of mythology is nothing other than what we speak of as "the nuclear complex of the neuroses"... Two of my pupils, Abraham in Berlin and Otto Rank in Vienna, have ventured upon an attempt to invade the territory of mythology and to make conquests in it with the help of the technique of psychoanalysis and its angle of approach. But we are amateurs, and have every reason to be afraid of mistakes. We are lacking in academic training and familiarity with the material. Thus we are looking about for an enquirer whose development has been in the reverse direction, who possesses the specialized knowledge and is ready to apply

to it the psychoanalytic armory that we will gladly put at his command..." (Freud and Oppenheim 1958: 13-14).

Freud asked Oppenheim, "Can it be that you are willing to be this man we are longing for? What do you know of psychoanalysis?" Freud's letter was in response to Oppenheim's having sent him an offprint of an article on folklore which contained references to psychoanalytic theory. Oppenheim accepted Freud's invitation and the two collaborated on a joint paper around 1911. The paper, unfortunately, never appeared, presumably because Oppenheim soon afterwards resigned from the Vienna Psychoanalytic Society to join the ranks of Adler. Oppenheim had selected folktales, mostly from two folklore journals *Anthropophyteia* (1904-1913) and *Kryptadia* (1883-1911) which served as outlets for the publication of "obscene" folklore. The raw data was sent to Freud for his comments. Freud then presumably returned the manuscript to Oppenheim, but because of Oppenheim's subsequent disenchantment, the jointly written essay was not formally presented. Oppenheim died in a concentration camp in World War II, but his wife survived and took the manuscript to Australia, to which she emigrated. In 1956, Oppenheim's daughter brought the manuscript to the attention of a New York bookseller. It was acquired for the Sigmund Freud Archives and published for the first time in 1958 under the title *Dreams in Folklore*.

In the Freud and Oppenheim essay, one finds a significant confirmation of the importance of folklore for psychoanalysis as well as the importance of psychoanalysis for folklore. In the tales chosen by Oppenheim there were dream episodes. The symbols in these dreams told in the tales were interpreted either explicitly by the tales' dramatis personae or by the denouement of the plots. The theoretical point of interest is that the dream symbolism in the tales corresponded exactly to so-called Freudian interpretation of dream symbols outside of folktales. Specifically, feces as treasure or money, and a finger-ring as vagina occurred in a number of folktales. Clearly, the symbolic equivalents in folktales were entirely independent of any a priori theory, Freudian or otherwise. The original creators and later transmitters of the folktales, whoever they might have been, lived long before Freud was even born. As Freud himself puts it in a letter of 26 June 1910 to Friedrich Krauss, founding editor of *Anthropophyteia*, speaking of the materials appearing in that journal, "Its value may even be increased, perhaps, by the circumstance (not in itself an advantage) that the collectors know nothing of the theoretical findings of psycho-analysis and have brought together the material without any guiding principles" (1910: 234). Admittedly, the congruence of folkloristic articulations of symbolic meaning and the Freudian approach to symbolism does not necessarily "prove" the validity of the symbolic exegesis. In theory, both the folk and Freudians could be in error. Still, the correspondence is something which must be dealt with by critics of psychoanalysis who often argue that symbolic readings constitute little more than doctrinaire, ex cathedra pronouncements simply asserted rather than seriously documented. It is clear that Freud was delighted with the results of this essay, as it did offer unequivocal evidence in support of his understanding of symbolic materials.

From Freud's own investigations of folklore, we can see that the interrelationships between folklore and psychoanalysis are truly twofold. On the one hand, the materials of folklore offered substantive data corroborating insights obtained from the practice of psychoanalysis, and on the other hand, the application of psychoanalytic theory to folklore made possible new and increased understandings of myths, fairytales, customs, and the like. Jokes, for example, are a form of folklore, and if we recall Freud's brilliant analysis of jokes in *Jokes and Their Relation to the Unconscious* (1905), we can see just how helpful psychoanalytic concepts can be in content analysis. (For an interesting analysis of Freud through the jokes he selected for discussion, see Oring 1984.)

In view of Freud's genuine fascination with folklore, it is easy to understand why so many of Freud's first disciples were encouraged to explore elements of folklore. It should also be remarked that even before Freud there was psychiatry, and in the earlier psychiatric literature there were hints that folklore was relevant to the study of mental illness. In 1889, Ludwig Laistner suggested in his *Das Rätsel der Sphinx* that mythology originated from dreams, especially nightmares. Even more interesting was the work of Eugenio Tanzi. Tanzi, evidently one of the pioneers in the development of psychiatry in Italy, seems not well known except to Latin American scholars (Ramos 1958: 144; Carvalho-Neto 1972: 22; Sequin 1972: 79). Among Tanzi's publications are "Il folk-lore nella patologia mentale" (1890) and "The Germs of Delerium" (1891). In the latter essay, for example, Tanzi claims that " all the germs of paranoia, without exception, pre-existed in primitive man" (p. 80). In discerning would-be parallels between modern forms of mental illness and the myths and superstitions of so-called primitive man, Tanzi anticipated much of the theoretical thrust of the early Freudians. Karl Abraham, for example, wrote *Traum und Mythus* in 1909. He argued that myth reflected the childhood mental state or dream of primitive peoples while the dream is the individual's myth. In his words (1913:36) "The myth springs from a period, in the life of a people, long gone by, which we may designate as the childhood of the race...The myth is a fragment of the repressed life of the infantile psyche of the race. It contains (in disguised form) the wishes of the childhood of the race." Abraham was particularly concerned with analyzing the Prometheus myth. Also in 1909, Otto Rank published his ground-breaking *Der Mythus von der Geburt des Helden* in which he interpreted the standard Indo-European and Semitic hero pattern (i.e., the virgin mother, the father's attempt to kill his newborn son, etc.) in convincing Oedipal terms. Rank had presented his findings initially at a meeting of the Vienna Psychoanalytic Society on 25 November 1908, and although it was Rank himself who evidently wrote the minutes for that meeting, the report indicates that Rank's provocative study stimulated a lively discussion, especially on the part of Freud (cf. Nunberg and Federn 1967: 65–72). In other essays, Rank saw parallels between creation myths and the modern dreams of individuals. Some of these essays were gathered together in Rank's *Psychoanalytische Beiträge zur Mythenforschung* in 1919, a book which has yet to be translated into English. The first decade of the twentieth century was apparently a propitious period for the psychoanalytic study of folklore. Other early works include Franz Ricklin's *Wunscherfüllung und Symbolik im Märchen* in 1908 in which the existence of wishful thinking in fairy tales was forcefully demonstrated. In all of these writings, as Karl Johan Karlson put it in his doctoral dissertation in psychology of 1912, entitled "Psychoanalysis and Mythology," "The argument of the Freudian school...[is] that the laws of myth-formation and of the formation of fairy tales are identical with those in accordance with which the dreams are formed" (1914: 203). Incidentally, this dissertation, written under the direction of G. Stanley Hall of Clark University, who was in 1909 the first to invite Freud to lecture on psychoanalysis in the United States, is probably the first thesis devoted to the psychoanalytic study of folklore, although the bulk of it consists of surveying other theories of myth. The thesis is actually minimally psychoanalytic, being superficially derived from the writings of Freud, Rank, and Ricklin, but it is significant that a dissertation discussing the psychoanalytic approach to myth and fairy tale could have been written at all, especially in 1912.

In addition to encouraging his own students to investigate folklore, Freud also tried to enlist contributions from folklorists. One of these was Friedrich S. Krauss, a Serbian Jew residing in Vienna, who was an expert in the folklore of Yugoslavia and the leading force in founding and publishing the journal *Anthropophyteia* in which Freud and Oppenheim found such rich data for *Dreams in Folklore*. Krauss, anxious to defend his journal from charges that it contained pornographic and obscene matter, solicited and obtained in 1910 a letter of support from Freud who understood perfectly that he was being asked to bear witness "to the fact that material of this kind is not only useful but indispensable" from the standpoint of a psychologist (1910: 233). Krauss published the letter in *Anthropophyteia* as part of his "editorial" on behalf of the journal. Freud's willingness to endorse Krauss's efforts to provide a badly needed outlet for the publication of obscene folklore is also indicated by the appearance of his name as a member of the editorial committee for *Anthropophyteia* for volumes 7–9 (1910-1912). Freud presumably knew that his name appeared on the official masthead of the journal.

Freud would also accept Krauss's invitation to write a special introduction to the German translation of Bourke's *Scatalogic Rites of All Nations* in 1913. In turn, Krauss was occasionally invited to speak to the Viennese Psychoanalytic Society. The minutes reveal that he presented "The Corset in Custom and Usage among the Peoples of the World" on 15 March 1911 (Nunberg and Federn 1974: 194–200). Krauss also published several Serbo-Croatian versions of the Oedipus folktale in *Imago* in 1935. (For an English translation, see Edmunds and Dundes 1983: 10–22.)

There were other psychoanalytic studies of folklore in the initial decades of the rise of the psychoanalytic movement. The writings of Silberer (1910, 1912, 1914), Maeder (1908, 1909), and Storfer (1912) are representative, concentrating as they do on fairy tales and myths. Actually, almost every single major psychoanalyst wrote at least one paper applying psychoanalytic theory to folklore. It is not hard to document that folklore, especially mythology, constituted one of the most attractive areas for applied psychoanalysis almost right from the beginnings of the movement. In 1913, Otto Rank and Hanns Sachs teamed up to write *The Significance of Psychoanalysis for the Mental Sciences*. After an initial chapter on the nature of the unconscious, Rank and Sachs devoted each of six chapters to such topics as folklore, religion, ethnology and linguistics, esthetics and art, philosophy, ethics and law, and finally pedagogy and characterology. Not only is the subject of folklore the first to be discussed, but the forty pages allotted to "Investigation of Myths and Legends" almost dwarfs the other chapters: religion (eleven pages), ethnology and linguistics (thirteen pages), etc.

But if one had to single out the most important and influential contributors to the development of a psychoanalytic approach to folklore apart from Freud, one might well settle upon Ernest Jones and Géza Róheim. Although Ernest Jones seems to be best remembered for his extensive biography of Freud, his superb studies of folklore continue to be read. His paper on "Psycho-Analysis and Folklore" presented to the Jubilee Congress of the English Folk-Lore Society in September of 1928 fell on deaf ears, but it is notable insofar as Jones made a concerted effort to introduce psychoanalytic theory to folklorists. (Psychoanalysts who write on folklore in the standard psychiatric professional journals cannot assume that their works are read by folklorists.) Jones's lengthy essay "The Symbolic Significance of Salt in Folklore and Superstition" (1951: 22–109), first published in *Imago* in 1912, demonstrates Jones's impeccable scholarly methodology. This is hardly a patient's free association to an instance of spilling salt at table, but rather a conscientious, detailed investigation of the available literature on salt customs, eventually concluding that "salt is a typical symbol for semen." Similarly, Jones's book devoted to the creatures of nightmare, e.g., incubus, vampire, and the like, reveals a careful examination of the conventional sources. Although *On the Nightmare* was not published in book form until 1931, it was in fact written "in the years 1909 and 1910" (Jones 1971: 5), which further confirms that time period as a critical one for the development of the psychoanalytic study of folklore.

In contrast to Jones, Géza Róheim started out as a folklorist. Born in Budapest, he began a lifelong interest in folktales and myths which continued even after he discovered psychoanalysis. Fieldwork in Somaliland, Central Australia, the Normanby Islands, and with the Yuma Indians in Arizona, thanks in part to financial support from Princess Marie Bonaparte, allowed Róheim to become perhaps the first psychoanalytic anthropologist. A prolific writer, Róheim wrote dozens of essays applying psychoanalytic theory to folklore. No one has written more on the subject than Róheim. Unfortunately, his chaotic and undisciplined writing style (almost like free association!), coupled with a rather dogmatic way of asserting what a given item's symbolic meaning is, has tended to put off most readers, even those favorably disposed towards psychoanalytic interpretations. So it is that some of his speculations can make even an avowed Freudian flinch. Nevertheless, there are countless brilliant insights in Róheim's works and a careful reading of them reveals that a good many points made by later writers such as Kardiner or Bettelheim had already been stated or anticipated by Róheim. No one with a serious interest in the psychoanalytic study of folklore can afford to miss such books as *The Gates of the Dream* (1952) and *Magic and Schizophrenia* (1955), plus some of his many essays devoted to folktale and myth (e.g., 1922, 1940, 1941, 1953).

One has only to consult Grinstein's *Index of Psychoanalytic Writings* or the second edition of Kiell's *Psychoanalysis, Psychology, and Literature* (1982) to gain some idea of the enormity of Róheim's prodigious output.

Róheim had the great advantage of being familiar with conventional comparative folklore scholarship. So when he investigated a particular custom like the evil eye or a folktale like Frau Holle (Aarne-Thompson tale-type 480), he, unlike the typical psychoanalyst, used more than a single version, e.g., the Grimm version, for his analysis. Róheim, like Jones, presented a paper at the 1928 Jubilee Congress of the English Folk-Lore Society, his entitled "Mother Earth and the Children of the Sun," but it had little if any effect. One finds no reference to Róheim in mainstream folklore scholarship. Part of this is no doubt due to the understandable resistance to anything even remotely psychoanalytic in nature, but some blame must also be laid at Róheim's door insofar as his somewhat elliptic and cryptic writing style is not one to encourage any but the most daring to follow the twists and turns of his argument.

One of the principal theoretical difficulties in applying classical psychoanalytic theory to folklore from Freud through the works of Abraham, Rank, Jones, and Róheim is the assumption, explicit or implicit, that the theory is universally applicable. Freudian concepts and mechanisms are generally thought to be cross-culturally valid. What is even worse, psychoanalysts are willing to postulate absolute universality on the basis of a scattering of case histories—all typically from Western cultures. This cavalier disregard of cultural relativism, the notion that each human culture is to some extent a unique, noncomparable entity, has bothered anthropologists, for example, and has prevented psychoanalytic theory from being seriously considered by many potentially sympathetic scholars. To be sure, the opposite view is equally absurd. In applying the concept of cultural relativism to Freudian theory, one comes up with the still all too often heard comment that psychoanalytic theory applies only to Viennese Jewish culture. Any theory of culture developed in any particular cultural context may or may not apply to other cultures. It should and must be tested in other cultural contexts in order to determine whether or not it has cross-cultural validity. This, generally speaking, is what psychoanalysts have failed to do. This failure is understandable insofar as psychoanalysts are for the most part medical practitioners with their practice consisting largely of patients from Western cultures. There was therefore little incentive for psychoanalysts to venture among the "exotic" peoples of the world encountered and studied by anthropologists. With the few rare exceptions like L. Bryce Boyer, who has spent several decades studying the folklore of the Mescalero Apache, psychoanalysts have not often considered the folklore of non-Western peoples (cf. Boyer 1979). This is why there are dozens upon dozens of studies and restudies of selected Grimm tales, classical myths (especially Oedipus), and tales from the Old Testament, but almost no in-depth analysis of folktales from Africa or Oceania.

The universal versus cultural relativism issue was actually resolved in theoretical terms back in the late 1930s and early 1940s. At that time, psychoanalyst Abram Kardiner, in cooperation with anthropologists like Ralph Linton, organized a joint seminar at Columbia University to consider the interrelationships of psychoanalysis and anthropology (Harris 1968: 435). From this healthy cross-fertilization of disciplines came two important books from the pen of Kardiner. They were *The Individual and His Society* (1939) and *The Psychological Frontiers of Society* (1945). We know that Kardiner was heavily influenced by Freud because he himself reports on his analysis with Freud in his book of reminiscences (1977).

The gist of Kardiner's adaptation of Freudian theory was to culturally relativize it. He distinguished what he termed primary institutions (e.g., feeding techniques, weaning, toilet training, etc.) and secondary institutions (including such projective systems as religion, ritual, folktales, and myth). Retaining the Freudian notion that there is a logical connection, perhaps causal, but at any rate correlative, between infantile conditioning and adult projective systems (as in Freud's 1928 *The Future of an Illusion*), Kardiner argued persuasively that to the extent that infantile conditioning varies in different cultures, there will be correspondingly different projective systems. In other words, the folklore of a particular culture would be parallel to or isomorphic with the infant care of that culture.

One of the participants in the Columbia University seminar organized'by Kardiner was Cora Du Bois, an anthropologist who was an expert on the Alorese. She in effect served as an informant for the seminar. Kardiner noticed that among the Alorese, good maternal care ends the fourteenth day after the birth of an infant—the mother returns to work in the fields. The child is cared for at random by older siblings or relatives. The "maternal" care is sporadic, inconsistent, and undependable. Kardiner remarks that although the child may get enough nourishment in terms of calories, "it lacks the consistent image of one person with whom it can associate relief of hunger tensions." Kardiner then suggests that this might be related to the fact that the donor figure in Alorese folktales is either anonymous or one of many. In these tales, a stranger or "good being" appears from nowhere to bring relief (Kardiner 1945: 146–149). Kardiner also finds data supporting his theory from traditional Alorese art. "So slight is the tendency to idealize parental imago that the effigies by which the Alorese represent the ancestral spirits are made in the most careless and slipshod manner and are used in the most perfunctory way and then forthwith discarded" (1945: 167). The important point here is not so much the validity of Kardiner's analysis of Alorese folklore, but the fact that psychoanalytic theory can be empirically tested in diverse cultural contexts. Either there is some kind of demonstrable isomorphism between infantile conditioning in a culture and that same culture's projective systems or there is not. This possible relationship can be empirically investigated. In this way, the validity of Freudian theory can be established or disproved. Unfortunately, Kardiner's ingenious adaptation of Freudian theory had little or no impact upon the direction of folklore scholarship.

In the years since Kardiner's attempt to synthesize cultural relativism with psychoanalytic theory, there has been disappointingly little in the way of advances in the psychoanalytic study of folklore. Folklorists on the whole have ignored Kardiner just as they ignored Freud before him. Psychoanalysts seem even less well read than Freud and the early Freudians. At least Freud read the anthropology of his own day. Psychoanalysts continue to expend their considerable exegetical talents on reanalyzing Oedipus, and it is invariably the literary version of Sophocles which receives their undivided attention. The host of folkloristic tales of Oedipus, of which there are dozens, are probably not even known to most analysts. The story is still to be found in oral tradition, as a 1971 Gypsy version collected in Italy attests (cf. Edmunds and Dundes 1983: 23–27). How fascinating it is that in many oral versions, the hero kills his father while guarding the family garden or orchard. The father who goes to check on the hero to see if he is really alert (awake) is typically shot by the boy who thinks the intruder in the garden is a burglar in the night. The parricide is much more common in the garden than in an encounter with a carriage. It is not that psychoanalysts have necessarily misinterpreted the Sophoclean version, it is rather that there have been literally hundreds of attempts to plumb the depths of this one literary text (cf. Edmunds and Ingber 1977) with virtually no consideration of the numerous oral versions of the tale (Aarne-Thompson tale-type 931), even though the oral version is surely antecedent to Sophocles' rendering of the story (cf. Hägglund and Hägglund 1981, for an analysis of Finnish oral versions).

One can find occasional anthropologists, sympathetic to psychoanalytic theory, exploring the contents of non-Western folklore, e.g., Jacobs 1952, 1959; Barnouw 1955; Ehrlich 1961; etc. In one interesting short study, a content analysis of Zuni tales was compared with the results of Thematic Aptitude Tests (TATs) administered to Zuni subjects (Kaplan 1962). The conclusion was that folklore functions as a kind of natural (as opposed to artificial, imposed, a priori) projective test for a culture. The idea of folklore as projective text or rather projective test for a culture goes right back to Freud. In *The Psychopathology of Everyday Life* (1901), Freud remarked, "In point of fact I believe that a large part of the mythological view of the world, which extends a long way into the most modern religions, *is nothing but psychology projected into the external world*" (1901: 258). From a Kardinerian perspective, one would add only that there are culturally relative mythological conceptions of the world which reflect culturally relative differences in psychology. To the extent that folklore differs in different cultures, so psychological constellations and mental illnesses will also vary. What is constant is that in every culture there is a close relationship between the folklore of that culture and the dream content of individuals in that culture, between the folklore and the culturally relative forms of mental dysfunctioning, between the folklore and the particular form of infantile conditioning practiced.

One key theoretical problem with the Kardiner reformulation of the original Freudian idea of the relationship of folklore to infantile conditioning is essentially that he is describing a type of chicken-and-egg situation. It would be wrong to assert that infantile conditioning *causes* adult projective systems (including folklore) because that assumes erroneously that infantile conditioning exists in a cultural vacuum. Who is it who imposes infantile conditioning? Parents. And parents are surely influenced by their projective systems with respect to what infantile conditioning is imposed. So one could argue that adult projective systems affect the kind of infant care existing in a culture. That would be equally one-sided. The point is that it is always fallacious to assume that any one element of a cultural system is logically (or psychologically) prior to all other elements. There is an intellectually dangerous circularity in claiming that infantile conditioning *causes* adult projective systems and that adult projective systems *cause* a particular type of infantile conditioning. All we can infer is that there is a correspondence or correlation, not necessarily causal, between infantile conditioning in a culture and adult projective systems in that culture. From the ontogenetic perspective—and psychoanalysts normally deal with individuals, not whole cultures—it does appear that infant experiences do cause specific adult personality configurations. But from a cultural perspective, it is fairly clear that infant experiences are largely dictated by cultural values imparted and imposed by parents or parent surrogates.

Cross-cultural studies in psychiatry suggest that mental illness is culturally defined. There are different demons in different cultures and the defenses against them vary as well. For a psychiatric practitioner to be effective, the doctor and his or her patient must share the same worldview (Torrey 1972). It is difficult to exorcize ghosts if one does not believe in them. Ghosts and other demons are part of folklore. They are the subjects of legends. It is unfortunately part of ethnocentrism to believe that all other peoples think just the way we do (only typically not quite so well!). We come once again to the plaguing question of universals. Don't all men eat? Yes, but what they eat, when they eat, how they eat, with whom they eat, etc., varies widely from culture to culture. Universality cannot simply be assumed or asserted without proof. In folklore, for example, I know of no single folktale or myth which is universal. Even the flood myth, which is extremely widespread, is totally absent in sub-Saharan Africa. It is not that black Africans don't have myths. They do. They just don't happen to have the flood myth (except where it was obviously introduced by a Christian missionary). If there are truly universals, then with all the data that has been so assiduously gathered for the past several hundred years by travelers, missionaries, colonial administrators, and more recently by anthropologists and folklorists, it really ought to be possible to document such universals.

I do think it might be possible to demonstrate, for example, that men everywhere envy women, especially their procreative ability. The widespread distribution of the custom of couvade in which men pretend to go through the motions of parturition would support this possibility. What is interesting is that Western male psychoanalysts have long claimed that it is women who envy men. *Penis envy* is a standard idiom in the psychoanalytic lexicon. Yet while there is plenty of folkloristic evidence of men desirous of bearing children without the help of women—the range runs from Athene being Zeus's brainchild to knee babies to the sowing of dragon's teeth, etc.— one finds almost no folkloristic data demonstrating a female wish for a penis. There are plenty of castration tales, but a woman's destroying a man's phallus is not to be confused with a woman's necessarily desiring one. If one understands that most of the key psychoanalytic constructs have close analogues in folklore—remember that it is no accident that Freud chose the tale of Oedipus to name the complex—then one has to take account of the absence of such analogues for certain alleged psychoanalytic truths. One could conceivably regard the concept of penis envy as a form of male projection! Men envy women, but are not willing to admit this. So instead they assert that it is women who envy men. Bettelheim in *Symbolic Wounds* reviewed the anthropological evidence from initiation rites which reveal that men in secret act out being women, even to the extent of making their subincised penises bleed and then calling them vulvas (Bettelheim 1962: 105). In initiation, males are born anew from males. Where is the comparable ritual evidence suggesting that women want to be men? Even the relatively limited clinical data on penis envy is somewhat suspect. If a patient is being treated by an analyst who believes in the existence of penis envy, then a patient's associations might well have been induced. I don't say categorically that there is no such thing as penis envy. I say only that it is curious how little penis envy folklore has been recorded or reported.

If one looks at the relatively few works treating psychoanalysis and folklore in the mid-twentieth century, one sees few advances. Carvalho-Neto's *Folklore and Psychoanalysis* (1972) is an English translation of a work published in Spanish in 1956 which in turn was largely inspired by Carvalho-Neto's Brazilian mentor Arthur Ramos, who devoted three chapters of his *Estudos de Folk-lore* (1958) to a review of early psychoanalytic studies of folklore. (Ramos's chapters originally appeared as essays in *Revista Brasileira* in the 1940s.) Most of the essays appearing in the psychoanalytic journals tend to be Oedipal analyses of the same small corpus of myths and folktales (cf. Glenn 1976; Edmunds and Inger 1977). This led anthropologist Melville Herskovits to charge that the undue emphasis upon father-son dynamics had tended to obscure the undeniable elements of sibling rivalry in folklore (Herskovits and Herskovits 1958: 85–95).

One significant psychoanalytic study of folklore is Bruno Bettelheim's *The Uses of Enchantment: The Meaning and Importance of Fairy Tales*. He offers brilliant readings of individual European fairy tales (mostly from the Grimm canon) arguing persuasively that such tales are often critical for the mental health of children as they pass through puberty to adulthood. With such a positive evaluation of fairy tales, Bettelheim differs radically from such earlier psychoanalytic negative assessments as those of Brill who claimed (1921: 304) "Fairy tales are also very harmful to the normal psychic development because they are primitive and archaic modes of expression; and catering as they do, to the primitive impulse, they encourage primitive modes of thought and action in the individual." With their components of sadism and masochism, fairy tales have the most pernicious influence upon the child, Brill went on to say. Brill had gone on record opposing the effect of fairy tales as early as his 1914 article "Fairy Tales as a Determinant of Dreams and Neurotic Symptoms" in the *New York Medical Journal*. Similarly, Lorand in his 1935 paper "Fairy Tales and Neurosis" suggests on the basis of a case history that "under certain circumstances the fairy tale may cause harm and produce a traumatic effect" (p. 234). In this light, Bettelheim's advocacy of fairy tales for children represents a noteworthy departure from earlier views.

Yet Bettelheim is no folklorist. He claims that Cinderella "is the most popular of all fairy tales and is distributed worldwide" (1977: 253). Once again, we find the conventional psychoanalyst's claim of universality. Cinderella (Aarne-Thompson tale-type 510A) is *not* reported among the North and South American Indians, in black Africa, in Oceania, in aboriginal New Guinea and Australia, etc. It *is* widely reported in the Indo-European and Asian traditions. The oldest recorded versions seems to be from ninth-century China, but it is hardly "worldwide" in distribution. (For an entry into the extensive Cinderella scholarship, see Dundes 1983.) Bettelheim claims that Cupid and Psyche is a myth, not a fairy tale (1977: 294). This is wrong. It is a standard folktale (Aarne-Thompson tale-type 425A). Also somewhat strange is Bettelheim's insistence that fairy tales can serve children's emotional growth only if their unconscious, latent content is not revealed. ". . . fairy tales can and do serve children well. . . as long as the child doesn't know what they mean to him psychologically" (p. 57). "One must never 'explain' to the child the meanings of fairy tales" (p. 155). If one of the aims of psychoanalysts and folklorists is to make the unconscious conscious, then this would seem odd counsel. One could just as well argue, I should think, that fairy tales ought to be explained to children so that the underlying emotional traumas with which they deal may be less threatening. Bettelheim does cite some previous psychoanalytic treatments of fairy tales, but there is no mention of Ricklin's pioneering work of 1908 or of the many essays by Róheim who has offered in-depth analyses of a number of the tales discussed by Bettelheim.

While on the subject of Bettelheim's book, I cannot forbear making a somewhat personal comment. In his lengthy analysis of Cinderella, Bettelheim discusses the shoe-fitting episode as follows:

> While in Perrault's Cinderella a gentleman of the court tries the slipper on, and in the Brothers Grimm's tale the prince only hands it to Cinderella and she herself puts it on her foot, in many stories it is the prince who slips the shoe on. This might be likened to the groom's putting the ring on the finger of the bride as an important part of the marriage ceremony, a symbol of their being tied together henceforth...A reflection on a universally accepted part of the wedding ceremony may lend support to this idea. The bride stretches out one of her fingers for the groom to slip a ring onto it. Pushing one finger through a circle made out of the thumb and index finger of the other hand is a vulgar expression for intercourse...The ring, a symbol for the vagina, is given by the groom to his bride; she offers him in return her outstretched finger...By having the ring put onto her finger, the bride acknowledges that from now on, her husband to some degree will have possession of her vagina, and she of his penis... (1977: 265, 271, 272).

In 1967, some years earlier, I accepted an invitation to comment in the *Psychoanalytic Forum* on an essay on Cinderella by Beryl Sandford. With respect to the prince carrying the glass slipper to Cinderella, I offered the following observation:

> He then places the female genital symbol upon her foot. Since feet are usually phallic symbols, one has the male manipulating a female symbol and female extending a male

symbol. In achieving the perfect fit, it is the prince's control over the unbroken glass (= virginity) slipper coupled with the heroine's desire for the union which assures success. This ritual act in which the participants appear to manipulate the other's genitals is probably just as appropriate symbolically as our wedding ritual in which the man places the "female" genital ring upon the outstretched phallic finger of his bride! In marriage, one has access to and control of the genitals of the other sex (1967: 141).

While Bettelheim does indicate in an early footnote in his book en passant that he has read the Sandford essay on Cinderella (1977: 313, n. 11), he makes no other reference to it. Of course, I am flattered that Bettelheim thought enough of my analysis to borrow it.

Before concluding this overview of the history of the development of the psychoanalytic study of folklore, I must mention briefly several other important contributions. One is *The Glory of Hera* (1968) by Philip Slater. This is an insightful application of psychoanalytic theory to Greek mythology. If mythology represents a projection of critical child-parent relationships, then it should be possible to reconstruct such relationships by reading back from the mythology. Using Greek myths as his corpus, Slater elucidates the parent-child relationships in the ancient Greek family structure with special attention to the mother-son relationship. Although the study is once again limited to Western peoples, it is nonetheless an exciting, stimulating essay, particularly in gauging the effect of sexual segregation in Greek (and other Mediterranean) societies. With the men out in the taverns, the neglected women lavish their love and attention instead upon their sons, thereby exacerbating the inevitable Oedipal situation.

Another major contribution to the psychoanalytic study of folklore is Gershon Legman's comprehensive treatment of dirty jokes in the Western world (1952, 1968, 1975). His erudite and psychoanalytically informed content analyses of hundreds of standard jokes is the folkloristic extension of Freud's pioneering work *Jokes and Their Relation to the Unconscious* (1905) and Martha Wolfenstein's ingenious study of children's jokes and riddles first published in 1954.

In *Childhood and Folklore: A Psychoanalytic Study of Apache Personality* (1979), L. Bryce Boyer brings his psychoanalytic acumen to bear upon field data he and his anthropologist wife Ruth have gathered from the Mescalero Apache over a period of two decades. Most psychoanalysts analyzing folklore have tended to be armchair workers rather than field workers, preferring instead to rely on folklore texts collected by someone else. In Boyer's case, he is analyzing data gathered by him from informants known to him. Boyer's rare combination of folklore fieldwork and psychoanalytic expertise is nearly unique. Not since Róheim has there been an analyst who has spent so much time in the field working with folklore materials.

These representative works by Bettelheim, Slater, Legman, and Boyer indicate that the impetus provided by Freud with respect to examining the contents of folklore in the light of psychoanalytic theory has not died out. It should be mentioned that revisionists of Freud, or neo-Freudians as they are sometimes labelled, have not made much of a contribution to the study of folklore. Erich Fromm's *The Forgotten Language: An Introduction to the Understanding of Dreams, Fairy Tales and Myths*, published in 1951, offers an analysis of Little Red Riding Hood (Aarne-Thompson tale-type 333) and a Babylonian creation myth, but he depends heavily for his interpretation upon a rigid evolutionary notion of initial primeval matriarchy supplanted by patriarchy, a theory popular in the nineteenth century. A few attempts have been made to apply "ego psychology" to the study of myth (cf. Aarlow 1961; Bergmann 1966), but without great success. The failure of ego psychology to illuminate folkloristic materials may be attributed to the fact that folklore represents primary-process or id products. The relatively uncensored nature of folklore (as opposed even to dream contents) would suggest that ego psychology might not be all that relevant. (I am indebted to Dr. Kato van Leeuwen for this observation.) Still, to the extent that individuals draw upon folklore for their own personal psychological needs, ego psychology may yet be proven useful in the analysis of folklore.

A Jungian stream of scholarship devoted to folklore has continued to flourish. Marie Louise von Franz has published a series of books (1970, 1972a, 1972b, 1974, 1977, 1980) attempting to illuminate fairy tales and myths in the light of analytical psychology, following along the lines laid down by Jung in his essay "The Phenomenology of the Spirit in Fairy Tales" and his "The Psychology of the Child Archetype" previously quoted, but this does not really belong in a discussion of psychoanalysis and folklore. There are also various mishmashes of Freud and Jung, or Freud, Jung, and Anthroposophy (cf. Hedwig von Beit 1952, 1956, 1957; Heuscher 1963; and Dieckmann 1977, for samples of such approaches). I have not attempted in this overview to list every single book or article which contains psychoanalytic treatments of folklore. Readers interested in further sources should consult such surveys as La Barre 1948; Giehrl 1970; Carvalho-Neto 1972; or such standard bibliographical reference aids as the *Internationale Volkskundliche Bibliographie* (1917–); Grinstein's *Index of Psychoanalytic Writings* (1950–), the *Chicago Psychoanalytic Literature Index* (1920–).

Finally, I should like to mention briefly several of my own works in order to demonstrate my long-standing conviction that the psychoanalytic approach to folklore offers great and as yet untapped opportunities for both psychoanalysts and folklorists. For example, in considering Kardiner's adaptation of Freudian theory, I began to think about the possible underlying rationale of ritual fasting. Why should fasting be considered a foolproof method to ensure contact with the supernatural? Why should an American Indian initiate a fast for four days before going on a quest to find his guardian spirit? A Yale-educated Winnebago Indian born circa 1884 reported "Fasting is a universal practice among Indians. Sometimes they go without food from four to ten days at a time. The purpose of these fasts, in which I often took part, is to gain the compassion and the blessing of some spirit, in order that he may come and reveal himself." Typical explanations of fasting in the literature include the removal of impurities from one's body so as to be more pleasing to the deity. The question is why is food, which evidently does not offend the deity on other occasions, suddenly deemed impure? And why should the deity care in any case if the supplicant has an empty stomach or not? Another explanation is that fasting weakens one so that hallucinatory experiences are more likely. This struck me as being a post-hoc type of explanation. Yes, fasting might well encourage hallucinations, but that seemed improbable as an impelling cause for the practice. The practice continues even in our own society with various political activists engaging in so-called hunger fasts intended to influence those in power to bring about nuclear disarmament or prison reform. Here then is a typical example of a standard custom or practice which has been reported in the folkloristic literature for decades. How can the application of psychoanalytic theory help us understand this customary behavior?

In my analysis (Dundes 1963), I suggest if the infant is to the parent as the adult is to his or her deity, then we have a possible explanation. Since the human neonate cannot live unaided, he or she must be fed in order to survive. Early on, there must be an association between feeling hunger pangs and the coming of a powerful, large figure who brings nourishment. Hence in the transformation of this infant-parent relationship, it is logical to assume that if an adult wants a deity to approach, he should make himself hungry. Furthermore, the hungrier he gets, the more likely it is that the deity will approach. One may usefully re-read the Winnebago statement in this light. I believe this Freudian-Kardinerian explanation of ritual fasting is an eminently reasonable one. If one wished to speculate further, then one might surmise that in societies where infants are fed often— whether they cry or not, perhaps in accordance with a prescribed schedule of frequent feelings, fasting ought not be a popular practice. If a parent freely provides without an infant having to feel hunger pangs, then in that society adults might well not feel that fasting was a necessary or efficacious means of soliciting divine or supernatural aid/intervention.

Using comparable psychoanalytic reasoning, I have tried to explain the underlying significance of subjects as varied as the earthdiver myth (1962), the bullroarer (1976a), the potlatch ritual (1979), and American football (1978). In the latter instance, I sought to show how the game involves a homosexual ritual battle in which one group of males tries to get into another group's endzone more times than that group is able to penetrate the first team's endzone.

One of the psychoanalytic constructs which I have found especially helpful in the study of folklore is projection (1976b). I have tried to distinguish between straightforward projection and what I term inverse projection. In the simpler form of projection, a cause of anxiety is translated more or less intact onto another plane. Here one can find the Oedipal constellation displaced upwards as it were to the Christian religious family. Jesus is born of a Virgin Mary—if one's mother is a virgin, this constitutes the ultimate repudiation of one's father who thus had no part in the son's conception, although with the doctrine of consubstantiation with father and son the same, Jesus as God is his own begetter, again an Oedipal ideal, as Otto Rank pointed out long ago in his *The Myth of the Birth of the Hero*. As an Oedipal projection, the story falls short insofar as the son does not conquer the father, but rather yields and suffers symbolic castration when he is nailed to a phallic cross (plus suffering additional penetration by males in authority by having his side pierced). However, the Oedipal triumph occurs when Jesus rises from the dead and this "erection" (resurrection) is first observed by a harlot who bears, coincidentally, of course, the same name as that of Jesus' mother: Mary. The Oedipal or rather Electral component of the Christian family plot has something for females, too, as we have a virgin impregnated miraculously by a heavenly father (cf. Dundes 1981, for a fuller psychoanalytic consideration of the life of Jesus).

Secular as well as sacred folklore offers occasions for projection. So the life of George Washington, according to legend, has him chopping down his father's favorite cherry tree and having to confess his crime "I cannot tell a lie." The folklore insists, up and down the East Coast, that "George Washington slept here," which is appropriate enough if Washington is truly the father of his country. The particular monument erected by a grateful country to memorialize their founding father also attests to the nature of the priapic projection. The Oedipal cast to the legend is also appropriate insofar as a then young republic was throwing off the yoke of an old English king.

Projective inversion, in contrast, involves a transformational shift. As Freud put it in his 1911 paper "Psycho-Analytic Notes upon an Autobiographical Account of a Case of Paranoia," "I hate him" becomes transposed to "He hates me". Otto Rank's marvelous insight in his classic study of the Indo-European and Semitic hero pattern was that the inevitable father-king's attempt to kill his newborn son was a projection—I would call it an inverse projection—of the son's wish to kill his father. But Rank and other early Freudians were not equally perceptive with respect to female projection. Thus the father-king's act of locking up his daughter to protect her was seen by Freudians only from the point of view of the father. Rank claims (1959: 80): "The father who refuses to give his daughter to any of her suitors, or who attaches to the winning of the daughter certain conditions difficult of fulfillment, does this because he really begrudges her to all others, for when all is told he wishes to possess her for himself. He locks her up in some inaccessible spot, so as to safeguard her virginity." Strange really that Rank and others understood male inverse projections so well and female inverse projections so poorly. Ricklin, at least, in his discussion of tales in which fathers attempt to marry their own daughters, correctly understood that the initial death of the mother (queen) reflected wishful thinking on the part of the daughter (princess) (1915:65, n. 1, 70). In the context of the folktale plot underlying Shakespeare's *King Lear*, I have suggested that Freudians are mistaken in assuming that a father's wish to marry his own daughter (as found in a number of standard folktales) was simply a reflection of a male father's wishful thinking. Rather, it is the daughter who would like to marry her own father. The daughter's wish to marry her father is transformed through projective inversion into the father's wish to marry his daughter, just as the son's wish to kill his father is similarly transformed into the father's wish to kill his own son. Both transformations leave sons and daughters guilt free. Fairy tales, after all, are always told from the child's point of view, not the parents'. I concluded that King Lear was essentially a girl's fairy tale told from the father's point of view (1976c).

The distinction between projection and projective inversion is not always made clear in psychoanalytic discussions of projection. This is why it may be useful to draw upon the folkloristic data available. Projective inversion is often found in legends, for example. Consider the all too common urban legend in which black youths are said to have castrated a white boy in a public school bathroom, a legend told by whites, not blacks. This legend appears to be a projective inversion of the whites' wish to castrate blacks which the white stereotype depicts as being hyperphallic. The white fear of superphallic blacks is also manifested in a 1983 legend in which two older women on an elevator watch a tall black male with one or two dogs in tow enter. In most versions, the man commands his dog, "Sit bitch!" whereupon the two women immediately sit down on the floor of the elevator. Later when the women go to check out of the hotel, they are told that some famous black athlete (Reggie Jackson or Wilt Chamberlain) has paid their bill.

This is a brief sampling of instances of how I think psychoanalytic theory can greatly illuminate folklore, but I am equally convinced that folklore can be of service in extending the boundaries of psychoanalytic theory. For example, one of the theoretically most troublesome areas of psychoanalytic interpretation is symbolism. Psychoanalysts depend heavily upon symbolic readings of behavior and objects, but often little in the way of concrete evidence is offered for a given symbolic interpretation. The analyst simply asserts that a particular object has a particular symbolic meaning. Occasionally, he or she may say that the statement is made on the basis of long clinical experience, which hardly provides testable documentation as far as sceptics are concerned. Even more commonly, an authority is cited, as "proof," for the correctness of the symbolic reading. Usually the authority is some other analyst, preferably Freud. Symbolic interpretation sometimes gives the appearance of being a matter more of faith than of science! Folklorists, not all that disposed to accept psychoanalytic interpretations on faith, are often genuinely perplexed by discrepancies in these interpretations. For example, one psychoanalytic reading of the folktale of Jack and the Beanstalk (Aarne-Thompson tale-type 328) claims that the beanstalk is Jack's phallus: "Pursued by the menacing ogre for his thefts, Jack castrates himself: the beanstalk shrivels at the first touch of the hatchet, and the threatening father image disappears" (Desmonde 1951: 288). Róheim in *The Gates of the Dream* (1952: 359) states that the beanstalk is *both* Jack's penis and the father's penis. The analysts do agree that the beanstalk is a penis; the question is whose?

The suspicion of what are perceived to be somewhat arbitrary symbolic formulaic interpretations of data—the charge is typically that symbolic meanings are read into data rather than being read out of data—has even led to folklore reflecting this mistrust. A sentence with veritable proverbial status is attributed to Freud himself: "Sometimes a cigar is (just) a cigar." I can find no evidence that Freud ever said this, but whether he did or not, it is significant that critics of psychoanalytic symbolic readings insist on quoting Freud to counter a given suggested interpretation. Another piece of folklore springing from the same source of anxiety comes in legendary form. In this perhaps apocryphal story—it is often cast with Bettelheim as the analyst—a psychoanalyst is supposedly giving a public lecture and is bothered by a woman sitting in the front row of the audience busily knitting. Finally the annoyed analyst interrupts his lecture to address the woman, saying, "Don't you know that knitting is a form of symbolic masturbation?" The woman replies scornfully, "When I knits, I knits, and when I masturbates, I masturbates."

The serious and legitimate question at issue here really is: can one demonstrate empirically that a given object or act does have a particular symbolic meaning? If Freud was correct in his tenth lecture of the *Introductory Lectures on Psycho-Analysis*, "Symbolism in Dreams," when he said, " 'Pulling off a branch' as a symbolic representation of masturbation is not merely in harmony with vulgar descriptions of the act but has far-reaching mythological parallels" (1916: 164, 156)—cf. "jerking off" in American folk speech—then can we assume that Frazer's undoubted fascination with the passage in Virgil's *Aeneid*, in which a hero aspiring to become "King of the Wood" had to first pluck a golden bough, has an onanistic import? If so, writing a twelve-volume magnum opus, *The Golden Bough*, surely the longest footnote in the history of scholarship, might constitute a symbolic form of mental masturbation. Such assertions could only be convincing to those of an analytic persuasion. Is there any way of making the study of symbols less seemingly arbitrary and subjective?

I have developed a methodology combining the comparative method and structuralism designed to provide a more reliable means of isolating possible symbolic equivalents in a given culture. Vladimir Propp's innovative *Morphology of the Folktale*, first published in Russia in 1928, demonstrated that standard European fairy tales consist of some thirty-one sequential plot units. He called these functions, but I have relabelled them motifemes. Comparative studies of fairy tales have assembled as many as a thousand versions of a single tale. If one aligns all the versions of a single fairy tale along a structural matrix so-to-speak, one can by empirical inspection observe the range of variation within a particular motifemic slot. The range of allomotifs shows what the folk consider to be functional equivalents for a specific episode in the tale. These equivalents are, in my view, symbolically equivalent as well, and, it should be pointed out, these symbolic equations are made with no help from any a priori theory, psychoanalytic or otherwise. I have sought to demonstrate this methodology by analyzing a standard European folktale, the Rabbit-herd (AT 570). The interested reader should refer to this essay (Dundes 1982 and chapter 6 of this volume) for this new approach to the study of symbols.

As another example of how folklore and psychoanalysis can be mutually beneficial, let me cite my research on identifying German national character through folklore. Starting with German folklore, I found an enormous number of proverbs, folksongs, and jokes dealing with anality. This penchant for *scheisse* is also observed in the writings of Luther and Mozart, not to mention Günter Grass and Heinrich Böll. From early toilet training (beginning as early as five months) and a long tradition of swaddling (in which infants were left immersed in their own feces for periods up to twelve hours), one can see a consistent pattern. There are more jokes about anality then genitality in German culture.

Some of the striking relevant data from German culture includes the construction of the German toilet (with a porcelain platform upon which the feces falls—to be inspected), to the candy *dukatenscheisser* (folk figure who excretes ducats or money), to the monstrous iconographic figure of the *Judensau*, found only in German-speaking areas, which shows Jews suckling from pigs who are considered dirty because they eat feces. With the help of such psychoanalytic constructs as reaction formation, one can better understand the German love of order, cleanliness, and thrift. The Freudian-Kardinerian notion of the critical importance of infantile conditioning led me to conjecture about the possible connection between swaddling techniques (and the infrequency of changing the swaddling clothes) and the prominence of "shitting in pants" and "shitting in bed" in countless folk rhymes. A German proverb itself proclaims the relationship: "Life is like a children's nightshirt: short and shitty." I used a variant of this proverb as a title for my monograph "Life is like a chicken-coop ladder." So psychoanalysis proved essential for my analysis of German national character through folklore. But the research also revealed how folklore can illuminate psychoanalytic theory. It was no accident, in my opinion, that it was a German or Austrian who first identified anal erotic character. The alleged characterological features of the classic anal erotic are in fact identical to the list of supposed national characteristics of the Germans and Austrians. When Freud wrote his famous anal erotic character essay in 1908, he even pointed to the well-known example of the *dukatenscheisser* (again using folklore to make his point), but in the English translation, a note had to be added explaining the *dukatenscheisser* to a non-German speaking audience.

It is interesting that in all of the huge literature devoted to German national character, stimulated in part by two world wars, there is little or no mention of the German love of feces. Moreover, within the psychoanalytic literature, there is an enormous scholarship devoted to anal erotic character, but in none of these books and articles is there any mention of Germans and German character. One reason for this is probably that so many of the early analysts and their patients were German and Austrian. It was simply assumed in traditional ethnocentric fashion that the way they were was the way the world was. In fact, on the basis of a number of folk rhymes proclaiming a specific connection be-

tween orderliness or cleanliness and toilet training, I have specu-
lated that Freud may first have gotten the idea for the association
from folklore. (See Dundes 1984 for details.)

From this combination of folklore and psychoanalysis, I believe I was enabled to explain something about German national
character. One can now better understand the German love of
sausages (stuffed intestines), wind instruments, mud baths, even
some of the unspeakable horrors of antisemitism as practiced in
Nazi Germany. One Nazi goal was to make Germany *Judenrein*,
that is, *clean* of (dirty) Jews. So Jews were cruelly ushered into
showers—why showers?—and in one particularly vicious experi-
ment actually transformed into soap. The literalization of a metaphor changing dirty Jews into clean soap constitutes a
singularly cruel and savage way of eliminating a scapegoat, but
there is an undeniably aggressive component of anality (e.g.,
dropping bombs from the bowels of airplanes). It is difficult to
summarize years of research in a few paragraphs, but I suggest
that the study of German national character through folklore
does show how folklore and psychoanalysis can both be utilized
in a common analytic effort.

Let me conclude this extended consideration of folklore and
psychoanalysis on a more pleasant note. Unlike the Germans,
Americans prefer genitality to anality. We turn briefly to popular
culture rather than folklore. Popular or mass culture includes tel-
evision, motion pictures, detective stories, the Western, science
fiction, etc. It differs from folklore in that it does not manifest multiple existence or display variation. Each time one sees
Star Wars, it is the same. It does not change. I would argue that
just as psychoanalytic theory can be an indispensable aid to the
analysis of folklore, it can serve equally in the study of popular
culture.

Star Trek is a popular science fiction series, now often shown
on syndicated reruns. In *Star Trek,* a space ship on patrol visits
alien peoples. They make uninvited rather than invited visits to
these peoples. Typically, these alien people pose some kind of
threat to the space ship. Often the ship is caught by a hostile
force field which rudely shakes the ship's passengers, making
them hurtle from one side of the ship to another. Clearly, some-

thing has to be done about the alien people. Occasionally, the people can be reasoned with. One merely beams down and exports a bit of democracy, Christianity, the secret ballot, or the like. Sometimes the aliens can be successfully converted, but sometimes they prove to be incorrigible. In such cases, one has no choice but to annihilate them.

Who is in command of the space ship? Kirk. What kind of a name is Kirk? It is an Anglo-Scottish name and it just happens to mean church. Who are the other leaders? Spock may be another breed with his uncharacteristic ears, but his name is a good German one. The other leaders include Scotty and McCoy, again good Wasp names. When the order is given to come right to course so and so, or to commence firing, who actually turns the helm or pulls the trigger? Is it Kirk? No, it is Sulu or Uhura or other members of the ethnic support group. In any case, once the alien people is suitably pacified or destroyed the ship is once again set free. Free—what's the name of the ship? Enterprise! Free Enterprise. So United Star Ship (which just coincidentally happens to yield the initials USS—as in United States Ship) continues on its merry way, arriving uninvited among alien peoples, feeling free to convert or destroy them to keep enterprise free. Is this not an example of projection, perhaps unconscious projection?

Star Wars also falls in the science fiction genre. But it has a folklore base. A hero raised by foster parents (cf. Rank's *The Myth of the Birth of the Hero*) finds a damsel in distress. In folktale, the hero finds a lock of a princess's hair, but in this modern version, it is a remarkable piece of technology which provides the impetus, as Princess Leia's message of "Help me, Help me—This is a recording!" comes from a robot computer bank. The hero meets an old donor figure who just happens to have the hero's father's old sword which he dutifully presents to the hero. An appropriate villain named Darth Vader (death of the father?) must be overcome by the hero. The hero's name, incidentally, is Luke Skywalker, rather an unusual name for a hero until one remembers that the creative genius behind the *Star Wars* films is named Lucas. (Lucas evidently is well read in folklore, but was the selection of the hero's name conscious or unconscious?) Other names are suggestive, e.g., Princess Leia (as in "lay ya"), who is obviously no conventional fairy-tale princess, passive, submissive. Rather at one point, this hip princess takes the "guns" away from the two heroes and shows that she is well able to use these ordinarily male weapons. Something no doubt for the women's liberation members of the film-viewing audience. Also she doesn't marry Luke as fairy-tale heroines normally do, partly because there is going to be a sequel. Nor does she marry the other reluctant hero, whose name is a curious Han Solo, which has a bit of an onanistic ring about it.

But fairy tales are not enough to ensure a box office success. So World War II films have been superimposed on the fairy-tale plot frame. The enemies are storm troopers, dressed in white. Another enemy appears briefly in the marvelous barroom scene in which Han Solo is encouraged to pay his debts. The enemy speaks in a foreign tongue—it is the only time in the film when subtitles are used. The enemy is short and colored. Whether the language is Swahili or Nahuatl, it sounds to most audiences like an oriental language. If the Germans and the Japanese were the enemies in World War II, what about Luke's allies? One is Threepio, an effete robot who speaks with a pronounced British accent. A helpful polyglot who knows many languages, but not quite a man—he is an android, but a useful ally. The dogfight aerial scenes are also updates of World War II battles and movies.

Yet fairy tales and World War II are not enough to guarantee success either. So we must look at the unconscious content of *Star Wars*. What is the nature of the hero's magic weapon? It is the famous force which happens to come packaged in the form of a cylindrical light sword. Luke initially has trouble controlling his father's life force, but eventually it helps him perform the arduous task required to destroy the Death Star, the enemy stronghold. The task, as most who have seen the film will recall, consisted of flying down a long, long channel or passage in order to drop a capsule down a hole. The enemy is bent on keeping Luke out of the channel, but after he closes his eyes (surely a strange way to fly!) to get in touch with his feelings, he succeeds in navigating the long, treacherous channel. It is only in the successful transit that he momentarily conquers the father-villain. In the later sequel films, we learn that Luke is the son of the villainous Darth Vader and to this father-son combat we have the hint of brother-sister incest as Luke and Leia turn out to be siblings. Popular culture may be new in form, but it is old in content insofar as it, like folklore, provides an important outlet for the projection of Oedipal and sibling rivalry tensions.

Finally, let me conclude with an example not from fiction but from fact just to remind readers that projections into the stars always start on earth and are concerned with earthy matters. Certainly, one of the highlights in the life of anyone living in the second half of the twentieth century has to be the lunar landing. It truly represents one of the great triumphs of man and technology. It was a thrill for all those privileged to watch it and to participate in it vicariously. To show how folklore pervades our daily life and also how psychoanalytic thinking can enrich our understanding of that daily life, let us recall what the name of the famous lunar mission was: Apollo. In theory any name could have been chosen, but the actual name selected was Apollo.

According to *Origins of NASA Names* (Wells et al. 1976: 99), Abe Silverstein, Director of Space Flight Development, proposed in July 1960, the name Apollo "because it was the name of a god in ancient Greek mythology with attractive connotations and the precedent for naming manned spaceflight projects for mythological gods and heroes had been set with Mercury. Apollo was god of archery, prophecy, poetry and music, and most significantly he was god of the sun." NASA approved the name and announced "Project Apollo" at a July 28–29 conference.

What the discussion in *Origins of NASA Names* does not allude to is Apollo's relationship to the moon. The goddess of the moon is Artemis or Diana. Apollo and Diana are brother and sister. Apollo is the sun (homonymic with *son* in English) whose goal was to be the first to land on the moon. (Diana is associated with hunting and chastity.) One problem with the rocket launching was to build up enough "thrust" to escape the gravitational pull of (mother) earth. One folklore idiom for masturbatory behavior—to have a rocket in one's pocket—supports this symbolic reading. (Shades of Han(ds) Solo and pinball/video games!) So the son has to get up enough thrust to escape from the attraction of mother earth in order to make it to the moon. The moon has many female images associated with it—it has a cow jumping over it, it is made of green cheese, it has an intrauterine "man in the moon," etc.

On 20 July 1969, the first men landed on the moon. Who was the first man to set foot on the surface of the moon? Armstrong. Curious name for a body extremity. It wasn't simply alphabetical coincidence because by strict alphabetical order it should have been *Aldrin*, which comes before *Armstrong*, who was first. Collins, the third man, did not have a name beginning with A. Millions of fascinated viewers saw the leg emerge from the capsule to take a "giant step for mankind." What is the first thing the astronauts did upon arrival? They erected the flag, as countless generations of explorers had done before them to claim virgin land.

The Apollo program concluded with Apollo 17 in December 1972, after putting twenty-seven men into lunar orbit and twelve of them on the surface of the moon. Who remembers the names of the second group of astronauts to land on the moon? Nobody knows; nobody cares. The moon could be violated only once. What did Armstrong and his cronies bring back with them? Rocks, pieces of moon to show off back on earth, especially to the Russians that we had (masculine) proof of our conquest of lunar space.

One can only wonder what Freud, Abraham, Ricklin, Rank, Jones, and the other pioneers in applying psychoanalytic theory to folklore would have thought of such data. My guess is that they would have thoroughly enjoyed it. I can but echo the final sentence of Freud's letter to Friedrich Krauss written 26 June 1910: "It is therefore safe to hope that the psychological importance of folklore will be more and more clearly recognized, and that the relations between that branch of study and psychoanalysis will soon become more intimate."

2   Heads or Tails

A Psychoanalytic Study of Potlatch

One of the best-known examples of ritual behavior is the institution labeled, rightly or wrongly, *potlatch.* The term allegedly derives either from Chinook jargon meaning "to give" or from a Nootkan word *pa-chitle,* meaning the same thing (Goldman 1975, n.5; Clutesi 1986:9–10). It has been observed somewhat facetiously that this is perhaps the only point of agreement among all the numerous students of potlatch (Drucker and Heizer 1967:8). In any event, this celebrated behavioral complex is reported in various forms from many of the tribes of the Pacific Northwest Coast with cognate forms among tribes as far away as Alaska and northern California. Potlatch has been the subject of a great many essays, and indeed whole books have been devoted to attempts to decipher its function, structure, and meaning. It has intrigued a host of European scholars (e.g., Adam, Bataille, Birket-Smith, Davy, Lenoir, Mauss) as well as a succession of distinguished American anthropologists going back to Franz Boas. Generations of anthropology students who are inevitably exposed to discussions of potlatch in introductory anthropology survey courses, plus the millions of readers of Ruth Benedict's classic *Patterns of Culture* (where it is described at some length), have helped bring the term into standard American English usage and dictionaries. Yet despite all that has been written about potlatch, the fact remains that it is simply not well understood. Even those who have written at length about it are forced to concede that much of its meaning remains obscure.

47

The majority of the would-be explanations of potlatch are framed either in terms of economics or in terms of social structure. A few scholars have sought to comprehend potlatch as a religious phenomenon. Virtually the sole psychological interpretation ventured was that offered by Ruth Benedict, who unfortunately tended to describe the Kwakiutl practitioners of potlatch in rather superficial Freudian terms such as paranoia and megalomania (1946:169, 195). Anthropologists themselves have frequently recognized the inadequacy of their theoretical efforts to explain the rationale of the apparently irrational potlatch behavior, e.g., destroying wealth, i.e., coppers, as a means of shaming a rival. George Peter Murdock's remarks at the beginning of his short monograph *Rank and Potlatch among the Haida,* published in 1936, are still applicable:

> The potlatch of the Northwest coast, though extensively treated in the literature, has always remained something of an ethnological curiosity. Whether viewed in psychological terms as an exaggerated and institutionalized expression of vanity or narcissism, or in economic terms as a disguised form of investment, insurance, or exchange, or even in sociological terms as the conventional road to social recognition and prestige, the seemingly reckless distribution or destruction of property has appeared at best, only partially understandable. To call the potlatch the product of historical accident under unique circumstances does not, of course, dispose of the question; it merely begs it. (1936:3)

Murdock then proceeds to articulate a fivefold Haida potlatch typology in which he distinguishes housebuilding, totem pole, funeral, vengeance, and face-saving types of potlatches. Concern with classification is a well-known academic technique which succeeds in avoiding the more fundamental questions of meaning and significance. Murdock does suggest, however, that the potlatch is functionally a means of establishing and confirming individuals' rank and status in the society. More recently, it has been argued that one did not acquire status through potlatching so much as confirming or validating hereditary status by this ritual means (Drucker and Heizer 1967:134).

In failing to consider the possible symbolic aspects of pot-latch, Murdock was following the Boasian approach to potlatch, and for that matter to anthropology generally. Boas, who consistently refused to speculate about symbolic implications of his rich Northwest Coast data, was very matter-of-fact about what he thought was the significance of potlatch. In his 1895 report, *The Social Organization and Secret Societies of the Kwakiutl Indians,* Boas wrote:

> Before proceeding any further it will be necessary to describe the method of acquiring rank. This is done by means of the potlatch, or the distribution of property. This custom has been described often, but it has been thoroughly misunderstood by most observers. The underlying principle is that of the interest-bearing investment of property. (1897:341; 1966:77)

Although Boas's notion of gift-giving as a culturally sanctioned form of loan-sharking has been largely discredited (e.g., Barnett 1938:353; Goldman 1975:164), the idea that rank or status is validated through displays or distributions of wealth remains the dominant explanation of potlatch (Drucker and Heizer 1967:153; Irvin 1977:75).

It is easy enough to find examples of such explanations. Rosman and Rubel in their paper "The Potlatch; A Structural Analysis," see potlatch as a ritual occurring at "critical junctions which mark the rearrangement of the social structure." The ritual involves "host and guests where the latter serve as witnesses to the statement of the new arrangement of personnel in the structure" (Rosman and Rubel 1972:669). Paul Bohannan in his textbook *Social Anthropology* begins his discussion with this statement: "Occasionally an economy is so bizarre as to seem unexplainable: the potlatch which is one of the most widely known American Indian institutions, seems to be such." He then proceeds to suggest that potlatch can be "quite easily understood when it is seen as hyperdevelopment of conversion" in which large numbers of blankets can be 'converted' into coppers which in turn can be 'converted' into rank and prestige. "The motivation of the individual Kwakiutl," says Bohannan, "then was to get as many blankets as he could, to turn his blankets into coppers, and ultimately to destroy the coppers and turn it all into the purest value: reputation" (Bohannan 1963:253, 258). Bohannan, like most of the proponents of an economic or social structural view, seems merely to *describe* the process rather than explain it.

Economic anthropologists are aware of the difficulties of purely economic explanations. Andrew Vayda, for example, cited a number of specific scholarly views of potlatch as "topsy-turvy, nonadaptive, nonfunctional, absurdly wasteful, and little related to problems of livelihood" (1961:618, 623), but he himself favors a hypothetical notion that potlatch provided for the redistribution of wealth among people who might have suffered temporary scarcity of food. In this he was following Suttles's suggestion that in terms of the total socioeconomic system, the potlatch's "most important function is to be found neither in the expression of the individual's drive for high status nor in the fulfillment of the society's need for solidarity, neither in competition nor in cooperation, but simply in the redistribution of wealth" (Suttles 1960:303), and Piddocke's idea that potlatch encouraged food and wealth sharing to enable "a larger population to live in the Southern Kwakiutl country than would otherwise have lived there" (1965:261). These highly speculative musings have been criticized (cf. Orans 1975). Drucker and Heizer remark, for example: "That these or any other Northwest Coast people lived with the specter of starvation perpetually leering over their shoulders is absurd.... Thus in short, Piddocke's construct of the famine-ridden Kwakiutl does not make sense" (1967:148–149).

But if potlatch cannot be fully explicated in terms of economic principles, how then is it to be understood? Lenoir (1924:260) may have been on the right track when he hinted that the economic function of potlatch, assumed by most scholars to be essential, might only be secondary and perhaps even problematic. Goldman has followed this line of reasoning by claiming:

> It takes little "deep" analysis to discover that "potlatches," even as they deal in "property," even as they bind outsiders into formal exchanges, even as they reflect on the prestige

of chiefs, are basically and decidedly religious actions....
The "potlatch" is a religious phenomenon, a complex ritual involving human relations with other realms of life, in
particular animals and trees. (Goldman 1975:8, 24)

Several writers have argued that the potlatch belongs to an area
lying between religion and economics (Bataille 1967:113; Irvin
1977:75), but this suggestion has not really illuminated the many
details of potlatch ritual.

If the economic and legal contractual elements of potlatch are
but a facade, then it might be reasonable to consider potlatch in
psychological terms. In this context, one should note that Codere's theory of potlatch was derived from early statements made
by informants cited in Boas's reports. According to these informants, potlatch was a substitute for warfare and "fighting with
property" was a less harmful form of aggressive behavior (Boas
1897:343; Codere 1950). Several scholars sophisticated in psychiatry have considered the Kwakiutl (Kardiner 1939:116–121; Róheim 1952; Parker 1964), but Kardiner suggests only that
"Frustration in Kwakiutl culture probably involves cravings for
dependency" (1939:120), while Parker is unable to decide
whether the potlatch and winter ceremonials provide an
adjustive-cathartic outlet and control for aggression, or whether
the potlatch and winter ceremonials themselves contribute to an
increase in interpersonal conflict (Parker 1964:155).

There seems little point in citing additional anthropological
theories of potlatch. Not one of them even attempts to elucidate
such fundamental questions or details as, Why are coppers used?
What is the reason for their shape and form? Whey are they destroyed and in some instances thrown into water? Why was copper thought by the Kwakiutl to have a smell? Why are Kwakiutl
offices embodied in "seats"? How is it that shame can be "wiped
off" one's body by giving a potlatch? Why is it that giving blankets to a tribe was called "swallowing" that tribe? I do not intend to argue that potlatches may not serve as a means of earning
or redistributing wealth, of achieving or validating social status,
but I do mean to suggest that previous general economic and social structural theories do not sufficiently take into account the

metaphorical and symbolic aspects of potlatch. It is one thing to say that potlatches entail fighting with property (Codere); it is quite another to explain why coppers were used rather than any one of a hundred other possible cultural artifacts. And why would the destruction of property (coppers) by one individual shame a rival? No theory is adequate unless it can offer at least some explanation of particular details in the data being considered. I submit that none of the previous theorizing about potlatch has even begun to probe the phenomenon in terms of the total system of Kwakiutl metaphor and symbol. Only the surface or most superficial characteristics of potlatch have been considered, while the symbolic elements have been ignored. Understanding a metaphor literally is one of the bases of riddling and, I believe, this is precisely why potlatch has remained a riddle to anthropologists.

During the same years that Franz Boas was faithfully documenting the potlatch and other cultural features of the Northwest Pacific Coast, Sigmund Freud and his followers began to delineate features of what was termed anal erotic character. Freud's own paper "Character and Anal Eroticism," first published in 1908, suggested that the three traits of being orderly, parsimonious, and obstinate might stem from the sublimation of anal eroticism. Of particular importance was Freud's observation that "money comes into the closest relation with excrement," and it is noteworthy that he supported this symbolic association with folkloristic evidence, e.g., the "superstition which associates the finding of treasure with defecation." Feces is the first present or gift from an infant to a parent. The parent teaches (through toilet training) that the feces is worthless (and should not be retained or handled). But the parent's very concern with the infant's feces also confirms its value. Making a deposit ensures a parent's interest. Other papers extended Freud's initial insight, e.g., Ernest Jones's "Anal-Erotic Character Traits" in 1918, Karl Abraham's "Contributions to the Theory of the Anal Character" in 1921, and William Menninger's "Characterologic and Symptomatic Expressions Related to the Anal Phase of Psychosexual Development" in 1943. Several essays were especially concerned with the symbolism of money, notably Sandor Ferenczi's "The Ontogenesis of the Interest in Money" in 1914, and Otto Fenichel's "The Drive to Amass Wealth" in 1938. The evidence from Indo-European folklore for the connection between feces and money was impressive. Even in contemporary American folk speech, one can hear such expressions as "filthy rich," "to be 'rolling' in it" (referring to someone's being very wealthy), "to make one's pile" and "to have money up the ass." Payday among federal civil service employees and members of the armed forces is referred to colloquially as the day the "eagle shits."

There is no doubt that the anal erotic character is one of the most convincing personality portraits of all those drawn by Freudians. The question is: to what extent, if any, does it apply cross-culturally? The typical objection raised is that the alleged feces-wealth equation is strictly a European one, or perhaps even more narrowly, a Viennese Jewish one with no relevance whatsoever to American Indian or other cultures. Certainly anthropologists have been wary, to say the least, of testing Freudian hypotheses concerning the possibility of cross-cultural symbolism. Psychologists and anthropologists alike, with a few notable exceptions, have little use for Freudian theory. A recent survey of "Cross-cultural Studies and Freudian Theory" remarks at the outset (Kline 1977:51): "We shall straight away admit that it is essentially unscientific because it lacks quantification, fails to distinguish between data and interpretation and employs hypotheses and constructs so vague as to make clear refutation impossible." In the present essay, we are not necessarily concerned with the cross-cultural validity of all Freudian constructs but rather to see if the ones treating so-called anal erotic character can be usefully applied to the Pacific Northwest Coast.

It will obviously not suffice to simply assert that a particular tribe or group of tribes demonstrate anal erotic characteristics. Melville Jacobs, for example, claims that: "Very likely all northwest states people had an intense anal preoccupation" (1959:238). Similarly, Alfred Kroeber remarked that "the anal-type description...seems to agree pretty well with the average or modal personality produced under certain cultures. This holds for instance for the Yurok or native California and their co-tribes of the same culture" (1948:618). One needs concrete ethno-graphic data. Actually, anal themes have been documented among the Yurok (Erikson, Posinsky), the Mohave (Devereux) and the Chippewa (Barnouw 1977:240–243), but the existence of such themes among the Kwakiutl and related peoples, and its possible relevance to potlatch, remain to be demonstrated.

Consider the account of a supernatural figure, "Wealth Woman," from the Tagish who live on the headwaters of the Yukon river. The sound of the crying of Wealth Woman's baby can bring good luck. McClellan reports the following:

> Today Patsy knows just what to do if one hears the crying of Wealth Woman's baby. One strips off all clothing and metal ornaments, throws urine at the woman and seizes her child, refusing to return it until the mother scratches one deeply four times with her golden finger nails and defecates four golden colored balls. These will become pure gold if one first returns the baby to the mother and then carries out proper ritual procedure, e.g., keeps silent about the encounter, fasts and bathes for four days while making special wishes for wealth, etc. (1963:123)

Here we have an explicitly infantile situation involving the equivalence of gold and feces. It is the crying of a baby which signals the possibility of new-found wealth. Removing the baby from the mother makes the mother defecate wealth (in the form of four golden colored balls). This looks very much like a transformation of the proposition that removal of the mother from the baby makes the baby defecate. That is, the baby defecates to bring the mother to it. Feces, the first present or gift, so-to-speak, accomplishes the goal of receiving maternal attention. Baby and mother are reunited through "payment" of fecal offerings. McClellan does not interpret this data psychoanalytically, but notes that Wealth Woman is known in identical form among the Haida and Tsimshian and that she may stem ultimately from the interior rather than the coast: "an ultimately interior origin is suggested by her close association with copper" (1963:124,n.7).

The association of wealth, in the form of copper, with feces is absolutely critical to an understanding of potlatch. A Kwakiutl tale tells of a proud daughter of a chief of high rank who refuses to marry. One day the girl, named "born to be copper-maker woman," stepped on the droppings of a grizzly bear. She complains about the dirty creature having left filth for her to step on. (In other versions of the tale she curses the bear.) Later she is punished for her "bad words against that Grizzly bear." To avoid the difficulties, she is counseled to dig a hole on the beach secretly and to defecate in it. Then covering it well, she is instructed to leave one of her copper rings there. The Grizzly bear people find the ring and say: "It is little wonder she talked so proudly...Her excrement is copper!" (Curtis 1915:273). Even though this tale contains a pseudorationale for the confusion of copper and feces, the symbolic association is explicit. Incidentally, it should be noted that this is no isolated narrative. It is in fact one of the most popular tales told on the Northwest Pacific Coast. Boas listing ten versions (1916:836) called it "The Girl Who Is Taken by the Bear," while more recently McClellan devoted a short monograph (1970) to eleven versions she collected. In a Tlingit version entitled "The Origin of Copper" (Swanton 1908:252-261), it is finally a character named "Garbageman" who pounds out copper and becomes rich. No one ever really explained the appropriateness of the symbolic linkage between garbage or feces, and copper in this tale type.

The principal supernatural figure associated with copper is an undersea being known as "Wealthy" or "Copper-Maker" (Boas 1935a:128, 68). His house, according to one tale, is reached by a canoe passing through "the door of the underworld," a cave through which the tide rushes out (Boas 1935a:129). The door of the *under* world might well be a metaphorical description of the anus. Boas remarks: "In one tale, his house is described as situated west of the ocean and reached by canoe after passing the places to which charcoal, sand, driftwood and toilet sticks go" (1935a:128). This latter detail may well account for a narrative element in another tale in which an individual "obtains copper which drifts ashore attached to a stick" (1935a:69). In another tale (Boas 1910:485), a man goes to the place where his children have drowned and finds a stick with a copper attached. Since "people ease themselves on the bank of a river" (Boas 1935a:27), one can understand how one might encounter sewage floating on the water. Moreover, if copper is symbolic feces, then one can understand how: "A man who is training for power finds a copper plate floating on the water of a pond" (Boas 1935a:68). We are dealing here with fantasy since obviously a copper plate cannot float on water!

The only scholar to have suggested that potlatch had an anal character was Géza Róheim in his review of Helen Codere's *Fighting with Property.* He suggested that "copper and other valuables have the same latent content as gold (money) in our own culture," and that "this is clearly shown by folklore." But his citation of a single version of Bungling Host, in which Raven tries to imitate a small bird's pulling enough fat out of mountain goat's rectum to feed a crowd, is not a very convincing piece of evidence to support his assertion. Raven pulls out blood or excrement rather than fat and is put to shame. It is not at all clear how this tale demonstrates that copper is symbolic feces.

Yet there is evidence in Northwest Coast ethnography that feces signifies wealth or good fortune. For example, Swanton reported the following incident among the Tlingit (1908:454–455): "When people were out halibut fishing and saw a cormorant flying about they said, 'Squeeze your buttocks this way.' Then, after it had shaken itself and defecated, they said, 'It has done so now,' and they expected luck." If copper is symbolic feces, we can understand better the significance of the following Kwakiutl belief (Boas 1932:228): "Copper is a means of putting an end to both lucky and unlucky events. It stays the run of fish, disease and life. Some people claim that the effect of copper is due to its smell." Lucky and unlucky, copper, like feces, is both valueless and valued. Also, like feces, copper is said to have a strong smell.

Coppers can also be equated to menstrual blood. In one Kwakiutl account, a man celebrates his daughter's first menses by giving a potlatch. "My daughter has her monthly, and I am going to give potlatches" (Ford 1941:149). After the coppers are brought,

> he put two of them on the ground in the house and put two
> of them on the back and called his daughter to come out of
> the house and sit on the coppers, and lean her back on the
> others.... He picks up the broken one that is his own and
> told the people that this is the blood of his daughter, that
> he is going to give it to one of the chiefs. (1941:150)

Menstrual blood, like feces, is a form of body discharge and so it
is reasonable that it is equated to a copper in the light of the
present argument. Menstrual blood is also red, the same color as
other Kwakiutl ritual symbols: red cedar bark, salmon, and coppers (cf. McLaren 1978:83).

But simply stating that the Kwakiutl and other tribes from
Alaska to northern California have anal erotic character traits or
that copper is symbolic feces does not really explain the dynamics of potlatch. In order to understand potlatch, I submit
that one must take account of two principles of Kwakiutl worldview. First, the world and all objects in it are perceived to have
heads and tails, or to put it more bluntly, mouths and anuses.
The second principle, clearly related to the first, is that the
mouth (face, head) is highly valued while the anus is not. Power
is achieved by participating in the normal "movement" from
mouth to anus in the manner of food becoming feces. The interruption of the movement can cause harm or dismay to an enemy
or rival. Thus if an enemy is swallowed, he is transformed first
into food and ultimately into the end product, feces. If an enemy
loses his head (literally), he is reduced to being merely an anus,
incapable of participating fully in the life process of moving
from head to tail. If an enemy is forced to vomit, this too interrupts the normal flow. The food initially incorporated is not retained but is rather forced to move in a reverse direction, that is,
backwards up the throat and out of the mouth. Making an enemy vomit, therefore, is to transform his mouth into a pseu-
doanus. Symbolically speaking, in potlatch competitions, the
winner succeeds in reducing his opponent to an anus or to feces
coming out of the winner's anus.

Let us consider the first principle. In the Kwakiutl metaphorical system of perceiving the world, a wide variety of objects were considered to have heads and tails. For example, if rivers, inlets or other similar *bodies* of water had mouths in Kwakiutl thought, they also had "hind ends," as Boas decorously phrased it in his extensive compilation of *Geographical Names of the Kwakiutl Indians.* The root is "!xsd," hind end (Boas 1934:14). One finds numerous examples of "forehead beach" and "beach at hind end" (1935:45–46). This psychogeographical data supports the thesis that the Kwakiutl transferred the human body's conversion of food into feces to the world at large. Canoes were also said to have rear or hind ends. (Boas 1966:21). In one tale, one man in a canoe is said to have "struck the cheek" of another canoe, meaning one of the sides of the bow (Boas 1935b:59). Even fishing nets had similar denominations for their parts. Boas (1909:466) reported that among the Kwakiutl: "The various parts of the net are called by the Indians 'the mouth of the net'. . . and the end, finally, 'the tail of the net.'" In like fashion, the final portion of a song was called the "tail" (Curtis 1915:171).

If objects were indeed perceived metaphorically to have heads and tails, then it should come as no great surprise to learn that coppers exemplified the very same patterning. Even if coppers were a late addition to Kwakiutl culture from European sources, as some scholars claim (cf. Richard 1939, and Couture and Edwards 1964), they were clearly made to fit into a preexisting cultural configuration. Boas specifically says that the top part of the famous coppers used in the potlatch was called "the face" and the lower part the "hind end" (Boas 1897:344; 1966:82), and it is not that difficult to see the lower part of coppers with its typical linear ridge down the middle as a relatively straightforward symbolic representation of the buttocks area. (For excellent photographs of a variety of coppers, see Keithahn 1964.) We might note that Goldman was correct when he reminded us (1975:84) that: "The copper is like a person. It has a human torso shape. Its upper section is considered the head and face." But he is definitely mistaken when he says "the longer lower section" is "the body." It is not the body so much as the buttocks! And this is significant in the light of the underlying dynamics of potlatch.

We should now consider the second principle, for the point is not simply that the Kwakiutl world consisted of objects having heads and tails, but rather that the world, like Kwakiutl society itself, was ranked. In terms of body imagery, head is high status while buttocks is low. In the division of whales, for instance, one began by cutting at the head for chiefs, and proceeding to cut away from the head towards the tail for people in order of their rank (Codere 1957:481). Similarly, only chiefs eat the "plucked cheeks," so-called from the head of the dog-salmon, while the poor people eat the pectoral fins, anal fins, and tails (Boas 1921:329). Goldman discusses the same social ranking pattern.

> Among the Kwakiutl, the chief is called *gyigame,* which means literally 'being in front.' *Gyiu* refers to the prow of a canoe and to the forehead. Thus the seniors are in the forefront. The imagery of chiefs as the heads, as the forward parts of the body, is repeated in the ritual distribution of an animal at a feast. The front is reserved for high chiefs, the middle section for lower chiefs, and the hind quarters and tail for the common people. (1975:49–50)

For example, in the distribution of a seal, Boas reports (1921:750–751) "they have given the tail of the seal to people lowest in rank." We have already noted that patterning in canoe terms. The Kwakiutl word for a canoe's stern, *o'qtle,* derives, according to Boas (1893:76), from the root *qtle,* meaning 'hind part.' In the same way, social order is perceived in terms of heads and tails. Thus the youngest son, that is, the last born son, is in Kwakiutl *wala'qtle,* from -*qtle* meaning 'hind' (Boas 1893:46, 75). The perception of birth order in terms of heads and tails is also signalled in a custom connected with twins. According to Boas, as soon as a woman gives birth to twins, the name of her elder or preceding child is changed to Salmon-Head. If the preceding child is a girl, the name becomes Salmon-Head Woman (1921:681–682). In contrast, the next child to be born to a mother of twins is given the name of Salmon-Tail if it is a boy, Salmon-Tail Woman if it is a girl (1921:692).

Even the dishes used in feasting are subject to the same patterning principle. One of Drucker's key informants, Ed Whonnuck, drew attention to this important metaphorical feature in Kwakiutl culture when he observed, "Feasts cause lots of problems; sometimes I think they are more difficult than potlatches. Take my tsonoqua dish, for example, I have to be careful how I seat the chiefs to eat from it, because no one wants to eat from the hind end" (Drucker and Heizer 1967:123–124). I suggest that this might explain why so many serving dishes in the Northwest Pacific Coast often took the form of two-headed animals. With dishes having heads at both ends, no one would have to suffer the indignity of being served from a dish's hind end, so to speak.

The possible rationale behind two-headed serving dishes may well also be applicable to the celebrated *Sisiutl* or double-headed serpent so prominent in Northwest Coast art (Boas 1935a:146–148). Boas translates *Sisiutl* as meaning 'mouth at each end' (1893:68, 73). It is interesting in this connection to speculate about the phonetic similarity of the Kwakiutl words for mouth, *qstē* and for anus, *qstēe* (Boas 1893:37, 63). In any case, this hypothetical interpretation of the double-headed serpent as a denial of the anus might explain why the mere sight of the serpent could cause severe body contortions (Boas 1930:75, 81, 88, 91). An individual without an anus might very well feel sufficient bodily discomfort to make him writhe in considerable pain. To my knowledge, no one has ever offered an explanation for the rationale underlying the Sisiutl's possessing two heads. But in Kwakiutl culture where so many objects are explicitly perceived as having both a head and a tail, and since snakes in reality do have both a head and a tail, it is quite reasonable to assume that the double-headed serpent could represent a fantastic denial of the anus. The Sisiutl is a supernatural figure who is literally all head and no tail.

Armed with this facet of Kwakiutl metaphorical thought, we can now consider another important feature of potlatch ritual: swallowing. The symbolic association of the digestive act to potlatch was made explicit by Boas in his interesting report on ritual questioning during the Kwakiutl Winter Ceremonial (1897:558; 1966:192). References to defecating or vomiting wealth confirm that the contents of the stomach or intestine were highly valued. In the ritual, a leader asks each participant, "What is in your stomach?" The answers were "Kwakiutl," "Four Tribes," meaning the four tribes of the Kwakiutl, and "The Kwakiutl, the Koskimo, and all other tribes." Then Boas reported as follows: "When he asked the next one, he acted as though he was vomiting. This means that he was vomiting the property that was to be distributed at night. The fifth one said to the speaker that he had gone from tribe to tribe through the whole world swallowing the tribes." Boas in an explanatory footnote (1897:559,n.1) offers: "That means giving away blankets. When blankets are given to a tribe, it is called swallowing the tribe." I am not aware that any of the various theoretical explanations of the potlatch offered in the past one hundred years have shed any light on this metaphor. Curtis (1915:239) did report one Kwakiutl's name as meaning "constantly eating, that is, destroying and distributing property," but this merely confirms that eating property is consciously understood by the Kwakiutl as a metaphor for destroying and distributing property. Postal in her fascinating comparison of body-images among the Kwakiutl and Hopi does identify "incorporation" as a motif in Kwakiutl culture (1965:458; cf. McLaren 1978:84), but she does not relate it to potlatch. She suggests that one theme in Kwakiutl culture involves the failure to retain what is incorporated. She claims that many Kwakiutl tales mention "the running of things from mouth to anus" with strong disapproval, citing specifically the tale in which Wren insults Grizzly Bear by saying: "You ugly hollow stomach, you ugly one whose food goes from end to end." Grizzly Bear swallows Wren, but: "Wren just went from end to end through the intestines of Grizzly Bear and jumped out his anus" (Boas 1935b:20–21). One cannot help but recall a detail of the Kwakiutl Winter Ceremonial in which one dancer "pretends to be the rectum of the Grizzly Bear" while the head Sparrow is named "All-Excrement" (Boas 1930:100). The tale of a bird flying from mouth to anus is also found among the Yurok, where in one version (Erikson 1943:286) it ends with the explanatory: "That's why the bear has such a big anus and can't hold his feces." In a Bella Coola version (McIlwraith 1948:430), Grizzly Bear tries to block Winter Wren's exit by plugging up his anus, but the wren makes a fire in Grizzly Bear's stomach. "Then he removed the plug from the anus and flew away." The "end-to-end" metaphor also occurs in other Kwakiutl contexts. For example, in one tale, a protagonists's younger brother constructs a house of cedar-sticks, which Boas explains in a footnote (Boas and Hunt 1908:192,n.1) are: "Small cedar sticks used in place of toilet paper." When the house made of toilet-sticks was finished, "it had the name Wind-blowing-from-End-to-End and Face-out-of-Sight" (Boas and Hunt 1908:193, cf. Boas 1935b:1). I believe Postal may have overemphasized the oral incorporative act or rather underestimated the significance of the anal excretory act. The triumph of Wren is that he foils Grizzly Bear's attempt to (literally) incorporate him. Wren does not remain incorporated, but instead he forces the Bear to defecate against his will.

From the present psychoanalytic perspective, the potlatch host is reducing his rivals to feces by swallowing them. By swallowing them, he has in effect "eliminated" them (cf. Erikson, 1943:296,n.10). Swallowing was almost certainly a metaphor for aggressive behavior. A particularly warlike group of Kwakiutl, the Lekwiltok, enjoyed a great reputation for ferocity, and they exacted tolls from canoes which passed through their waters. According to Curtis (1915:105): "As one old man expressed it, 'they were like a great mouth, always open to swallow whatever attempted to pass.'" Boas reported that it was considered bad manners among the Kwakiutl to open the mouth wide (1909:423, 427). This would be consistent with the idea that opening the mouth was perceived as an aggressive act. The swallowing metaphor also occurs in the naming of baskets used in berry-picking. The largest basket is called a "swallowing basket," and when the smaller basket is filled with crabapples, currants, or salal-berries, it is dumped into the swallowing basket (Boas 1921:205–206, 208, 216).

Another illustration of the swallowing metaphor is found in the Kwakiutl symbolism surrounding the house. The Kwakiutl speak of the body as the "house of the soul" (Boas 1921:724; cf. Goldman 1975:64). In terms of the house-body equation, we note the following report (Curtis 1915:8, 264n.): "In the fantastically figurative thought of the Kwakiutl the house is represented as a face with the door a great mouth ready to swallow the guests of the master." Boas (1935a:2) remarked: "The door of the house is often described as the mouth of an animal or monster." It may be that the house represented only the head of a body, e.g., Boas reports that "the rear of the house is called its 'forehead' (1909:415), but if the dwelling can be construed as a symbolic body, then it may be relevant that among the Tlingit, the corpse is placed at the back wall of the house and eventually removed through the back wall (Krause 1956:157). In another account of Tlingit ritual, "the corpse is hoisted out through the smoke hole" (Olson 1967:59). If the smoke-hole were a symbolic anus, then it might be noteworthy that the Kwakiutl claimed that the word *Kwakiutl* meant "smoke of the world" (Boas 1897:330). It would be perfectly appropriate that a people so concerned with wealth would believe their very name derived from a waste product. Boas (1897:330,n.1), however, dismisses the conjecture as folk etymology. Folk etymologies nevertheless, despite their philological inadequacies, may provide important clues for students of symbolism. In any event, the Tlingit death custom is suggestive. Death and feces are both end products of living, and so one might suggest that the corpse is in effect defecated out of the back of the house (or excreted through the smoke-hole). In Nootka potlatch ritual, a chief giving a potlatch might receive material assistance from tenants as well as kinsmen. Drucker reports (1951:381): "When one of the chief's tenants had some property, he would often 'give it to the rear of the house.'" Of interest here is the notion that the property is given to or amassed metaphorically by the rear of the house from where it will be given out (excreted?).

Boas (1935a:27) notes a tale in which people ease themselves "on the side of a hill so that the excreta fall on the roof of a small house of a despised member of the tribe." If the door of a house is a mouth, then the roof might well represent the top of the head. Thus to defecate upon a despised person's roof would be analogous to defecating upon his head. In another Kwakiutl tale, one individual complains, ". . . we are no longer men. . . . Only dirt is thrown upon us by our tribe.. We are not men now. Nothing, we are the poorest. We have for our firewood toilet sticks that were thrown away" (Boas 1935b:179). Men having to use the equivalent of used toilet paper as fuel are clearly demeaned. The dumping of feces (or wealth) upon a rival to humiliate or embarrass him is essentially what we are suggesting lies at the heart of the potlatch ritual. In one potlatch song, the singer says it makes him laugh to see little, insignificant individuals who "always rush up to my face, the little ones who rush against (?) (pieces of copper) thrown against my chief here" (Boas 1921:1284).

If A can conquer B by orally incorporating him, it is also true that A can embarrass B by forcing him to vomit, that is, to reverse B's normal oral incorporation process. Forcing a rival to vomit is in fact part of potlatch strategy. The idea is "to set before the guests so much that all cannot possibly be eaten and the chiefs of the rival gens (or tribe), in their efforts to avoid the disgrace of leaving food and thus acknowledging the wealth and power of their host, may incur lasting disgrace by vomiting in the feast" (Curtis 1915:153). Boas (1897:356) reports a Kwakiutl potlatch song which includes the host's exhortation against the rival: "...give him plenty to eat, make him drink until he will be qualmish and vomits." Other Kwakiutl feasting songs include such lines as: "It is only said he made them vomit" and "Let your guest die of vomiting, chief!" (Boas 1921:1293–1294). If one makes one's rivals vomit, this reverses the normal alimentary direction and dooms the rivals' would-be incorporation to failure.

Erikson in his analysis of Yurok worldview coined the term "double-vector situations" to describe significant direction reversals. By this he meant "configurations in which an object entering a canal turns around and leaves it and by doing so creates a magic event of either beneficial or dangerous character" (1943:263-264). He notes that: "With respect both to vomiting and to sorcery, it is the one-way flow through the nutritional tube which is obstructed or averted" (1943:300). I believe this direction reversal notion is also applicable to Northwest Coast cultures.

The tubular view can also be relevant to folk theories of childbirth, particularly with respect to the proper exit. Snyder reports (1964:192) that

> the Skagit believed that anal deliveries were possible in women and viewed them with horror, as they did all unnec-

essary contacts with the anus and fecal matter. Deliveries in which there was tearing of the perineum may have appeared to them as being through the anus. In any case, births like those were shameful to mother and child. Possibly, they suggested anal intercourse, which...Skagits may have believed causal to pregnancy in both sexes. Informants were unable to tell about persons though, who were disgraced by such accidents, since a precaution was always taken against them. This was having the mother during labor sit on a woven cedar-bark pillow which was provided with a projecting knob, a sort of plug, that was slipped into the anus, thus forcing delivery through the proper channel.

Among the Yurok, Erikson reported: "During birth, the mother, who is lying on her back and bracing her feet against an assistant, must shut her mouth; this makes it easier for the child to pass the vagina: apparently another manifestation of the tube configuration" (1943:284). Presumably, closing the mouth meant the only exit was the vagina (or anus). This same directionality theme may also be reflected in the Kwakiutl custom governing the father-to-be's behavior. "During the whole period of labor, her husband must walk from house to house, entering slowly through the rear door, and going out quickly through the front door." Perhaps metaphorically through homeopathic magic, the husband is trying to guard against the child's coming out the wrong exit, that is, the anus. (Boas 1966:361).

Once one understands the importance of one-way directionality through the alimentary and other canals, one can comprehend the underlying logic of hostile attempts to obstruct or reverse the path. A mode of punishment allegedly practiced by a secret society among the Lummi of northwest Washington illustrates one means of producing such a reversal. Erring members of the society were punished as follows: "A long green stick is heated in the fire and forced up the victim's rectum all the way to his throat forcing blood and flesh to come out of his mouth" (Stern 1934:86).

A more common means of preventing an enemy from oral incorporative acts, leading to the desired one-way directionality, is the removal of his head. This may help explain the custom of taking the heads of slain enemies. The Kwakiutl were headhunters (Curtis 1915:98). By taking an enemy's head, one has reduced that enemy to an anus. The enemy cannot incorporate any more since his head (and mouth) have been removed. Boas (1897) reported that slaves were formerly killed in potlatches, and buried under house posts or totem poles. Later they were given as presents rather than being killed. "Whenever this was done, the inverted figure of a man or an inverted head was placed on the pole" (1897:357). This might represent the inversion process with the head becoming a tail, so to speak.

The idea that potlatch ritual might be analogous to attacking one's rival's head is explicit in at least one account. Curtis, in his remarkably detailed 1915 account of the Kwakiutl, criticizes the simplistic notion of the potlatch as a form of economic investment. Referring to Boas's earlier theorizing, Curtis observed: "It has been said of the potlatch that 'the underlying principle is that of the interest-bearing investment of property.' This is impossible. A Kwakiutl would subject himself to ridicule by demanding interest when he received a gift in requital of one of like amount made by him. Not infrequently at a potlatch a guest calls attention to the fact that he is not receiving as much as he in his last potlatch gave the present host; and he refuses to accept anything less than the proper amount. Even this action is likened to 'cutting off one's own head,' and results in loss of prestige" (Curtis, 1915:143). If cutting off one's own head means a loss of prestige, then it follows that cutting off the enemy's head means a loss of prestige for the enemy. In this context, it may be worth noting several of what Boas refers to as swear words (which we would probably nowadays term slurs or insults). One example is: "Your head has been cut off," while the retort to this is: "You are a body without a head" (1921:794). Similarly, among the Haisla, Olson (1954:222) notes that a person may jokingly swear at another by calling him "big rectum."

If we are correct in our contention that the alimentary tract provides a fundamental metaphor for Northwest Pacific Coast interpersonal relations, including those involved in potlatch ritual, then we would expect to see evidences of this symbolism throughout the cultures in question. And in fact we find such data. A striking anal erotic ritual reported among the Nootka by an informant in 1921 is related by Sapir without comment. According to the informant, a group of boys began to dance in a circle around a fire after singing such songs as: "Let the anus be sticking in the eye of the little old people." Following instructions given in a series of song lines, the boys proceeded to stand up straight, bend over, place their hands on their buttocks, pull their buttocks apart, point at their buttocks, insert their index fingers into their buttocks, smell their fingers, and finally put their index fingers into their mouths. "Some of the gullible children really insert their fingers into their mouth, but others are afraid because their fingers smell of dung" (Sapir and Swadesh 1955:38). Presumably, the gullible ones are duped into reversing the normal "food-into-feces" process. They are shamed by acting as though feces were food.

An interesting confirmation of the ritual role of vomiting in a contest situation is provided by a detailed Kwakiutl account of a lunar eclipse (Curtis 1915:63; cf. Boas 1930:179). It was believed that some creature first swallowed the moon and later disgorged it. Here is the account:

> About the year 1900, an eclipse of the moon was visible at Fort Rupert, and Pawili, the oldest man of the village, was aroused. "Is it all swallowed?" he inquired. They said it was not, and he declared: "Then I will make him vomit it!" He ran outside where all the people had assembled, ordered them to build a fire, and each person to throw into it some portion of his clothing or hair. Then he began to sing over and over, while the people, as they caught the air, joined in: "Vomit it, vomit it, or else you will be the younger brother of Pawili!" The old man danced slowly around the fire. After a while he called, "Is he vomiting it?" When the moon reappeared, he said proudly: "I made him vomit it! Now he is still my elder brother."

The usage of younger and elder brother in connection with vomiting in this account strongly suggests sibling rivalry. The creature who swallowed the moon is told to vomit it, to give it up, or else he/it will be the younger brother. It is presumably only the younger sibling rival who is allowed to keep down what he has eaten. The older sibling has to give up what he once swallowed in favor of the younger nursling. In the above account, Pawili takes credit for making the creature vomit the moon; thus the creature is Pawili's *elder* brother. In terms of potlatch rivalry, one may recall that sometimes the person honored in a potlatch assumes a *new* title or name. In other words, he makes others vomit or give it up.

Perhaps the most fascinating ritual parallel to the notion that the ideal movement is from mouth to anus, without being interrupted or blocked, is found in the Kwakiutl Winter Ceremonial. In his discussion of the Winter Ceremonial, Boas notes a distinction between "winter-ceremonial-that-does-pass-through" and "winter-ceremonial-that-does-not-pass-through." He explains in a note (1930:180,n.2) that the terms have reference to the mythical house in which novices are supposed to be initiated. The "going through" ceremonial involves passing through the door of the house and into it; the "not-passing through" stays on this side of the door and does not pass through the door into the house. Maybe it is only coincidence that the leader who owns the "privilege of getting the eagle down of the supernatural power of the winter-ceremonial-that-does-*not*-pass through" is named "Closed-up Backside"! (Boas 1930:149). With respect to the latter name, it may also be relevant to remark the great frequency of Kwakiutl folk medicines which serves as laxatives, e.g., water hemlock, yellow dock root, etc. (Boas 1930:210–213, 222, 228-229).

We may now turn to one of the Kwakiutl words used to refer to potlatch. Codere states that the usual word for potlatch was *p!Esa,* to flatten, and that it came to mean to flatten a rival under a pile of blankets or "means of flattening" (1950:120, cf. Curtis 1915:142; Boas 1935a:40). However, Goldman, in a study notable for its praiseworthy concern for the nuances of Kwakiutl metaphor, suggests that *pasa* means to flatten a soft basket from which objects had been removed (1975:133). He goes on further to say that *pasa* introduces a concept of self-divestment, of emptying out in behalf of a name, the contrary of flattening an opponent. This would seem to strongly imply an emptying or a sense of evacuation. In this context, we can now understand in a new way the possible significance of a particular copper being named "to clean everything out of the house" (Ford 1941:169; Codere 1950:73). The potlatch ritual is thus not fighting with property but rather fighting with feces. The person who can give away or destroy the most "property" (or divest himself of it) demonstrates the most prestige. To prove one has taken in (orally) the most, one must defecate the most. The destruction of property, e.g., a copper, is the ultimate demonstration in Kwakiutl culture of wasting wealth.

Feces can represent good luck and thus the act of defecating can be construed as a good luck producing act. If this is so, then it follows that withholding feces would be an act likely to produce bad luck. If wealth and property are symbolically equivalent to feces, then distributing or spending would bring good luck while holding back or being miserly would cause bad luck. In northern Tlingit funerary ritual: "Every bit must be given away, since this is the only way in which the dead can receive its benefit in the spirit world. Should any of the collected goods be withheld, the host sib will suffer 'bad luck'" (McClellan 1954:81). Failure to spend can cause a loss of social position. Among the northern Tlingit, even inherited high position can be "lost through niggardly ceremonial participation" (McClellan 1954:93). Among the Nootka, generosity was valued and a "niggardly individual was looked down on" (Drucker 1951:322). The Nootka also say: "A chief who is stingy is laughed at" (Sapir and Swadesh 1955:334). Similarly, among the Bella Coola (McIlwraith 1948:I:190): "A chief must never appear stingy."

The fecal underpinnings of wealth explain why wealth can be both bad/valueless and good/valuable at the same time. Feces is a waste product, but parents reward the infant's act of presenting it, especially if it is disposed of properly. We can now offer an explanation of a problem noted by Goldman (1975:78) when he observed that the Kwakiutl word for the material property given in potlatches was referred to in the texts as *yaklelwas,* a term translated, by Boas's faithful coworker George Hunt, as "bad things" (cf. Boas 1925:291,n.1, 343,n.1). Goldman bothered to say: "The term has not been explicated, and Boas did not speculate as to the sense in which these valuable are to be considered as 'bad.'" Goldman in his interesting compilation of words derived from the root *yaq* or *yak* or *yax* (1975:245,n.6), includes *yaq,* (to distribute); *yaqwas,* (give away); *yaxwede,* (give away property); *yaq,* (to lie dead); *yaq,* (dead body); and *yak,* (bad); but he neglected to include *yaxyegil,* (intestines) (Boas 1921:1393). How can the same root refer to property, dead body, distributing, bad, and intestines? Feces and death, as noted previously, are both end products of living. Feces is given to a parent by an infant, but its value (to the parent as perceived by the infant) lies in its being given away or given up. The parent indicates that it is bad material, from the intestines, but that he or she apparently values receiving it!

One may ask, in the absence of comprehensive ethnographic data on toilet training among the Kwakiutl and other Northwest Coast peoples, how one may know how parents felt about infant defecation. There is admittedly only indirect evidence. Before the turn of the twentieth century, Deans, an early observer of the potlatch, commented: "It has been from remote ages the custom of our aborigines, at least those living near the northern coasts, to at first give their children filthy names, which they could not be otherwise than ashamed of in riper years, and endeavor by all means to obtain a better one" (1896:329). It is a great pity that Deans failed to cite any specific examples. De Laguna, in describing Tlingit infants' pet names and nicknames, does report that typical examples include "Stinker" and "stinking little girl" (1972:787). The custom of giving infants "dirty" names may very well be relevant to the potlatch insofar as one typical occasion for a potlatch was the bestowing of a new name. Nootka informants said, for example: "It gave a good name to potlatch," meaning that it gave one honor and a good reputation (Drucker 1951:377). A recent book-length study of the potlatch was in fact entitled: *To Make My Name Good"* (Drucker and Heizer 1967). If potlatching provides a means for making one's name good, it would seem to imply that without a potlatch, one's name might be bad.

The scatological tenor of joking names is also found in the

play potlatch tradition. Codere reports that Boas was given the play potlatch name of "Where-the-southeast-wind-comes-from," which alludes to the foul smell of the wind in question. The folk explanation for the smell is contained in a Kwakiutl narrative in which the owner of the wind causes it by constantly breaking wind (Codere 1956:344). Boas (1935a:27, 140) observes: "The flatus of the Southeast Wind is so strong that nobody can endure it. It blows out of the door of his house." The imagery pattern is no doubt related to the Kwakiutl "Prayer When Overtaken at Sea by a Gale," which begins: "Stoop down on the sea for me, Summer-Woman, our dung on the sea, Summer-Woman, our bad smell on the sea, Summer-Woman" (1930:183). Boas, characteristically, offers no explanation, but perhaps the logic is that an act of supernatural defecation will end the passage of dangerous wind, that is, the gale.

If one assumes that shame may have been employed by parents to toilet train infants, then one can understand the curious repeated references in Northwest Coast ethnography to wiping away shame by potlatching, by giving. It is the strikingly consistent usage of the English word *wipe,* which is encountered in nearly every ethnographic account of potlatch, that I think may be relevant. Boas in his essay "Metaphorical Expression in the Language of the Kwakiutl Indians" noted that: "A name given during a potlatch is fastened to its owner. A person who is ashamed 'wipes off (the shame) from his body' by giving a potlatch" (1940:239). Most of the scholars writing about potlatch do specifically refer to the "wiping" metaphor, but they fail to offer any comment whatsoever on it. Birket-Smith, for example, observes (1964:7) that "if a man was insulted or suffered from a stroke of bad luck, it was a disgrace that could only be wiped off by giving a potlatch." Among the northern Tlingit, high ranking individuals considered potlatch for "wiping off a 'shame' such as a physical blemish or awkward incident..." (McClellan 1954:78). Murdock in describing Haida potlatching remarks: "The object of the potlatch seems, consequently, not too much to take vengeance against an opponent as to wipe out a slight and uphold the prestige of the donor" (1936:15). But what is the logic or rationale behind the notion of wiping away shame *from one's body?* Ruth Benedict, in her classic description of the Kwakiutl in *Patterns of Culture,* used the same wiping verbiage:

> All accidents were occasions upon which one was shamed. A man whose axe slipped so that his foot was injured had immediately to wipe out the shame which had been put upon him. A man whose canoe had capsized had similarly to "wipe his body" of the insult. People must at all costs be prevented from laughing at the incident. The universal means to which they resorted was, of course, the distribution of property. It removed the shame; that is, it reestablished again the sentiment of superiority which their culture associated with potlatching. (1946:190)

(For the canoe capsizing incident, for which a potlatch was used to wipe off the shame, see Boas 1925:133). If the infantile prototype of shame were the fecal soiling of self, then it would make perfect sense to speak of "wiping" away the shame. And if the shame can be wiped off by giving a potlatch, then in some sense giving a potlatch must represent in symbolic form a means of ridding oneself of feces.

The idea that shame can refer both to an embarrassing situation or feces can be found in other cultures, that is, non-Northwest Coast cultures. For example, in Papua New Guinea, shame at being caught in a culpable act or in not having fulfilled obligations or *in having been observed in the act of defecating* is referred to as being shame "on the skin" (Strathern 1975). The equivalence of shame with anality is also signaled in Kwakiutl metaphor. Boas in his account of the Winter Ceremonial tells how an individual defeats the Wolves by displaying the double-headed serpent (which we have earlier suggested may represent a symbolic denial of the anus). Seeing the double-headed serpent causes severe body contortion. The Wolves were defeated and "for shame they went into the woods and they really became wolves after this." An explanatory note for the wolves' defeat says: "Literally: to pass off wind. In the winter ceremonial any mishap or mistake (which is considered shameful) is so called" (Boas 1930:81,n.2). (Although Boas shied away from symbolic

interpretation, it is greatly to his credit that his excellent ethnographic glosses and footnotes provided the necessary data for the
present interpretation.) In other words, any mistake in the conduct of the ritual was termed metaphorically passing wind. This
surely suggests that the Kwakiutl tended to define embarrassment or mistake in anal erotic terms. If mistakes are anal acts,
then they certainly could be appropriately atoned for or removed
by a ritual act of wiping off the body. If the potlatch constitutes
such a ritual means of wiping off shame, then in some sense the
potlatch must represent the elimination of feces. This is why the
destruction of property in general, and coppers in particular,
makes sense. It is making waste and giving it to one's rivals. One
gets rid of one's shame by shaming someone else.

Giving a potlatch may provide a means of wiping away shame,
but it is also clear that giving potlatch creates shame. Lines from
a Kwakiutl song declare: "Shame is caused by the large amount
of this great potlatch of our chief, tribes," and "I am the great
chief who makes people ashamed" (Boas 1921:1289, 1291). Other
lines say: "Our chief brings shame to the faces...Our chief
makes people cover their faces...Only at those who continue to
turn around in this world, working hard, losing their tails (like
salmon) I sneer..." (Boas 1921:1291). One shames one's rival
by swallowing him (and thus metaphorically transforming him
into feces) and/or by completing an unsurpassable anal act.
Boas reported:

> The rivalry between chiefs and clans finds its strongest ex-
> pression in the destruction of property. A chief will burn
> blankets, a canoe, or break a copper, thus indicating his
> disregard of the amount of property destroyed and showing
> that his mind is stronger, his power greater than that of his
> rival. If the latter is not able to destroy an equal amount of
> property without much delay, his name is "broken."
> (1897:353-354)

In Anglo-American equivalent slang, we might say the defeated
individual's name is "mud," an obvious fecal substitute.

Are we justified in claiming that potlatch ritual represents, in symbolic form, an alimentary metaphor in which the preferred movement is from head to tail? The notion is not so different from what scholars have suggested in other related cultures. Among the Skagit, Snyder has observed an eqiuvalence of anality and orality. "Symbolically, feces equaled foods, clearly expressed in several of the Skagit myths" (1975:159). And she refers to a system, apparently comparable to the one attributed to the Yurok by Erikson, in which the two zones, anal and oral, are part of one overall alimentary complex. Farfetched as some may find the idea, the metaphorical equivalence of potlatch ritual to the natural transformation of food into feces is almost explicit if one reads the ethnographic record carefully. From the Bella Coola we learn that: "After a fourth potlatch a man is accorded a position of eminence, and is termed a *numitl* chief. *Numitl* is an untranslatable word with the significance of 'passage,' an allusion to the amount of goods which have passed through his hands. Jealous and vulgar-minded persons pun on the word applying it to the digestive tract" (McIlwraith 1948:I:173-174). In a Bella Coola glossary, *numitl* is defined as 1—A passage, especially the digestive tract. 2—Laudatory adjective applied to chiefs, referring to goods distributed. (McIlwraith 1948:II:597). What the Bella Coola have said in jest, we say in earnest.

In terms of the relevance of the metaphorical equation to potlatch, I suggest it is incorporation which is highly valued. As a guest, one obtains prestige and rank in the potlatch according to how much wealth one is given. Thus the more one incorporates, the more status he has. But the ultimate proof of how much one has incorporated is how much one defecates. The more one defecates, the more one has obviously incorporated. Thus giving a potlatch provides the most prestige. The more one gives away (defecates), the more prestige he obtains. This is why the last resort of competitive potlatching is to destroy or waste an object, e.g., a famous copper. To break a copper and perhaps throw it in the water is supposedly a symbolic act intended to shame a rival. No one has hitherto, to my knowledge, offered an explanation of why the broken coppers are specifically *thrown into water* as a final act of destroying or wasting wealth. Economic theorists cannot claim that this is an instance of distributing or redistributing wealth. Rather it is an act of destruction. But I would argue that to make waste is precisely the symbolic code involved. Throwing the broken copper into the water might well be analogous to depositing waste (feces) in water. (Even in Anglo-American culture, we have the notion of a big spender trying to make a big splash!) Thus one can "waste" a rival, to use current American slang, by breaking one's copper. And there is a logic underlying Kwakiutl copper-o-philia!

Another illustration in Kwakiutl culture of how one proves what one has incorporated by either defecating or vomiting is found in an account of supposed ritual cannibalism. A hamatsa ate or pretended to eat human flesh, including the skin. Curtis reported the following:

> The hamatsas do not vomit the pieces of skin. Men have told me that they cannot disgorge them, no matter how much water is drunk and vomited. The number of pieces swallowed is carefully counted, and the excrement is examined to see that the full number is voided. Men say that after swallowing the pieces, there is great pain in defecating. Each piece passes separately, but only after the exertion of the greatest effort, and it is accompanied by blood and the sensation of red-hot iron passing through the rectum. While the pieces are in the stomach there is considerable pain, for they lie in a compact mass. (1915:228)

Whether or not such cannibalistic rituals actually occurred, the fact that informants recounted such details to Curtis is itself of ethnographic interest. The account is slightly reminiscent of a narrative, cited by Boas (1897:364), in which a cannibalistic suitor is forced to vomit to show the bones of all the previous suitors he had eaten. Comparing the count of pieces swallowed with pieces excreted does suggest a numerical concern, which is also obviously found in potlatch ritual in which gifts received (swallowed) must later be returned (vomited, excreted).

A facet of Kwakiutl potlatch ritual not yet considered concerns the notions that power or rank are embodied in "seats" (Curtis 1915:137–138; Boas 1897:339; Rosman and Rubel

1972:665). To my knowledge, no one has offered any explanation why Kwakiutl offices should be centered in seats. Among the Kwakiutl, Curtis (1915:138) tells us: "Ordinarily a man does not transfer his most important name to his heir and step aside in his favor, but retains his own place until death; but he may give his principal seat to his son when the young man has reached an age of about thirty-five years; and himself step down to a position 'at the tail.'" In the fall of 1876, the Reverend M. Eells observed a potlatch on a Skohomish reservation, and he remarked that two rows of men with each row twenty-five feet long faced each other and the men were sitting down, "a very unusual form for men, as they almost always stood, though it was a common form for the women" (1883:143). In the conduct of a Nootka potlatch, the host announced through his speaker a number of salient facts, e.g., the person and occasion being honored by the potlatch, how much wealth was being given away and the source of that wealth. He might, for example, indicate how much "came from his potlatch seat" (had been given to him in potlatches), (Drucker 1951:379). The idea that the source of wealth was a "potlatch seat" would certainly not be incompatible with an anal erotic interpretation of the ritual. Among the Haida, Murdock reported the following: "When the children had returned to their places, the hostess called back her son, as well as two of her husband's nephews, and they all retired behind the curtain. Here her husband made his son sit on a large 'copper' which his nephews lifted upon their shoulders. The curtain was then thrown open, and all the Eagles applauded while the nephews marched back and forth with their burden, followed by the proud parents. When the applause ceased, the procession stopped, and the host explained to the assembled people that he was bestowing upon his son the name of his father, who had been cradled in a 'copper' the day after his birth" (1936:10). From the present perspective, sitting on a copper is sitting on wealth, and the reference to being cradled in copper is an explicit reference to an infantile situation (in which the infant might be lying in his own feces). Also in light of the present argument, we may be better able to understand a Bella Coola idiom in which a man, feeling injured or slighted, decided with his wife to publicly give the donor of a potlatch $300 "to make clean where we sit" (McIlwraith 1948:I:416). Similarly, an elderly Bella Coola informant remembered an incident in which "the ground on which he was dancing was dirty, meaning, that it had not been made clean by the distribution of sufficient presents to justify his dance" (McIlwraith 1948:I:246). Again we see that potlatching, giving presents, wipes away dirt. Potlatching to make clean where one sits is certainly suggestive in the present context.

The lack of detailed ethnographic data describing toilet training among the Kwakiutl makes it difficult to substantiate the hypotheses upon which the extended argument has been made. And yet, there are a few piecemeal clues to be found. Evidently, one of the first events in a Kwakiutl neonate's life involves a laxative. Right after the newborn infant is wiped off with soft shredded cedar bark, a woman functioning as midwife puts a little red ocher in its mouth "in order to make its bowels move, so that the bad things in the belly of the child come out" (Boas 1921:652–653). Aside from the possible traumatic influences of such a ritual, the practice confirms the Kwakiutl's concern with eliminating the bad contents of the intestines. Another pertinent detail is that a child's first excrement is saved and stored in a cedar box which is then hidden (Boas 1921:670). This "saving" of the excrement would seem to support the Freudian hypothesis that feces is the first form of wealth or gift.

Actually, I believe the most telling evidence for the anal origin of potlatch may well be a curious detail in the Winter Ceremonial. In the Winter dance, one set of dancers acted as fools, and part of acting as fools included playing with feces. Curtis offered the following description:

> [These dancers] are characterized by their devotion to filth and disorder. They do not dance, but go about shouting wi..., wi..., wi...! They are armed with clubs and stones, which they use upon anything that arouses their repugnance for beauty and order. Excreta are sometimes deposited in the houses, and the "fools" fling nasal mucus on one another. This use of mucus is in fact the salient characteristic of nuhlimahla, in conformity with the myth of the

original nuhlimahla, who, returning from an encounter with some supernatural beings, would constantly smear the excretion of his nose over his body. In the initiation of a nuhlimahla the older members fling mucus upon him. (1915:215–216)

Boas has described the "fool dancers" as follows:

They were initiated by a fabulous people. Their village is believed to be on an island floating on the lake. They have enormous noses and their bodies are covered with snot. In olden times a man went beaver hunting and fell in with these people. He came back exhausted and "crazy." His nose was running all the time; he ate the mucus and smeared it all over his body. He urinated and defecated in the house, and only after a long time did the people succeed in restoring him to his senses. When a young man is to be initiated in this order, the old members will throw mucus from their nose on to him and thus "throw the spirit of the winter ceremonial into him." The fool dancer is filthy and acts as though he was out of his senses...Fool dancers do not dance, but when excited run about like madmen, throwing stones, knocking people down and crying. They turn to the right instead of to the left, and make the circuit of the fire turning to the left. Someone tries to correct them, but they grow only the more excited. They dislike to see clean and beautiful clothing. They tear and soil it. (1897:468–469)

Here we have a transparently infantile situation with an unsocialized infant running amok with his nasal mucus and feces. This is a ritual destruction of property—tearing and soiling clothing coupled with unmistakable anal themes. The initiation ritual involves a rebirth (cf. Locher 1932:41). After the rebirth, the initiates must be reminded of the socializing process by means of which the handling of body excreta is discouraged and eventually repressed. The ritual occasion, of course, provides a marvelous socially sanctioned outlet for regression to a pre-toilet-training era.

The rebirth ritual combined with anal features (feces, nasal mucus) suggests that this may represent male (as opposed to female) procreativity. In male creation myths and rituals, the production of feces is perceived as being functionally equivalent to female production of babies (Dundes 1962). One Kwakiutl song verse indicates that producing coppers is a form of birth: "I thought in vain that another one was making coppers for you, tribe! Behold, he is the one who brought it forth by giving birth in the house, the maker of coppers with unbroken backs all around this great house, the rich chief" (Boas 1921:1285). Among the Upper Tanana Indians, a man who gives a potlatch must observe taboos for one hundred days following the potlatch, e.g., he must scratch his face only with a scratching stick and he carefully caches his excrement in a tree to prevent dogs from getting it. For three days following the potlatch, he must sit constantly with his knees doubled up in front of him. This is apparently analogous to the Tanana woman's crouching during parturition. For one hundred days after birth, the new mother must refrain from scratching herself with her fingers and must use a scratching stick. Shortly after delivery, the midwife takes the afterbirth and buries it in the ground or hides it in a tree so the dogs cannot get it (McKennan 1959:137, 140). This Upper Tanana data would appear to equate male excrement with female afterbirth and thus make potlatch an anal equivalent to female parturition.

It should be noted that in symbolic terms in other cultures, nasal secretions are commonly substitutes for anal excretions (Ralske 1966). In a Bella Coola folktale (McIlwraith 1948: II:427), Deer, referring to wolves say: "They are bad people. They whistle through their nostrils which are like anuses." The equivalence of nose and anus in Kwakiutl culture is suggested by a song text in which one line speaks of curing the nose while the following line suddenly substitutes the anus: "He tries to cure me; curing the nose. You came trying to cure me. There is now no cause of fear curing the anus" (Boas 1935b:25). The Kwakiutl favored the perforation of the septum so that elaborate nose-ornaments could be worn (Boas 1909:454). In other words, an ornament, e.g., made of abalone shell, was suspended from the nose. From a psychoanalytic perspective, this might be construed as transforming nasal secretions into jewels. In this context, it might be recalled that the vast majority of examples of the narrative motif, "Birth from mucus from the nose," are reported from the Northwest Pacific Coast (Boas 1916:734). In terms of the anal origin of wealth, there is a striking Bella Coola legend of a supernatural weeping woman. "As she cries, she ejects mucus from her nose, which solidifies into a glass-like substance about a foot in length. Anyone who sees her should take the transformed mucus, and wrap it in some article of his own clothing; it will bring him good fortune" (McIlwraith 1948:I:535, 432). In the Kwakiutl Winter Ceremonial, the ritual playing with nasal mucus is equivalent to playing with feces.

The Winter Dance ritual also includes other prominent anal features, including the reversal of directions, going right instead of left, and going the opposite way around the fire. Ernest Jones, in his delineation of anal erotic character traits, specifically commented "upon the tendency of anal erotics to be occupied with the reverse side of various things and situations and upon the proneness to make mistakes about right and left, east and west; to reverse words and letters in writing..." (Jones 1961:423; cf. Abraham 1953:390). With respect to the special interest in the backside of things, one might cite a Kwakiutl tale in which a transformer paints the backside and face of one man who became a raccoon, puts white dust on another who becomes a deer: "that is the reason why the backside of the deer is white," and sticks a spear into another man's backside as a tail (Boas 1935b:2, 9). The tale ends with "backward talk" that is, "he said the opposite of what he meant" (Boas 1935b:12, 143). Backward speech, of course, is by no means peculiar to the Kwakiutl but has been widely reported throughout native North America (Ray 1945; Makarius 1970:61). Makarius suggests it is merely a symbolic representation of a reversal of normal, accepted behavior (1970:61, 69), but offers no psychological explanation for it or for reverse or contrary behavior in general. Her failure to see anal erotic factors in such behavior is also obvious when she says that the ritual use of such substances as "snot, saliva or mud" symbolizes blood (1970:66). The point here is simply that if anal erotic symbolism is indeed an element in Kwakiutl culture, one would expect to find it expressed in various forms of ritual behavior. The relatively overt references to feces, nasal secretions, and backward movements in the Winter Ceremonial dance would seem to support the general proposition that anal erotic factors are of importance in Kwakiutl worldview.

I have tried to show that there is ample evidence attesting not only the presence of so-called anal erotic character traits among the Kwakiutl and other Northwest Pacific Coast tribes, but that these traits are closely related to the dynamics of potlatch. From the perspective afforded by psychoanalytic theory, we can offer explanations why Kwakiutl offices are embodied in seats, why shame is said to be wiped off one's body by giving a potlatch, why coppers are thought to have a smell, and why they are destroyed or given away to validate status. I do not claim that the psychoanalytic approach to potlatch precludes other, more conventional approaches to potlatch, but I hope that the functioning of potlatch as a means of displaying wealth or venting aggression can now be better understood. The feces-wealth equation would seem to be applicable to the Kwakiutl data, and the dumping of wealth or feces upon a rival to humiliate him or the idea of swallowing him to reduce him to feces would appear to illuminate the nature of the venting of aggression. The potlatch, which has over the years been described as an "ethnological curiosity," "so bizarre as to seem unexplainable," "topsy-turvy, nonadaptive, nonfunctional, absurdly wasteful and little related to problems of livelihood," may make sense after all.

A symbolic ritual must be understood in symbolic terms, not solely in literal terms. If approached literally as a purely economic activity designed to give or validate status, the potlatch will remain a riddle to be solved. It is only, I suggest, when potlatch is perceived in terms of symbol and metaphor that some of its underlying dynamics may finally begin to emerge. And what's more, I believe the Kwakiutl themselves recognized some of the underlying symbolism of potlatch, even if literal-minded anthropologists did not. Codere (1956:344) reports an example of a so-called play potlatch—play potlatches were clearly intended to parody the whole potlatch ritual—in which: "When a clam buyer did not show up, a man caught with a surplus of clams gave a play potlatch in which everyone was presented with a sack of clams and a roll of toilet paper."

3 The Strategy of Turkish Boys' Verbal Dueling Rhymes

With Jerry W. Leach and Bora Özkök

The underlying strategy of specific traditional verbal encounters has not received much attention from anthropologists and folklorists. Anthropologists speak at length of joking or teasing relationships in general, but rarely do they describe in detail actual verbal duels or provide anything remotely resembling *explication de texte*. Folklorists, who tend to be text- rather than context-oriented, do at least present reasonably complete texts of insults, taunts, and retorts. However, more often than not, these texts are presented in no particular order other than the arbitrary one imposed by the collector. Given this presentation of the data, it is virtually impossible to reconstruct even an approximate idea of a live verbal battle in which the texts might appropriately be employed. For example, in Roger Abrahams's valuable study of the Dozens, the classic American Negro example of verbal dueling, he firsts lists thirty different Dozens insults ("raps") and then follows them with a separate list of twelve Dozens replies ("caps").[1] It is conceivable, of course, that it really doesn't matter which reply follows which initial insult. Yet, there is obviously a particular order or sequence in any one actual dueling encounter. For those students who are interested in understanding folk rhetorical strategy (for example, what strategic factors

1. Roger D. Abrahams, "Playing the Dozens," *Journal of American Folklore* 75 (1962): 209–220.

influence a verbal duel participant to choose one retort rather than another), it seems clear that knowledge of the particular sequence of exchanges is absolutely essential. Thus full transcripts of observed or at least participant-reported hypothetical verbal duels must be collected if we are ever to attempt to analyze underlying strategies.

The study of strategy in verbal duels is part of what has been termed "the ethnography of speaking folklore."[2] The ethnography of speaking folklore refers to the rules governing the use of both whole genres of folklore and particular exemplars of those genres. Thus it is not just a matter of describing the general function of one type of insult, but also of describing the particular rationale underlying the use of one particular insult by one particular individual to another particular individual on one particular occasion. Admittedly, the determining factors involved may not be in the conscious mind of the duel participants. Nevertheless, like so many of the "rules" of culture, they may be articulated after careful analysis. If there is to be any fruitful study of the dynamics of the transmission or communication of folklore, then the particulars of the processes in which folkloristic materials are employed must begin to receive the critical attention of folklorists and anthropologists. If folklore is a code, then folklorists must consider the rules of usage of that code by examining the concrete contexts of that code. As an illustration of "The ethnography of speaking folklore," we shall briefly examine one type of verbal duel found throughout Turkey.

Among Turkish boys from about the age of eight to around fourteen, there is a traditional form of ritual insult exchange which depends upon an individual's skill in remembering and selecting appropriate retorts to provocative insults. While it is possible that some of the initial insults or curses might be known by girls and women, it is quite unlikely that the retorts are similarly known. Moreover, in the absence of evidence to the contrary, it seems doubtful that the elaborate mechanics and tactics of engaging in these linked-retort contexts are familiar to many Turk-

2. E. Ojo Arewa and Alan Dundes, "Proverbs and the Ethnography of Speaking Folklore," *American Anthropologist* 66, no. 6, part 2 (1964): 70-85.

ish females. For that matter, the very existence of this verbal dueling tradition seems to be little known by professional students of Turkish culture judging by lack of allusions to it in the Turkish scholarly literature. Most probably, the same obscenity which keeps the tradition out of the reach of most Turkish women has tended to keep it out of the province of scholars. Still it seems incredible that none of the anthropologists who have conducted ethnographic fieldwork in Turkey have so much as mentioned the tradition.

One of the most important goals is to force one's opponent into a female, passive role. This may be done by defining the opponent or his mother or sister as a wanton sexual receptacle. If the male opponent is thus defined, it is usually by means of casting him as a submissive anus, an anus which must accept the brunt of the verbal duelist's attacking phallus. A more indirect technique is to disparage or threaten the opponent's mother or sister, which is a serious attack upon his male honor. Thus the victim either has to submit to phallic aggression himself or else watch helplessly as phallic aggression is carried out upon his female extensions, his mother or sister. Of course, the victim normally does not simply remain passive. Rather he tries in turn to place his attacker in a passive, female role. Much of the skill in the dueling process consists of parrying phallic thrusts such that the would-be attacking penis is frustrated and the would-be attacker is accused of receiving a penis instead. According to this code, a young boy defends and asserts his virile standing in his peer group by seeing to it that his phallus threatens the anus of any rival who may challenge him. It is important to play the active role in a homosexual relationship; it is shameful and demeaning to be forced to take the passive role.

The retort must end-rhyme with the initial insult. This is a critical stylistic principle as opposed to the overall structural or content requirement noted above. It clearly involves a fairly demanding and restrictive rule. In most instances, there are specific rhymed retorts for given insults, and, if one is the victim of such an insult, he is expected to come back with the most appropriate traditional retort. It is thus to an individual's advantage to memorize as many of such traditional retorts as possible inasmuch as such memorization arms him against any sudden attack. Failure to respond in rhyme will almost certainly invite a scathing comment from one's opponent. On the other hand, even worse than not answering in rhyme or in what is adjudged good rhyme is not answering at all. If one does not or cannot retort to a phallic insult, one essentially admits that he is reduced to the female receptive role.

Within the general necessary requirements of content (one's phallus must enter one's opponent's anus) and texture (the retort must rhyme with the immediately preceding insult) there is still some room for individual skill. This skill entails making editorial judgments upon the quality of the previous verbal thrust and also making a judicious selection of either another attack formula or a sufficient defense formula from the large fund of available formulas. So long as one fulfills the minimal content and rhyme requirements, one can continue to duel. In some of the fairly lengthy sequences of linked retorts, the participants must often be able to seize upon an actual or an alleged mistake in the attacker's previous text. Often it is just one word or the quality of the rhyme that forms the basis for the selection of an appropriate traditional response formula. In one sense, an individual is almost honor-bound wherever possible to take part of the previous text as the point of departure for the continuation of the duel. With such a folk esthetic principle, two evenly matched youths may produce quite an extensive series of linked retorts. Frequently, considerable word play may be required to keep the linkage going. In summary then, an important part of the strategy would seem to entail selecting a retort from the repertory, the selection to be based in part upon one or more "weak" elements of one's opponent's text as well as upon the exigencies of the rhyme requirement. At the same time, the retort should be sufficiently clever so as not to provide the opponent with potential ammunition for a good thrust in return. In addition, the pace is fast and the retorts are supposed to be quickly and flawlessly delivered.

Before examining some examples of the lengthier strings of

linked, rhymed retorts, it might be well to consider several brief exchanges:

Speaker A:	Ayı bear			
Speaker B:	Sana you to	girsin enter let it	keman violin	yayı bow

Ayı meaning "you bear" is a commonly used insult in Turkey. *Bear* connotes a clumsy, big, and supposedly stupid animal. The conventional reply, "May the bow of a violin enter your ass" illustrates the rhyme requirement: *yayı* ("bow" in the possessive form) rhymes with *ayı* (bear). In theory, there are many other word forms that rhyme with *ayı* and that could have been used. However, there are in fact only two traditional retorts that we know of to the *ayı* insult. The bow of a violin is particularly appropriate because of its length, its smoothness, its unusualness in this context, and possibly even because the nuances of the repeated bowing motion suggest the possibility of repeated penetrations of the opponent's anus. The motion of the bow thus gives it an advantage over more stationary potential phallic symbols such as a winnowing fork or a hoe. (Of course, the latter are ruled out by the rhyming pattern.) One informant, when asked to comment on the violin bow image, suggested that the most habitual homosexuals—that is, the ones with larger or extended anuses—would "require the longest and biggest instruments."

Another traditional retort to *ayı* is:

sana you to	koysun put let him	(speaker's own first name)	dayı mother's brother

which means roughly, "Let a real man like (B's name) put his prick in your ass." Incidentally, *dayı*, the mother's brother, in terms of the quality of the relationship is the familiar uncle, the uncle with whom one can joke. This is in contrast with *amca*, the

father's brother, the more formal uncle, to whom one must invariably show respect.

Another example of a brief exchange is the following:

Speaker A:	Hıyar	
	cucumber	
Speaker B:	Götüne	uyar
	Ass your to	fits

Hıyar meaning "you cucumber" is a pithy insult. There are, as a
matter of fact, a number of idiomatic usages involving the cucumber.

Hıyara	bak!
cucumber to	look at
Hıyarlık	etme!
cucumberness	act not

"Look at that cucumber" or "Don't act like a cucumber" are
representative. "Cucumber" is an insult, not because of any literal sense, but rather because of the cucumber's fancied resemblance to the male organ. "Cucumber" basically implies
stupidity. A speaker who is called a cucumber (somewhat analogous to being called a "prick" in American argot) must reply under pain of admitting that he is indeed a cucumber. By using the
traditional retort *Götüne uyar,* he neatly turns the insult back
upon his opponent inasmuch as he has asserted that the "cucumber" fits the insulter's anus. At this point, B, the second speaker,
having rhymed *uyar* with *hıyar* and having placed his phallus
deftly in his opponent's anus, has earned the advantage of the
verbal duel.

Although most of the brief exchanges do not involve a great
deal of choice on the part of the boy trying to retort, there are
some insults that may be answered by quite a variety of standard
responses. For example, if speaker A tells speaker B:

Has	siktir
Come on,	penised get

B may choose one of a number of possibilities. While *has siktir* literally refers to "getting penised," that is, "fucked," figuratively it is normally used to tell someone to "get the hell out of here." However, the second speaker will normally use the literal sense as the basis of his comeback. He might say:

Siktirdiğin	yere	mum	diktir!
penised got that you	place to	candle	set up

which means "put the candle at the spot where you got yourself fucked." The second speaker thus implies that his opponent has already been sexually assaulted, and he specifically tells him furthermore that the place where this occurred, for example, a particular room, a clearing in the woods, or wherever, should be memorialized by placing a lighted candle there. This mockingly sanctifies the "holy" place. The brief exchange may end at this point, but the first speaker could reply:

Ablan	varsa	bana	siktir!
older sister your	there is if	me to	penised get

which says, "If you have an older sister, let me fuck her." Here the first speaker wishes to avoid the passive role as signaled by having a lighted candle mark the spot where he was supposedly in the habit of accepting a male phallus. So instead he launches a would-be phallic attack against the older sister of the second speaker. A verbal sexual attack on a speaker's mother or older sister is a tactic commonly resorted to in these duels.

It should be noted that not all the traditional retorts to *has siktir* are in strict rhyme. One such alternative response is

Has	sik	istiyorsan	Istanbula	git!
good	penis	want if you	Istanbul to	go

which informs the initial speaker that if he wants a good penis, he should go to Istanbul, the latter presumably being the hometown of the second speaker. Once again, the obvious principle is that when one is confronted with the threat of being sexually assaulted, one attempts to sexually assault the attacker in turn.

Still another possible retort to *has siktir* is

Tabii	siktir	paçacı	kemiği	mi	zannettin?
Of	penis	butcher's	shinbone	(question	think did
course	it is			marker)	you

(*Paçaci kemiği* is the sheep's shinbone, obtained from a butcher, used to make broth.)

This might be rendered: "Of course it's a prick! Did you think it was a sheep's shinbone?" In this case, there is a play on the word *siktir* which can mean "get fucked" as the causative form of the verb *sikmek* (to penis) but which can also mean, "Indeed it is a prick." The second pretends to ignore the first and more usual meaning in favor of the second meaning. By so doing, the second speaker implies that the first speaker is stupidly unable to recognize a penis when he sees one.

It is perhaps worth noting that the retort tradition is so well entrenched that sometimes routine, innocuous statements are converted into excuses for an exchange such as the following:

Speaker A:	Hayrola		
	What's going on?		
Speaker B:	Götüne	girsin	karyola
	ass your to	enter let it	bedstead

In this instance, the simple innocent question "What's going on?" is answered with "Stick a bedstead up your ass." However, this is almost a play on the whole retort convention, and it probably would not be taken seriously as an invitation to duel by either participant. In true duels, there is a serious atmosphere of jousting insult. In this case, there was absolutely no offense meant by the initial remark and its utilization as an excuse for a retort is facetious. Nevertheless, the rules of the convention are observed: *karyola* (bedstead) rhymes with *hayrola* (what's going on?), and a large unlikely object is shoved up the victim's anus. Boys familiar with the retort tradition must always be alert for playful traps of this kind. In practice, almost any word or phrase can lead an unwary boy into committing himself to the dupe's role. For example, when one of the authors of this paper wrote to a friend of his in Turkey for examples of the retort tradition, the author himself was "victimized." The friend, after giving some examples of the tradition, ended his letter by asking, "Bora, you know this airplane that is bringing you this letter?" Bora naturally said yes to himself, expecting some comment about the airplane. The next line in the letter was

> Sana   girsin!
> you to   enter let it

meaning "May that stick up your ass." In casual conversation, the same danger prevails. The only defense is not to say *evet* (yes or yeah) when someone says, "Do you know the car we're driving in?" "Do you know the weather today?" If one silently nods rather than saying "yeah," the attacker cannot shove the car, weather, or other object up the prospective victim's anus.

Before proceeding now to the extended exchanges, it should be mentioned that in a few instances, the second speaker simply buries the first speaker with a list of rhymes. In these cases, the first speaker is not given an opportunity to reply at all. He must stand and take the punishment. One such example is afforded by the use of the precipitating insult *inek,* one of the many Turkish insults involving an animal term of abuse.

> Speaker A: Inek
>   cow
>
> Speaker B: Üstüne   binek
>   top your to   ride let's
>   Dağa   gidek
>   mountain to   go let's
>   Seni   sikek
>   you   penis let's

which freely translated would involve speaker A calling speaker
B a cow—a female animal—followed by B's reply, "Let me ride
you; let's go to the mountain; and there let me fuck you." In a
variant from Adana, the retort is

Üstüne	binek
top your to	ride let's
Halebe	gidek
Aleppo to	go let's
Halep	yıkıldı
Aleppo	flattened
Içine	tıkıldı
inside your to	stick in

which may be translated as

Let me ride you
Let's go to Aleppo
Aleppo was flattened
It [Aleppo] was crammed inside [your ass]

This implies that the opponent's anus is so large that not only
could an entire city fit in it, but a city totally flattened, with all
its ruins (collapsed walls), could be accommodated. Whether or
not the flattening of Aleppo is supposed to be caused by the se-
verity of A's sexual assault on B is open to question.

The burying or overwhelming of an initial attacker may consist of more than four lines. A fairly elaborate response of this
type is the following reply to still another domestic animal insult:

Speaker A:	Eşoleşek		
	son of a donkey		
Speaker B:	Eşşoğlu	Eşşek	baban
	donkey son of	donkey	father your
	Seni siken	coban	
	you penising	shepherd	

Coban	da	ben	
shepherd	so	me	
Aldin	mi	agzının	payını
get did	(question	mouth	share
you	marker)	your	
Yedin	mi	kıllı	dayımı
eat did	(question	hairy	brother
you	marker)	mother's	my
O	sözlerini	atlatırım	
that	words your	make jump I	
Götünü	patlatırım		
ass your	explode I		
O	sözlerin	havaya	
that	words your	air to	
Götün	tavaya		
ass your	frying pan to		
Köprü	altı	cam	cam
bridge	below	glass	glass
Seni	siken	amcam	
you	penising	paternal uncle my	
Köprü	altı	boy	boy
bridge	below	length	length
Seni	siken	kovboy	
you	penising	cowboy	

This, freely translated, runs as follows:

Your father is the son of a donkey
The shepherd who fucks you
That shepherd is me.
Did you get your mouth's share? [You sure got
    the answer you deserved]
Did you eat my hairy prick
Your words don't get to me.
I burst your ass [by means of a massive ejaculation]
Those words that you gave me go to the air
    [mean nothing to me]

Your ass goes into the frying pan.
Beneath the bridge is lots of broken glass
My uncle [father's brother] fucks you.
Underneath the bridge are varying lengths
The cowboy fucks you.

First of all, it should be noted that, although the whole retort can be used as a single reply, it actually consists of separate sections. Speaker B might well have paused after "Did you eat my hairy prick?" to see if A had anything to say. The following *atlatırım/patlatırım* couplet could be held in abeyance to squelch anything A did say. The same is true for the *havaya/tavaya* lines and for the final four lines concerned with *köprü* (bridge). In other words, B might elect not to use so much ammunition at once but rather save some of his salvos for the duel which may ensue. On the other hand, B's rattling off such a list of retorts might, tactically speaking, be the most effective course of action.

In this elaborate retort sequence are a large number of allusions that are not clear at first glance. The shepherd, for instance, seems to have special significance because he lives his life alone, often far from human society. Frequently he has only animals for companionship. According to one informant, it is the shepherds' presumed sexual relations with donkeys and dogs which are thought to make their penises larger than normal. Thus speaker B, by assuming the identity of a shepherd, takes on superphallic characteristics. (The same informant also indicated that it was a sin to have sexual relations with animals that one eats. Hence there was supposed to be no intercourse with cattle or sheep. Donkeys and dogs, however, are not eaten and thus may serve as possible sexual partners. Assuming that intercourse with any animal is in some sense a "sin," the distinction between animals one eats and animals that one does not eat is a most interesting one.)[3]

The reference to "mouth's share" in "Did you get your mouth's share?" refers to an answer in kind. In other words, your

---

3. For a consideration of the possible correlations between edibility and sexuality, see Edmund Leach, "Anthropological Aspects of Language: Animal Categories and Verbal Abuse," in Eric H. Lenneberg, ed., *New Directions in the Study of Language* (Cambridge: MIT Press, 1966), 23–63.

mouth issued a verbal challenge or insult; now it is being paid back in kind. It may or may not also refer to fellatio. Certainly the next line, "Did you eat my hairy prick?" does suggest oral-genital contact. However, the informant said that it was the anus that "ate" the hairy phallus. The allusion to bursting the victim's anus is a self-congratulatory bit of hypermasculinity. One's phallus is so large and so powerful that the opponent's passive anus cannot contain it and consequently the poor anus quite simply falls apart. The explosion *patlatırım* implies orgasm and more precisely it is the power of the orgasm or ejaculation that destroys the victim's anus.

The broken glass under the bridge is somewhat obscure. Possibly broken glass *cam cam* was introduced primarily for rhyming purposes. On the other hand, the area under bridges in Turkey—as elsewhere—is often a favorite trysting place for homosexuals and homosexual activities do occur there. The broken glass may suggest certain physical danger (castration?) to the body. Probably the varying lengths "under the bridge" refer to various sized phalluses which might also cause pain. The reference to the American cowboy may be like the reference to the shepherd. The cowboy, like the shepherd, spends much of his time alone with animals with whom he is thought to enjoy sexual intimacies. A cowboy is tough; he carries a gun; he has a large phallus. Thus B heaps ignominies upon A by having A submit to sexual attacks from shepherds, cowboys, and B's father's brother.

Having sampled several short examples of rhymed retorts, one may be better able to appreciate what is involved in an extended duel. Here is an example of such a duel. Individual A, angered at individual B, tells him:

> Ananın   amı
> mother your   cunt

This is a serious insult and B, the addressee, may respond in one of several ways. He may go and physically strike A; or he may reply using exactly the same words; or he may elect to respond with a retort. If he chooses the latter alternative, he has to end rhyme with *amı*. B could reply to A:

Babamın	kıllı	damı
father my	hairy	roof

This retort stresses the role of B's father as the protector of B's mother. The parts of the retort which carry meaning are "father" and "hairy." Together they mean that the retorting person has a father with a hairy penis and that this father, acting as the protector of the mother will sexually assault the first speaker as a matter of revenge. The word *damı* ("roof" in the possessive) is used primarily for the sake of rhyme. However, in the context of this retort, *damı,* following as it does the words *Babamın kıllı,* takes on the meaning of "phallus." Also, since a roof covers a house, the implicit reference may even be to A's having been "covered" by B's father, that is, the A has submitted to a phallic attack from B's father.

Now A is on the spot. Having started by mentioning the vagina of B's mother, he suddenly finds himself attacked by the hairy phallus of B's father. He must try to retort in turn. Examining B's rhyme, he quickly realizes that one part of it makes little sense. B said *damı,* which literally means roof, and this gives A an opportunity to criticize B's retort. A could say,

Onu	öyle	demezler
that	this way	say don't they
Paynir	ekmek	yemezler
cheese	bread	eat don't they
Ben	de seni	sikmezsem
I	too you	penis don't if I
Bana	[Speaker's name]	demezler
me to	[Speaker's name]	say don't they

This means roughly:

They don't say it that way
They don't eat bread and cheese
If I don't fuck you
They won't call me Ahmet [or whatever the
    speaker's name is]

A tense and fast-moving duel is now in progress. B must now come up with another answer. He realizes that now he himself as well as his mother is under possible sexual attack. A has criticized his preceding retort and has articulated the guiding principle of the dueling code: "If I (A) don't fuck you (B) they, the other males, our peers, will not honor me by calling me by my name." B, sizing up the situation, spots the weak point of A's rhyme. "They don't eat bread and cheese" as part of A's retort has little to do with the context. It apparently has neither literal nor figurative relevance and is there perhaps only because *yemezler* (they don't eat) provides a rhyming base for *demezler* (they don't call) in this particular rhyme scheme which involves end-rhyming in lines 1, 2, and 4. With this potential weak spot in mind, B mounts a new assault:

Uyduramadın		yan	gitti		
make up couldn't you		side	went it		
Ananın	amina	[*or* amindan]	kan	gitti
mother your	cunt to	[from]	blood	went

This may be translated: "You couldn't fit in the rhyme; it [what you said] went to the side [missed the target] and blood went to [came out of] your mother's cunt [in the process]."

This is a good thrust and a good rhyme. The only problem is that the same word *gitti* is used at the end of each line to produce the rhyme. Here is a good point upon which A might base his counterattack. A's retort, using the 1, 2, and 4 line end-rhyme scheme, could be:

Uyduramadın		yancığına
make up couldn't you		side its to
Bin	devenin	kancığına
ride	camel's	female to
Anan	çamasır	yıkarken
Mother your	laundry	washing while
Sabun	kaçmış	amcığına
soap	escapes	cunt her to

This may be rendered:

> You didn't make a very good rhyme.
> You ride a female camel;
> While your mother was washing clothes,
> Soap slipped into her cunt.

First, A tells B that his rhyme is inferior (referring to the double use of *gitti*). Then he insults him further by saying that B is not even able to ride a male camel, only a female one. The subsequent reference to B's mother implies that her vagina is so large that anything—even the soap used in washing clothes, can gain access to it.

At this point, B cannot argue about the quality of A's rhyme. It is clear that the rhyme in B's previous retort (which used *gitti* twice) was not up to par and that A has used a very good rhyme *yancığına, kancığına,* and *amcığına* in his last retort. B therefore changes tactics and retorts as follows:

> O   laflar   atlattık
> that   words   make jump did we
>
> Ananın   amını   patlattık
> mother your   cunt   blew up we.

which means:

> Those words don't have any effect on me.
> We blew up your mother's cunt.

It would appear that B is on the defensive. He may be running out of rhymes, and he is seemingly helpless against the onslaught of a good rhyme from A. This may be why, instead of basing his rhyme upon a selected aspect of A's previous rhyme, B retreats to the position that A's entire retort doesn't make sense, taking care to rhyme *atlattık* and *patlattık*. B does, however, attempt to burst A's mother's vagina. A, in replying to the challenge that his words don't make any sense and to the phallic attack on his mother, might offer the following:

O	laflar	havaya	
that	words	air to	

Taşaklar	tavaya	
testicles	frying pan to	

Bir	göt	ver	bana
One	ass	give	me to

Ahmet	[or speaker's name]	ağaya
Ahmet	[or speaker's name]	Mr. to

which may be rendered:

> Those words have no meaning.
> Testicles go into the frying pan;
> You give a piece of your ass
> To me, Mr. Ahmet [or speaker's name].

Note the high quality of the rhyme in this retort: lines 1, 2, and 4 with *havaya, tavaya,* and *ağaya.* A implies that B is no good and is so unmasculine that he does not need his testicles. B might therefore just as well cut off his testicles and put them in a frying pan and cook them. A thereby castrates B. Having emasculated B, A then completes the humiliating process by asking B to present his anus for penetration. A has thereby converted B from a male to a female. If B is unable to reply in kind to this excellent rhyme, then in some sense A is the "winner" of the verbal duel.

Let us now turn to the strategy of another extended verbal duel. Suppose A calls B *ibne,* which means passive homosexual. It is extremely important to note that the insult refers to passive homosexuality, not to homosexuality in general. In this context there is nothing insulting about being the active homosexual. In a homosexual relationship, the active phallic aggressor gains status; the passive victim of such aggression loses status. This distinction between homosexual roles in which it is only the passive, female role that brings discredit is not limited to Turkish culture. It is found, for example, in Mexican verbal dueling known as *al-*

bures.[4] In any event, B might respond to A's calling him *ibne* as
follows:

| Speaker A: | Ibne | | | |
| | passive homosexual | | | |

| Speaker B: | Sen | ibneysen | bana | ne? |
| | you | a queer if you | me to | what |

B could answer A's "You queer" with "What is it to me if *you* are
a queer?" Note that B ends with *ne* thereby rhyming with A's initial *Ibne*. As described earlier, the individual attacked tries to
make the initial attacker the victim of an attack instead. It is
analogous to children's disputes in American culture in that the
rhetorical device consists of repeating the initial insulter's pro-
noun so as to refer back to him. One child says to another,
"You're crazy." The second might reply, "That's right, *you're*
crazy," pretending that the first child's exact words are correct,
but correct only when uttered by the second child in reference to
the first child. The device is not terribly sophisticated, but it
seems to be reasonably effective. In this case, B says, if it is A
who is the one who is queer, what is that to me? In other words,
B not only calls A a passive homosexual, but he completely dis-
associates himself from A's problem. It is then A's turn. He
might, with a new tack not really connected to the preceding
couplet, insult B by using one of the many animal insults such
as:

| It | oğlu | it |
| dog | son of | dog |

A calls B a "son of a dog." If B is alert, he may reply:

| Iti | Allah | yaratmış |
| dog the | God | created |

4. John Michael Ingham, "Culture and Personality in a Mexican Village" (un-
published Ph.D. diss. in anthropology, University of California, Berkeley, 1968),
236.

Ananın	amını	kim	kanatmış?
Mother your	cunt	who	made bleed

This in free translation yields, "God created the dog. Who made your mother's cunt bleed?" The logic of B is that a dog is certainly (like all of us) a God-created, legitimate animal. There is nothing wrong with a dog. A dog is a legitimate being and the son of a dog is likewise a legitimate being. But while it is perfectly all right for Allah to make a dog, it is obviously not all right for anyone to make A's mother's vagina bleed. The vagina bleeds presumably because of the great phallic force applied to it. The implication is that A's mother is a prostitute who sleeps with anyone who comes along. A could parry this insult in the following way:

Anamın	sahibi	var
Mother my	owner	there is

Bacının	da	amı	dar
sister your	so	cunt	tight

Bahçeden	balcan	getirip
Garden from	eggplant	bring and

Bacının	amına	sokarlar
Sister your	cunt to	stick they

which might be rendered as:

> My mother has an owner [meaning A's father].
> Your sister has a tight cunt.
> They bring eggplant from the garden.
> They stick it in your sister's cunt.

First of all, we can see that A has duplicated the technique employed by B in B's last retort. Remember that B has responded to A's initial "son of a dog" insult in two steps. He began by setting the record straight with respect to being a son of a dog, and he ended by going on to attack A's mother. In this retort, A does much the same. He starts by correcting the record with respect to the question of the ownership of or access to his mother's vagina. A points out that his father is the one and the only one who "owns" A's mother and her sexual parts. Having answered B's attack, A goes on to an attack of his own, in this case an attack on the virginity of B's sister.

The virginity of a male's sister is almost sacred in terms of Turkish family norms. The honor of the family depends upon it. A penis enters her only when she marries, and the penis is that of her husband. When A refers to B's sister's tight vagina he is referring to her virginity, but when he mentions that an "eggplant" has entered B's sister's vagina, he is saying that B's sister is no longer a virgin. B's allusion to A's sister's initial virginity is not so much a compliment as a means of underlining the contrasting ruthless violation of that virginity. (The eggplant which grows in Turkey is long and thin.) B must now defend the honor of his family. Perhaps he can only muster the following rather mediocre retort:

> Bacıyı   karıştırma
> sister the   mention don't
>
> Ananın   amına   koydurma
> mother your   cunt   place cause to don't

This is almost an indirect admission by B of his acceptance of defeat. He asks A not to mention his sister. Still, he does make a last effort to insult A by saying that if A does mention (B's) sister, then B will be forced to retaliate by having intercourse with A's mother.

One final example of an extended series of linked retorts should suffice to demonstrate the nature of this extraordinary tradition. In this example, there are especially instructive instances of the use of metaphor and allusion. Frequently in verbal duels it is the nuance that is most important. It is the connotation, not the denotation, that may cause the greatest concern. Unfortunately, these subtleties are not always obvious from an examination of the text alone. This is why informants must be encouraged wherever possible to spell out "oral literary criticism," that is, their interpretations and understandings of particular words and phrases.[5]

In this example of an extended verbal duel, there are not only cryptic suggestive metaphorical descriptions that the uninitiated will probably not easily comprehend, but there are allusions to other specific verbal dueling routines. In other words, one of the duel participants may test his opponent's knowledge of the entire tradition by referring to one or more of the shorter discrete retort sequences, several of which have been discussed above. Readers of the following verbal duel may decide for themselves how much or how little they could understand from just the texts alone.

Two young boys, say about twelve years of age, are talking. The subject is their penises. One claims that his penis is big (an obvious point of pride among both boys and men). The other boy contends that his penis is just as big. Now the first boy, A, should say something else, something more about his penis, something "impressive." so he says:

Kara   kaşlı
black   eyebrowed

A says "black eyebrowed" meaning that his penis has black hair around it. The acquisition of abundant or at least sufficient pubic hair is another point of phallic pride among young boys. "Eyebrow" is immediately understood by the second boy, B, to refer to the hair around A's penis. He may be a little overwhelmed, but his answer, which rhymes with the first boy's boast, is just as impressive. He says:

Soğan   başlı
Onion   headed

This refers to another desirable phallic attribute, namely that the head of his penis is just as big as an onion. B has thereby

5. Alan Dundes, "Metafolklore and Oral Literary Criticism," *The Monist* 50 (1966): 505–516.

matched A's boast with a boast of his own. It is worth noting
here that there is a well-known boys' song that lists these phallic
characteristics:

Başı	soğan	gibi
head its	onion	like
Ortası	yılan	gibi
middle its	snake	like
Dibi	orman	gibi
bottom its	forest	like

Bam bili bili bili bom

Here is a valuable insight into Turkish body esthetics. The head
of a penis should resemble an onion. (It is too dangerous, by the
way, on the basis of a single Turkish text to speculate about the
Slavic and Moslem—not Turkish—architectural practice of placing an onion-like bulb on the tops of many minarets and spires.)
The middle of the penis should be as round and as smooth as a
snake. The bottom should have a "forest" of pubic hair around
it. The last line *Bam bili bili bili bom* is nonsense, but it does con-
note happiness. In this case, the happiness is that of a boy attain-
ing the three stated requisite attributes of an ideal penis. This
boy's song thus confirms the appropriateness of the terms of the
verbal duel.

In any case A, realizing that B has matched his boast *kara kaşlı*
with *soğan başlı,* tries a new gambit:

Ağzını	actı
mouth its	opened

"Opened its mouth" in this context means that the second speaker's female sex organ has opened its mouth as a gesture inviting

sexual intercourse. Since the second speaker is a male, the retort reverts to his wife. However, since B is too young to be married, the insult indirectly applies to his mother or sister. B immediately answers:

> İçine   kaçtı
> inside its to escaped it

Freely translated this means "it slipped inside." The retort means that the second boy suddenly sticks his penis into the "open mouth." He thereby changes the intended meaning of A's retort by making it sound as though A has said that his (A's) own mother's sexual organ had opened its mouth to him (B). A realizes that he is obligated to impress B with a new rhyme. He offers:

> Dedi   hastayım
> said   sick I

Dedi meaning "said" is a semiliterary word, a kind of formal quotative. It is especially used by wandering minstrels at the beginning of sentences in their poems. Here it has no significance other than that of a child imitating an elder. By saying "I am sick," A means that he is "sick" with love or as we might put it in American slang, sexually "hot" for B's mother or sister. However, B is quick to counter with:

> Dedi   ustayım
> said   expert I

Note that the rhyme requirement is strictly observed: *ustayım* rhymes with *hastayım*. B, by stating that he is the expert, tells A that he, B, is a great lover and that he would accordingly be greatly appreciated by A's mother or sister. One should realize that even though "mother" and "sister" are not specifically mentioned, they are definitely implied.

At this point, the duel may cease to be a matter of strategy and become more a matter of memory testing. In this form of the duel, there is no absolute winning or losing per se. Nevertheless, there are some governing unwritten rules with respect to gauging the outcome. It is the first boy who is the aggressor. He begins with an initial boast or insult. The second boy must come up with an appropriate rhymed retort or an acceptable portion thereof. The first boy can only "win" if the second boy fails to respond with a rhyming retort. So long as the second boy succeeds, the first boy must go on proposing other retorts, each time posing a different word which the second boy must counter with a proper rhyming word. The first boy is, however, obliged to use only traditional retort sequences. He cannot make up new retorts. Thus in effect, the first boy tests the second boy's knowledge of the verbal dueling tradition. The *Dedi* routine might continue in the following manner with A saying:

> Dedi   inek
> said   cow

A by calling B a cow is testing B's familiarity with the standard retorts to the cow insult. If B knows a retort, he will simply say:

> Dedi   binek
> said   ride let's

The "Let's ride" *(binek)* is the crucial rhyming portion of the traditional retort to the *inek* insult. B has "won" that portion of the match. A may continue:

> Dedi   siktir
> said   penised get

Again, if B knows one of the usual retorts he may reply:

> Dedi   mum   diktir
> said   candle   set up

In this unusual form of the duel, the retort need not be linked. In fact, the order of the retort couplets may be quite loose. In essence, A is simply testing B's knowledge of the whole tradition.

So what B needs at this point is a good memory rather than a good sense of tactics and strategy. Presumably only boys very familiar with the tradition and very well armed with a considerable repertory would conduct the duel in this fashion.

The fact that one boy can, in the course of a duel, test a second boy's knowledge of the different retort traditions supports the notion that these traditions are well established and well known. To be sure, there may be some Western-educated Turkish youths who are not familiar with this type of verbal duel, but there is evidence that the tradition has permeated Turkish male youth culture, including urban youth. For instance, the tradition finds expression in the graffiti found on bathroom walls, that is to say, in what has been termed "latrinalia."[6] Interestingly enough, the same kind of verse linkage so prominently characteristic of the oral encounters occurs in the latrinalia. A common latrinalia verse in Turkey, found written in various boys' public school bathrooms is as follows:

Bunu	yazan	Tosun
This	writing one	Tosun
Okuyana		kosun
writing one to		place let him

This boasting taunt, "This was written by Tosun; anybody who reads it is fucked by him," has both the rhyme and content features of the oral insult. *Tosun* is a man's name as well as a word for young male ox. It implies masculinity but it also has a slightly humorous connotation. Naturally, the key reason for using *Tosun* is that it conveniently rhymes with *kosun*.

Now if someone enters the men's rooms and reads the insult, he will if he is well versed in the tradition be tempted to reply. He would almost certainly write the following traditional retort:

Okudu	bunu	Molla
read	this	Molla

6. Alan Dundes, "Here I Sit: A Study of American Latrinalia," *Papers of the Kroeber Anthropological Society* 34 (1966): 91–105.

> Tosun götünü   kolla
> Tosun ass your   watch for

This means, "This was read by Molla; Tosun, you watch out for your own ass." Here are the familiar elements. The first verse contained the phallic attack. The reply warned the attacker that the attacker's anus might be the anus attacked. It is clearly the "my penis up your anus" strategy, and furthermore, like the oral duel, it may continue. A third person may enter the bathroom and take note of the exchange thus far. He may assume the role of the first writer and address a retort to Molla, the second writer. He might write:

> Oglum   Molla   sen   toysun
> son my Molla   you   inexperienced
>
> Tosun   sana   yine   koysun
> Tosun   you to again place let him

This gives the advantage back to the initiator of the exchange: "My son Molla, you are so inexperienced; let Tosun fuck you again." Notice the skillful word play. The original rhyme was on *Tosun* and *kosun*. This third verse rhymes *toysun* and *koysun*. Note also that the third person does not add a new name. Rather, since the duels are almost invariably dyadic and it is "Tosun's" turn to answer, the third person speaks on behalf of Tosun.

Still another indication of how well known the verbal duel rhyming tradition is may be found in a Hodja folktale. The Hodja figure is, of course, the national character of Turkish folklore, and there are scores of tales about him. In a striking example of metafolklore, the very nature of the dueling rhyme tradition becomes the subject of a humorous folktale.[7]

One day Hodja, riding his donkey, is coming home from the forest, with wood he had cut for the day. A friend of his stops him and asks what he is carrying. Hodja answers, *"Odun* [wood]." The friend immediately replies with a rhyme:

---

7. For a discussion of metafolklore or folklore about folklore, see Dundes, "Metafolklore and Oral Literary Criticism."

Ben	de	sana	kodum
I	so	you to	placed I

(So I fucked you.)

Hodja is really mad at his friend. But he just can't come up with a rhyme like his friend's in order to put him down. So finally he says,

Bugün	günlerden	ne?
Today	days from	what

(What day of the week is it today?)

His friend answers, *"Parzartesi* [Monday]*."* *"Ben de sana kodum* [So I fucked you]*,"* says the Hodja. The friend protests, "But Hodja, the rhyme doesn't fit." Hodja, red from anger, answers:

Uysada	kodum	uymasada	kodum
fit if even	placed I	fit not if even	placed I

(I fuck you if it fits; I fuck you [even] if it doesn't fit!)

As in so many of the Turkish Hodja tales, the Hodja, in childlike or fool fashion, is unable to operate successfully in the adult world. Yet he is no ordinary fool; he is a wise fool as are so many trickster figures. Although he is slow witted (he couldn't think of a rhyme), he is also quick witted (he made a good retort anyway). The opposition is exemplified with respect to the rules of verbal dueling. On the one hand, the Hodja takes it upon himself to ignore or violate the established norms; he forgets about the rhyming requirement. On the other hand, when questioned about this breach, the Hodja has the last word by which means he in fact conforms to the norm, that is, he successfully threatens placing his penis in the anus of his friend. Perhaps this suggests that the phallic thematic principle takes priority over the stylistic rhyme principle.

The Hodja narrative also tempts us to speculate that there may be a symbolic parallel between the rhyme requirement and the entire penis-in-anus image. One has to place his penis in his opponent's anus, but he has to make this threat in rhyme form. The rhyme form like the opponent's anus are the limiting boundaries into which the phallic thrust must go. Just as the penis must be bounded by the anus, so the verbal insult must be couched in rhyme form. With this reasoning, there does seem to be precedent for Hodja's violating the rhyme rule. Judging from some of the verbal duel texts previously cited, one can see that a particularly strong phallus is capable of bursting the anus. If bursting one's opponent's anus is an assertion of hypermasculinity, then the Hodja's breaking the rhyme convention may possibly be similarly construed. He is so phallic that he penetrates his opponent whether it ("it" being the content in the rhyme scheme and perhaps the presumably large phallus itself) fits or not.

At this point, regardless of the validity of the suggestion that the rhyme scheme may be symbolically parallel to the anus with respect to containing or restricting phallic thrusts, there can be no doubt whatsoever that the verbal dueling tradition exists in modern-day Turkey. In fact, there is evidence that a similar if not cognate tradition thrives in modern Greek folklore and northern African Arabic cultures. Most probably, this form of male verbal dueling occurs throughout the Near East. It also shares some features in common with verbal dueling in Africa generally and also with the African-derived form of verbal dueling found in the United States known as "playing the Dozens" among other terms. Philip Mayer's description of insult exchanges among young boys in an East African society clearly points to the African origin of this American Negro form of verbal dueling. Mayer even remarks that one of the greatest insults is the unequivocal "copulate with your mother." The striking similarity of the East African verbal ritual with the Dozens in terms of both form and content strongly supports an African origin hypothesis.[8] The Turkish custom is, however, apparently more similar to the Mexican *albures* than to the American Negro Dozens.[9]

It may be worth noting what seems to be an important difference between Turkish verbal dueling and the American Negro

8. Philip Mayer, "The Joking of 'Pals' in Gusii Age-Sets," *African Studies* 10 (1951): 27–41.

9. For an account of *albures,* see Ingham, 231–236.

Dozens. In the Dozens, the primary emphasis seems to be on attacking, sexually, one's opponent's mother. There are occasional allusions to homosexual activities, but they are relatively rare. In contrast, in the Turkish tradition, the major theme seems to be a homosexual one. Certainly there appear to be few insinuations in the Turkish duel that one's opponent is a "motherfucker," a common epithet in American Negro duels. One reason for this might be that to label a rival a motherfucker would be tantamount to acknowledging his phallic ability whereas, as we have shown, the strategy in the Turkish duel consists largely of denying any such activity. If this is a reasonably accurate partial comparison, then it becomes clear that the possible "universality" of verbal dueling is not more important than the content specifics of particular dueling traditions in particular cultural contexts.

The question of the distribution of verbal dueling among the peoples of the world is another matter altogether. Even if verbal dueling as a form were universal, the specific content would surely vary with individual cultures. The issue thus is the significance of the tradition as it is found in Turkish culture. What cultural-psychological needs does the tradition attempt to fill? Here we must enter the ever-treacherous area of interpretation. The empirical evidence of the tradition's existence is clear enough; the meaning of the tradition in the context of Turkish culture is not as obvious. Nevertheless, we assume that the thematic content of the linked rhyming retorts must be intimately related to Turkish psychology.

One of the most curious features of Turkish psychology or personality concerns an apparent paradox. On the one hand, Turkish worldview is said to be fatalistic, so that individuals are almost totally dependent upon the wishes and whims of a higher power, for example, the Will of Allah and the inevitability of Kismet (fate). On the other hand, there appears to be a very positive attitude toward aggression. Courage and strength are highly valued male ideals. One of the most popular national sports is wrestling, and military deeds are greatly esteemed. Many Turkish boys look forward with great anticipation to their military service. The question lies in determining whether Turks are fatalistic-dependent, actively aggressive, or both. Is it possible for an individual to be docile and obedient to his seniors, often to the point of what Westerners would regard as obsequiousness, and at the same time be actively engaged in proving his manliness through various socially sanctioned forms of aggression? Is there in fact a culturally caused insoluble problem arising from any attempt to reconcile these seemingly contradictory behavior patterns?

We believe that one of the origins of, or should we say, one of the contributing factors to the formation of specific worldview paradigms is the enculturating experience implicit or explicit in the dominant parent-child sets of relationships in any given culture. If the childhood experience is relevant to the study of worldview, then it is logical to look into the Turkish boy's childhood for possible precursors for the "dependent-aggressive" conflict. In the Turkish childhood experience, it is clear that sex and age are critical social factors. In Turkish culture, there is considerable sex segregation. Furthermore, men decidedly dominate women. Publicly women are definitely subordinate to men. There is also the factor of age. The young are subordinate to the old; children are subordinate to parents. How does all this affect the young Turkish boy?

The Turkish boy learns that, since men dominate women, he can assert himself with respect to his sisters and even his mother. In the world of women, even a little boy has status. But just as soon as this little boy leaves the world of women to join the segregated society of men he suddenly finds that he has junior, very junior, status. He is at the bottom of the social pecking order. He discovers that men do rank one another. For example, in the rural *oda,* the room in some village houses where men and only men congregate, he learns that ranking oneself with regard to one's peers is crucial and that even the seating order in the *oda* may reflect the public evaluation of any one individual's status.[10] Thus though the boy wants status, he finds he doesn't have much.

10. Paul Stirling, "Social Ranking in a Turkish Village," *British Journal of Sociology* 4 (1953): 31–44.

It is possible that the boy's extremely low status in the men's society is essentially equivalent or analogous to the low status of women. In other words, little boys learn that men should be aggressive and forceful with regard to male-female relations and they act so while they live in the world of women. But once having entered the world of men, the little boys soon realize that their own relationships to older men must, in fact, entail the assumption of a passive, deferential role quite similar to the role of women vis-à-vis men. Yet there is an additional critical feature of Turkish boyhood that may well bear upon the specific nature of the verbal duel pattern. This feature is circumcision.

The circumcision of boys was traditionally performed without anesthesia, typically when the boy was in the four- to eight-year age range.[11] There can be little doubt that this is a very important, probably traumatic, event in the life of a Turkish boy.[12] In this light it is entirely appropriate for Pierce to have begun his *Life in a Turkish Village* with an account of circumcision.[13] It has been suggested that circumcision performed at this age may be perceived by the child as an aggressive attack.[14] Cansever, in her interesting study of the psychological effect of circumcision on Turkish boys, suggests that circumcision, perceived by the child as symbolic castration, may lead to confusion concerning sexual identity such that boys may later tend to assume feminine traits.[15] Cansever also indicated that some boys regarded females rather than males as the perpetrators of the castrative circumcision, although circumcision is in fact performed by a male (in villages,

---

11. For details, see Orhan M. Öztürk, "Folk treatment of Mental Illness in Turkey," in Ari Kiev, ed., *Magic, Faith, and Healing: Studies in Primitive Psychiatry Today* (New York: Free Press, 1964), 343–363; and Gocke Cansever, "Psychological Effects of Circumcision," *British Journal of Medical Psychology* 38 (1965): 321–331.

12. Öztürk, 346.

13. Joe E. Pierce, *Life in a Turkish Village* (New York: Holt, Rinehart, and Winston, 1964), 4–8.

14. Cansever, 322, 236.

15. Ibid., 322, 325.

often by the barber). Cansever explained that the Turkish child's initial close contact with the mother in contrast with the child's relationship with a distant father (Bradburn's study[16] indicated that Turkish males find their fathers to be "stern, forbidding, remote, domineering, and autocratic") may partially explain why a female rather than a male is perceived as the primary castrator.[17] The great trust in the mother has been betrayed. She is blamed for having allowed the "castration" to take place. But whether it is the father or mother who is blamed for the traumatic ritual, the fact remains that the "higher powers" upon whom the child depended have betrayed his trust; and they have betrayed this trust with respect to a particular part of the body. It is the boy's phallus that is attacked by the "higher powers."

If circumcision is regarded by the young boy as a serious aggressive attack, and this is precisely what Cansever found from the results of standard psychological tests, then it is not illogical for the young boy to focus upon this part of the body as a means of combatting future forms of aggression. In fact, from psychological data alone, one might well be led to hypothesize that boys would want to punish attacking males by demonstrating to these males their considerable priapic prowess. Thus to gain status among one's male peer group, one would need to prove that one's phallus was in perfect working order and in fact was sufficiently powerful to place one's opponents in the passive, feminine position. In addition, if some old men as practicing pederasts demand that young boys assume the female position, then as these young boys become older and seek to attain a man's status, they must insist in turn upon the active, male role. In other words, the shift from the boy's female passive role to the man's male active role is an intrinsic part of the process of becoming an adult male.

There is another facet of the circumcision experience which may be related to the verbal dueling tradition. If Cansever is correct (and she does have supporting data) in stating that it is fre-

16. Norman M. Bradburn, "N. Achievement and Father Dominance in Turkey," *Journal of Abnormal and Social Psychology* 67 (1963): 464–468.

17. Cansever, 328.

quently females who are perceived as the castrators,[18] then it would be perfectly appropriate for a young male to perform some act of retaliatory, damaging mutilation upon an analogous portion of the female anatomy. One such technique might be causing a vagina to burst or fall apart. Another might be to have the original injured party, the phallus, cause the vagina to bleed. After all, the bleeding of the newly circumcized phallus of the young boy was thought to have been caused by the castrating mother. Certainly the repeated references to making mother's vagina bleed can be more logically explained by this than by, say, references to menstruation.

Circumcision does then appear to be a critical factor in the boyhood of Turkish males. And one cannot help but notice that it usually occurs at an age immediately preceding the initial participation in the verbal dueling tradition. Cansever puts the problem caused by circumcision among Turkish youth in this way: "The Turkish male, with his strivings toward, on the one hand, bravery, courage and endurance to pain, and on the other hand total submission to authority, particularly father figures, might represent a good example of the conflict between masculinity and homosexuality."[19]

In the light of all this, there does seem to be some basis for maintaining that the verbal dueling pattern among young Turkish males is a vivid dramatization of the whole dilemma. It is in quasi-ritual form a concretization, an externalization, of what is undoubtedly a crucial internal psychological dilemma for most young boys. The problem is that to belong to the world of men in Turkish culture, a boy needs to prove that he is a man, not a woman, and one of the ways of proving this is to demonstrate through act or symbolic words that one has a powerful aggressive phallus. Yet the difficulty is that to exist as such in the world of men necessarily involves the danger of being put in the female position by a more powerful male. Just as women in the male-dominated society can do little more than serve as passive vic-

18. Ibid.

19. Ibid., 329.

tims of male aggression, so boys and weak men may be forced by the same society into similar passive roles. Young boys, threatened by the fear of having been castrated, a fear culturally induced by the misreading of circumcision, must do their best to avoid being like women in serving as helpless victims of male phallic aggression. In this sense, Turkish male personality is not unlike that of Algerian males as described by Miner and De Vos. In analyzing the psychological characteristics of Algerians, Miner and De Vos remark that "the fear of retreating into passive homosexuality is one of the dangers besetting an individual who retreats from genital masculinity in the face of subconscious castration threat," and they also comment on the Algerian male's unconscious fear of being penetrated as would be the case if one assumed a passive homosexual role.[20]

Turkish male verbal dueling serves in part as a kind of extended rite of passage. Like most if not all puberty initiation rites, the duel allows the young boy to repudiate the female world with its passive sexual role and to affirm the male world with its active sexual role. The fact that the repudiation of the female role seems to involve the partial enactment of that role by males is in accord with Bettelheim's general theory of initiation rites in which males, envious of female organs, seek to usurp female sexual powers and activities.[21]

The verbal duel, then, offers the opportunity of penetrating one's fellow male but also the danger of being penetrated in turn by that same fellow male. The homosexual relationship involves dependence coupled with mistrust: dependence upon friends who will not attack but mistrust in the fear that they might attack. Just as the "higher powers" upon whom the young boy depended suddenly launched an emasculating attack (circumci-

20. See Horace M. Miner and George De Vos, *Oasis and Casbah: Algerian Culture and Personality in Change,* Anthropological Papers, Museum of Anthropology, University of Michigan, no. 15 (Ann Arbor, 1960), 141, 138. See also Ingham, 236, for a similar statement.

21. Bruno Bettelheim, *Symbolic Wounds: Puberty Rites and the Envious Male* (New York: Collier, 1962), 45. See also Roger V. Burton and John W. M. Whiting, "The Absent Father and Cross-Sex Identity" *Merrill-Palmer Quarterly* 7 (1961): 85–95.

sion), so one's peers upon whom one depends may suddenly threaten one's masculinity. In the verbal duel, a boy must try to aggressively hand out at least as much as—and hopefully a bit more than—he is forced to take. To the extent that Turkish worldview contains an oppositional contrast between fatalistic, passive dependence and individualistic, active aggression, the presence of both kinds of behavior in the verbal dueling situation makes sense. The Turkish proverb, "Some said he was *deli*, some said he was *veli*" says much the same thing. *Deli* means "insane," referring to destructive, aggressive behavior, while *veli* means "saint" with connotations of passivity and stability.[22] The point is that an individual must be both. The inconsistency is consistent. Each Turkish male must be both *deli* and *veli*.

One last detail concerns the Turkish male concept of friendship. The most commonly used word for "friend" is *Arkadaş*. Without presuming etymological expertise in Turkish, one is nevertheless tempted to remark that *"arka"* means among other things the backside of the body and *daş* is a suffix implying fellowship or participation. A friend is thus literally a back participant or a backfellow. It is, in short, someone who is trustworthy and who can therefore be allowed to stand behind one. One must be careful whom one allows to enter one's back zone. A nonfriend might take advantage of such a position to initiate an aggressive attack. Only a true friend or "backer" can be trusted not to do so. To trust to the protection of someone is

> Birine   arka   vermek
> Our to   back   give to

or to, literally, give one's back to someone. This and many other traditional metaphors involving the *arka* root suggest that friendship is semantically related to a safe backside. Among the traditional words and phrases found in A. D. Alderson and Fahir Iz, eds., *The Concise Oxford Turkish Dictionary* (Oxford, Clarendon, 1959), and Mehmet Ali Ağakay, ed., *Türkçe Sözlük* (Ankara: Türk Tarik Jurumu Basimevi, 1966), which we might cite in support of our hypothesis are

22. Öztürk, 349.

arkasıpek—literally, he has a lot of back; figuratively, one who has protectors or one who trusts somebody or one who trusts in a strong place.

arkalamak—literally, to back, to support, or to back up someone; figuratively, to help by giving trust to someone.

arkadaş değil, arka taşı—literally, he's not a friend, he's a back stone (a stone in the back); figuratively, he's hardly a friend. This might be said about friends who do one harm.

ardına kadar açık—literally, open to the backside; figuratively, wide open.

birinin arkasını sıvamak—literally, to plaster (as in construction) someone's back; figuratively, to show genuine affection.

If these philological materials are relevant, and they would seem to be so, they would tend to support the idea that an active penis attacking a passive anus has been a critical psychological configuration in Turkish culture for some time.

In any event, whether the ritual phallic penetration of an opponent's anus is a long-standing tradition or not, it seems safe to conclude that as the verbal dueling technique exists in twentieth-century Turkey, in city and in village, it is hardly an isolated, unimportant bit of esoterica. Rather it is a dynamic functioning element of Turkish culture, an element which provides a semi-public arena for the playing out of common private problems. The duel affords the young Turkish boy an opportunity to give appropriate vent to the emotional concomitants of the painful process of becoming a man.[23]

---

23. Although almost all the materials in this paper were provided by one of the coauthors, Bora Özkök, who was himself an active participant in the tradition, spot checking with more than twenty other Turkish students revealed that the same or similar texts were common in Istanbul, Ankara, Adana, Erzurum, and Izmir. Professor Ilhan Başgöz of Indiana University also had personal knowledge of the tradition, and we are indebted to him for several useful comments on the paper. The undoubted popularity of the tradition tempts us to speculate about the possibility of its relationship to the alleged sexual indignities suffered by the famed Lawrence of Arabia when he was captured by Turkish forces at Deraa. (See John E. Mack, "T. E. Lawrence: A Study of Heroism and Conflict," *American Journal of Psychiatry* 125 [1969]: 1083–1092.)

The *Piropo* and
the Dual Image of Women
in the Spanish-Speaking World

With Marcelo M. Suárez-Orozco

Many of the major folklore genres have been studied extensively, such as myths, proverbs, and riddles, while others have been rarely considered and remain virtually unknown to folklorists. One such genre is the *piropo,* which is widespread in the Mediterranean world, and extremely popular in Spain (Machado y Alvarez 1883:484–486; Beinhauer 1934:111–163; Gómez Tabanera 1968:104–107; Fribourg 1980:15–51; Pitt-Rivers 1954:92), throughout Spanish America (Mafud 1965:177–178; Andrews 1977:49–61), and in Brazil.

Before considering texts, let us first define the genre. As with other genres of folklore there are emic, or native, definitions proposed by the informants themselves, as well as the more analytical formulations by the relatively few scholars who have written on the piropo. A Salvadoran woman informant defined piropo as sayings "that guys say to girls in the streets in order to flatter a girl," and as a form of "male entertainment." This definition is not unlike that given by Andrews (1977:49), who calls the piropo a "flirtation walk." The anthropological folklorist Joyce Bishop (1971) defined the piropo as "a verbal expression spoken by a man to a woman or about her in her presence, which directly or indirectly comments on her physical attractiveness." A Mexican male who is studying in Berkeley, California, described the piropo as verbal comments a man addresses to a woman on the street "to flatter and to impress her." An Argentine male characterized the piropo as "the masculine art" of addressing women on the streets with traditional "expressive remarks about their figures or their femininity."

The *Diccionario crítico etimológico de la lengua castellana* (Corominas 1954:806) defines the piropo as "palabra lisonjera que se dice a una mujer bonita" (flattering word told to a pretty woman). In his extended linguistic treatment of Spanish texts, "Über Piropos," Beinhauer (1934:111) writes: "*Piropos* sind Schmeicheleien, mit denen ein spanischer Mann weibliche Schönheit preist" (Piropos are flattering comments with which a Spanish man praises female beauty).[1] Eugenio D'or (quoted in Beinhauer 1934:111) defines piropo as "un madrigal de urgencia" (an improvised madrigal or lyric poem). For Beinhauer, the piropo exemplifies the Spanish national character trait of popular artistic sensitivity and creativity. Such statements, however, often fail to take into account a large number of highly insensitive and even offensively crude piropos.

Fribourg (1980:15) defines the piropo as "un compliment que l'homme espagnol adresse á une femme qu'il croise dans la rue et qu'il trouve belle ou qui a quelque chose qui lui plaît" (the type of compliment which a Spaniard pays to a woman whom he encounters in the street and finds beautiful or who has some quality which pleases him). Fribourg's conclusion about the meaning of the piropo resembles that of Beinhauer. She writes (1980:42): "Les *piropos* correspondent à la personnalité de l'Espagnol qui s'extériorise volontiers avec son humour et son imagination créatrice, qui aime le fête et qui essaie de la revivre chaque fois qu'il le peut, ne serait-ce que quelques instants" (Piropos reflect the personality of the Spaniard who likes to express himself freely, with his humor and creative imagination, and who enjoys festivities, trying to experience such festivities again, be it only briefly).

Pitt-Rivers, in his classic *The People of the Sierra* (1954:92), writes about the piropo in Andalusia:

1. We would like to express our gratitude to Rene J. Francillon, Santiago Luppoli, and Carola Suárez-Orozco for helping translate materials from the French, German, and Latin.

The appreciation of feminine beauty and the attitude of ready courtship which it inspires are expressed in the *piropo,* a word which means literally a ruby and also means a compliment paid to a lady. It is a tribute paid [by a man] disinterestedly to one [woman] whose presence is a source of joy and, theoretically at any rate, without any ulterior motive. It may be said publicly to an unknown lady as she passes down the street, for it requires no response from her, and the freedom and charm of such custom has done much to recommend the cities of Andalusia to the pretty tourist.

Gómez Tabanera (1968:105) defines the piropo as a "frase breve y recortada, especie de dardo encendido, metafóricamente hablando, que se lanza al paso de una mujer que con su belleza, figura y encantos produce pasmo y suspenso para el que la contempla" (a brief phrase that, metaphorically speaking, one "throws" like a burning dart to a woman whose beauty, figure, and enchantment produce a spasm and a sense of suspense in the contemplating man). Etymologically the word *piropo* derives from the Latin *pyr,* which means "fire," and *oops,* meaning "aspect," resulting in the combination "looking like fire" or "having the aspect of fire." Many piropos illustrate the metaphor that the "heat" emanating from the "hot" aspect of the passing woman is transmitted to the man, thereby eliciting from him the traditional verbal "burning darts." The implication is that women inflame the passing man and make him burn with desire.

As shown below, not all piropos, indeed not even the majority, are poetically flattering, nor do all comment on the physical attractiveness of a woman. Although there are piropos that do compliment the passing female, many are insulting, aggressively bold, and denigrating. A piropo might be more accurately defined as a traditional verbal comment addressed by a man (often in the company of other males) to one or more females (usually unknown to the *piropeadores*) in a public place such as a street, marketplace, plaza, beach, and the like. The comments— ostensibly complimentary, yet often insulting—typically tend to focus on certain physical attributes of the approaching female. Frequently the piropo appears to contain and reflect the image

the man forms of her, a shared male image which does not necessarily reflect reality. In other words, *the piropo articulates a collectively held male fantasy on the nature of women.* If we are to
explain the full range of the piropo we must be able to account
for both piropos of praise and those of denigration.

Reports from the sixteenth century indicate that denigrating
and "dishonest" piropos were rather common in Spain.
Rodríguez Marin (quoted in Beinhauer 1934:112) notes that "Ya
a mediados del siglo XVI era común este requebrar en la calle a
las mujeres con frases deshonestas de elogio" (By the mid-
sixteenth century it was common to deliver dishonest piropos to
women in the streets). Rodríguez Marin quotes Violante on this
point: "Las hermosas padecen ansimismo estas pesadumbres
que no pueden salir un paso que no oigan de mil gentes bajas mil
palabras torpes y señas deshonestas, que de necesidad, si son
honradas les han de dar pena y gran disgusto" (Beautiful women
suffer from the fact that they cannot set foot in the streets without hearing thousands of low words and dishonest signs from
thousands of low people, which must sadden and sicken them, if
they are virtuous).

So widespread and common were these offensive piropos that
during the first half of the twentieth century, Primo de Rivera
sought to prohibit their use in Spain. This led Curro Vargas, in
his comments on this controversy, to rather arbitrarily dismiss
those "dirty" verbal comments as "brutalities" and not genuine
piropos. In response to the campaign to brand piropos as offensive, Curro Vargas (quoted in Beinhauer 1934:113) proposed the
following florid and romantic characterization of the piropo:
"una flor madrigalesca de la galantería, un dedicado homenaje a
la mujer hermosa, un incienso romántico, que al pasar, pone
como un nimbo a su belleza. El ingenio, la hipérbole, la exclama-
ción admirativa, y, sobre todo, la feliz oportunidad de la frase, es
lo que constituye el piropo, restos de una gaya ciencia, de un ex-
altado y casi divinizado culto a la mujer" (a madrigal flower of
gallantry, a homage dedicated to beautiful women, a romantic
incense that is delivered as she walks by as a halo to her beauty.
Ingenuity, hyperbole, the admiring exclamation and, above all,
the happy occasion of the phrase, are that which constitutes the

piropo, the remains of a gay science, and of an exalting and quasi deification of women). Such peremptory dismissal of "dirty piropos," as Curro Vargas suggests, disregards or ignores a large part of the piropo corpus.

How old is the piropo? D. Américo Castro (quoted in Corominas 1954:806) traces oral piropos to a written form found in sixteenth-century Spanish poems, then written in Latin. Young students in the 1500s read poems such as this:

Pinge me egregiam
Vultu formaque puellam,
Cuique gena roseo surgant de lacte colore
Lumina, stellanti denigrent luce pyropum.

(Paint me a girl
With a beautiful face and a wonderful figure,
Whose cheeks could change their milky skin into a pink color
Which could black the starry light of the ruby [piropus].)

According to Castro (quoted in Corominas 1954:806), "these verses became engraved in the memory of young students." Clearly the word *pyropus* suggested a sensuous context to the "young students." Eventually, Castro argues, students began to call their girlfriends "my piropo," that is, "my ruby," "my jewel." Symbolically, the fiery look of the precious red ruby, or pyropus, is equated with the sensuous "hot" aspect of a woman, which stimulates strong sexual emotions. Many piropos contain this symbolism. For example, this Mexican piropo was told to a woman walking alone in México, D.F.:

Donde hay un bombero que esta mujer me está quemando.
Where is there a fireman that this woman me is burning.

The piropo freely translates: "Where is a fireman, this woman is burning me." Andrews (1977:53) reports this piropo (in English translation only): "Look at me (warm me with your glance). I'm cold." Beinhauer (1934:134–135) reports these piropos from Spain:

Con el calor que despiden sus ojos hay
With the heat that emit your eyes there is

suficiente fuego para poner una freiduría.
sufficient fire to open a frying store.

(Free translation: "With the heat emitted from your eyes
  there is enough fire to open a frying store.")

Morena, no me mire así,
Blackhaired, no me look that way,

que soy explosivo.
that (I) am explosive.

(Free translation: "Baby, don't look at me that way because
  I am explosive."[2])

Another piropo, collected in Mexico, employs heat symbolism:

No se aproxime mucho, Morena,
(Do) not approximate yourself much, Blackhaired one,

que no estoy asegurado de incendios
that no (I) am insured of fire.

(Free translation: "Don't get too close to me, I don't have
  fire insurance.")

The woman's heat radiates to endanger the life of the man. A
nice reversal is also enacted: The man's unspoken wish for the
woman to approach him becomes a terrified "get away from
me."

Regardless of whether Castro's *Gesunkenes Kulturgut* literary
origin of the piropo is correct, there can be no question that the
piropo tradition is all-pervasive in contemporary Spanish and
Spanish-American cultures. The piropo is so central to the life of
males in these societies that whole books of texts, presumably intended to guarantee success in approaching women by using the

2. For other Spanish piropos utilizing the heat metaphor, see Beinhauer
(1934:134–135) and Fribourg (1980:43–50).

collected piropos, are published throughout the Spanish-speaking world.[3] In Spain a play entitled *El piropo* was written by the Quintero brothers (Beinhauer 1934:114). Andrews (1977:59) observes that in Cuba the newspaper *La Semana* dedicated an entire column to piropos. The piropo is germane to any serious study of Spanish-speaking cultures, as it encapsulates collectively held male attitudes toward (and fantasies about) women with remarkable clarity.

Here are some of the basic social rules which govern the delivery of piropos on the street. First, all females are potential addressees of a piropo, even a girl as young as fifteen years of age.[4] For example: "Si a los quince sos un monumento ¿que serás a los veinte?" (If at fifteen you are a monument [a "bombshell"], what will you be like at twenty?). Andrews (1977:52) reports from Latin American texts: "You're still green, I'll wait until you mature [ripen]" (for a version from Spain, see Fribourg 1980:45). Older women may also be the object of a piropo. Andrews (1977:53–54) includes the following: "I hope your daughter is as lovely as you [are]" and "How I wish I were your son so you could hold me in your arms!" The latter piropo clearly articulates the Oedipal wish; furthermore, both texts allude to the age of the passing female. Older woman are also legitimate addressees in Spain. Beinhauer provides these examples: "Olé, viva el siglo pasado" (1934:149) (Olé, long live the previous century [when you were born]) and "Olé la fruta maúra [madura] y bien conservada" (1934:150) (Olé to ripe, well-preserved fruit). Although potentially all women may receive piropos, in practice attractive females from sixteen to forty-five years of age receive the most attention. The piropeadores are males ranging from puberty to old age; the latter are known as *viejos verdes* ("old green

3. See, for example, *Piropos criollos: método práctico para conquistar mujeres en cinco minutos (1958): Piropos seleccionados: requiebros de todos estilos* (1957, 1975a); *Piropos y requiebros* (1975b). These are all anonymous works.

4. Not only single and married women, but also nuns may be addressed. Andrews (1977:54) reports: "For you I'd become a friar!" All texts not otherwise acknowledged come either from the personal collections of the authors or from the University of California Folklore Archives.

ones," *green* meaning "risqué'" in Spanish just as *blue* does in English [Roppolo 1953; Chamberlain 1968]). When a group of young males encounters one or more attractive women it is almost certain that a piropo will be delivered.

Piropos are at times combined with kissing noises and/or a wolf whistle. However, actually touching the passing woman is not common. (The cognate form of this behavior in Italy may involve some touching, for example, pinching and grabbing, which also occurs in Italian neighborhoods in Argentina.) A piropo is seldom, if ever, addressed to a woman walking with a man who appears to be her mate, but women walking with children or old men are considered suitable targets. Here is a sample of representative texts. The following piropo collected in Lima, Peru, idealizes the passing female, likening her to the celestial firmament:

Mírame a los ojos rubia, que quiero
Look me to the eyes blonde (one) that (I) want

ver el cielo.
(to) see the heaven.

(Free translation: "Look at my eyes, Blondie, I want to see
    heaven.")

A common metaphor found in piropos is to compare the passing woman to a royal being, as in the following text from Caracas, Venezuela:

Reina el día que usted nació deben hacerlo
Queen the day that you were born must be made

fiesta nacional.
(a) festivity national.[5]

(Free translation: "Queen, the day you were born must be
    made a national holiday.")

The piropos comparing the addressee to celestial or royal beings

5. For other piropos containing the "queen" theme, see Andrews (1977:54).

also include those which literally place the women on a pedestal.[6]
A Peruvian piropo, recorded in Lima, beautifully illustrates this
fantasy:

> ¡Lindura! Miguel Angel al lado de su Papá es un
> Beauty! Michelangelo to the side of your father is a
>
> poroto, porque con seguridad no ha hecho en su vida
> pea, because with security no has made in his life
>
> una escultura tan perfecta como usted.
> a sculpture as perfect as you.
>
> (Free translation: "Beauty!, Michelangelo next to your fa-
> ther is nothing, because I am sure he never in his life
> made a sculpture as perfect as you.")

The passing woman is "put on a pedestal," and equated with a
perfect sculpture. This next Mexican piropo expresses a similar
thought:

> ¡¿Qué fue su padre?!
> What was your father?!
>
> Para mi que fue escultor.
> To me that (he) was (a) sculptor.
>
> (Free translation: "What was your father? I bet he was a
> sculptor.")

The following one-liner from Buenos Aires expresses the same
thought:

> ¡Qué monumento!
> What (a) monument!

Some piropos characterize the addressee as "divine." A Spanish text recorded in Beinhauer (1934:158) is a good example:

6. For Spanish text illustrating the "woman-on-a-pedestal" metaphor, see Fribourg (1980:45).

Bendita sea la Divinidad que sale a la calle
Blessed be the Divinity that goes out to the street

sin custodia.
without custody.

(Free translation: "Bless you, Divine, walking around without a chaperone.")

These piropos portray the Latin male's collective fantasies about
the nature of the ideal woman. The fantasies include images of
celestial beings, often incorporating a "descending" metaphor,
symbol of the wish for the ideal virgin to descend from her pedestal. In this traditional piropo, collected in Mexico City, we see a
group of women equated with celestial beings who have somehow descended to this world.

¿Qué pasará en el cielo
What could happen in the heaven

que los ángeles andan en la calle?
that the angels go in the street?

(Free translation: "What could be happening in heaven
that angels like you are walking in the streets?)

Another text from Lima, Peru, addressed to a woman walking
alone, utilizes similar images. In fantasy, the woman falls from
her celestial habitat and inspires a piropo:

Adios, Ricurita...parece mentira que Dios permita que los
Bye, cute one...(it) appears (a) lie that God permits that
the

ángeles que habían de estar en el cielo
angels that should be in the heaven

anden sueltos por la tierra.
go loose through the earth.

(Free translation: "It is unbelievable that God allows angels like you, who should be up in the heavens, to walk
about this earth.")

The following Argentine version,[7] told to a group of girls walking together in Buenos Aires, blames Saint Peter for the event:

¡Qué veo! San Pedro debe estar encanado por dejar
What (I) see Saint Peter must be jailed for letting

escapar tantos ángeles del cielo.
escape so many angels from the heaven.

(Free translation: "What am I seeing! Saint Peter must be
in jail for letting so many angels escape from heaven.")

The following Peruvian piropo illustrates the "descending" metaphor:

El día que tu naciste cayó un pedazo de cielo,
The day that you were born fell a piece of sky,

cuando mueras y allá subas se tapará el agujero.
when (you) die and there go up cover up the hole.

(Free translation: "The day you were born a piece of sky
fell down; when you die and return to heaven, that hole
will once again be covered.")

Interestingly, the hole, with its sexual nuances, is only covered up again when the woman returns to heaven after her death. A Mexican piropo utilizes the same celestial imagery:

En tu escalera mañana he de poner un letrero con seis
In your stairway tomorrow (I) will put a sign with six

palabras que digan "Por aquí se sube al cielo."
words that say "Through here (one) goes up to the heaven."

(Free translation: "Tomorrow I shall put up a sign in your
stairway which shall read, 'This is the way to heaven.' ")

The virginal angel falls from heaven to the profane world, thus losing that which makes her ideal.

7. For another version, see Andrews (1977:54).

These piropos all use imagery which equates women with celestial, angelic beings who have descended from heaven to in-
habit the profane world. The symbolism in these and many other
piropos is important in documenting the collective attitudes of
Latin males toward women. These attitudes include concerns
about the pure angelic nature of the ideal woman. They may also
be coupled with the unhappy realization of the unattainability of
such an ideal.

The piropos compare women to angels who escape from
heaven and descend to earth, suffering a considerable loss of sa-
credness and prestige in the process. The virginal angel is only at-
tainable when she abandons her ideal state, her pedestal. Thus
we see the Latin male's unresolvable quest for the ideal woman
being enacted in these piropos: to be ideal, a woman must be virginal, but to be conquered means that she will cease to be a virgin. The metaphor implicitly plays on the notion of a "fallen
woman," one who has fallen from grace through committing the
sexual act.

This Virgin–Fallen Woman paradox might be related to the
"Don Juan" and "Latin Lover" syndromes also found in Mediterranean Europe and Ibero-American cultures. In this cultural
syndrome the man's worship of the female reaches an intense
emotional peak just before she succumbs to his sexual demands.
After sexual contact, the man typically loses interest and respect
for the woman and renews the ritual courting process with another female.

This pattern, found in the piropos, is also expressed in the following traditional Argentine folk rhyme:

El sábado busqué novia,
The Saturday (I) looked (for a) girlfriend,

el domingo me casé,
the Sunday me married,

el lunes dormí con ella,
the Monday (I) slept with her,

y el martes la garroteé.
and the Tuesday (I) her clubbed.

(Free translation: "Saturday I looked for a girlfriend, Sunday I married her, Monday I slept with her, and Tuesday I clubbed her.")

The moment the woman gives in to his sexual demands she is no longer of interest to the Don Juan, who violently rejects her.

Pratt (1960:321–335), a psychiatrist who has written on the Don Juan syndrome, sees a correlation between Latin child-rearing and the Don Juanesque series of seemingly endless sexual conquests. The infancy of the Don Juan is characterized by the abrupt loss of his mother's attention after the birth of another child. Pratt found that "The particularly close contact between mother and child is broken off at the birth of the next sibling" (1960:330). This can be termed the "fallen baby syndrome." According to Pratt, a Don Juan rejects the women he conquers because of his fear of being abandoned as he was once by his mother. The fear of a reenactment of the first and most painful (maternal) abandonment spurs the Don Juan from conquest to conquest. Ramírez and Parres (1957:19) endorse this view of the dynamic of Don Juan psychology: "The abandonment that the mother inflicts upon the child at the moment [birth of a sibling] is the pattern that later on will condition the abandonment of the wife by the husband."

The "fallen woman" metaphor which recurs in the piropos might thus be an instance of what Dundes (1976:1521) has termed "projective inversion" in folklore. This consists of an ego-syntonic inversion of reality in fantasy. In reality, it is the infant Don Juan who "falls" from maternal paradise at the birth of another child, yet the piropos express the opposite fantasy of fallen women.[8]

This early family dynamic, reflected ego-syntonically in the piropo, forms the root of the Don Juan's attitudes and beliefs

8. For a profile of the Don Juan as a man insecure about his masculinity who "attracts, seduces and abandons women and then substitutes them with others in an inexhaustible experience of love," see Marañon (1940:86). For a psychoanalytic interpretation of the Don Juan, see Rank (1975:41), who views the syndrome essentially as "the many women whom he [Don Juan] must always replace anew [who] represent to him the *one* irreplaceable mother."

about women. Additional popular piropos provide a more complete picture of this image. The following Argentine piropo was recorded in Buenos Aires. As a young, attractive female wearing a mini-skirt was walking alone, she heard from a man in a passing car:

> Quien quisiera ser baldosa para mirarte esa cosa.
> Who would want to be (a) tile to look (at) your that thing.
>
> (Free translation: "I would really like to be the tile you step
>   on so I could see your thing.")

In this voyeuristic fantasy the man reduces women to "walking vaginas." The point to note about this traditional piropo, and about many piropos in this thematic category, is that they invalidate the argument which views piropos as being primarily a socially sanctioned device for "approaching" a woman. To believe that such piropos are used for this purpose would be naïve, as the only response they appear to elicit are cold looks from the female and retorts such as *sinvergüenza* (shameless), *atrevido* (bold), and *insolente* (insolent).

A more reasonable explanation is to view the piropo tradition as articulating a dual image of women. We suggest that this is an expressive manifestation of a collectively held male attitude toward women, which has as its central feature fantasies about the angelic, virginal purity of the ideal woman (and an unhappy realization of the impossibility of ever obtaining this ideal being). This coexists with aggressive, hostile feelings, and the frequent reduction of women to sexual objects. A synthesis of these contradictory feelings and ideas makes the piropo tradition a seemingly paradoxical cultural fact: many piropos worship women, yet many others are clearly hostile and denigrate them. But let us review other denigrating piropos before analyzing the possible source of this dual image more fully.

The following Cuban piropo is rather direct:

> Vieja, móstrame la de Fidel.
> Old (one), show me the of Fidel.
>
> (Free translation: "Why don't you show me Fidel's?")

The reference is to Fidel Castro's famous beard, which in this case is a metaphor for the woman's pubic hair. An earthy piropo from Buenos Aires:

¡No quieres ser mostaza para mi salchicha?
No you want to be mustard for my hot dog?

(Free translation: "Don't you want to be mustard for my hot dog?"

For the piropeador the addressee is the ideal condiment for his "hot dog" (penis). The following piropo, also from Buenos Aires, illustrates a Latin male fantasy about the sexual life of women:

Si los cuernos fueran flores, mi barrio sería un jardín.
If the horns were flowers, my neighborhood would be a garden.

(Free translation: "If horns were flowers, my neighborhood would be a garden."

A married woman must be the target of this piropo, as it reflects the Mediterranean belief that "horns" grow on the heads of men whose wives are unfaithful (Brandes 1980:87-91). This piropo expresses the idea that women, especially in the piropeador's neighborhood, are sexually active with men other than their husbands, which may be an instance of projective inversion. As discussed above, in the Latin world it is the man who is the sexually promiscuous Don Juan. A man who desires many women claims, through projective inversion, that women desire many men. This collective belief tells us more about an underlying dilemma in Latin male psychology (probably related to sexual inadequacy) than it says about women's sexual practices. Thus, these piropos vent male anxiety rather than mirroring truth about women.

The belief about the hypersexual nature of women is not only manifested in piropos, but also in other folkloristic items. A sample collected in Buenos Aires presents this view. A married man observes to a friend of his:

Todas la mujeres son putas excepto mi madre y mi
All the women are whores except my mother and my

esposa y de mi esposa no estoy seguro.
wife and of my wife no (I) am sure.

(Free translation: "All women are whores except my
mother and my wife...and I am not sure about my
wife.")

An Oedipal ideal seems to be realized by deliberately desexualizing the virginal mother and by displacing all hostilities toward women in general.

The dual image of women as either harlots or virgins, found in southern Europe (Saunders 1981:435–466), made its way to Latin America. We suggest relating the ontogenesis of this dual image of women to a culturally patterned resolution of the Oedipal situation. The Latin "Oedipus" develops intense attachments to his mother and the world of women. Summarizing the writings on socialization patterns of southern Europe, Saunders (1981:457) concludes: "The most frequently cited qualities of socialization are indulgence of the child, nearly unconditional love, an intense particularized and personal relationship, a high degree of protectiveness, and outright encouragement of dependence."[9] His paradisiacal existence in the world of women suffers its first serious blow "at the birth of the next sibling" (Pratt 1960:330; see also Rommey and Rommey 1966:105–106, and Lewis 1951:336–337). An abrupt weaning from a previously indulgent schedule is perhaps the central feature of this trauma.

As indicated earlier, some scholars view this first trauma as responsible for the development of the "Latin Lover" or Don Juan syndrome, which is a primitive attempt at mastering this first loss (Pratt 1960:321–335; Ramírez and Parres 1957:18–21). Other scholars emphasize the "engulfing" aspects of Mediterranean mothering styles. These scholars tend to point out the "double bind" nature of the early mother-son symbiosis. Although they

9. See Brandes (1974:35–47) and Ramírez and Parres (1957:18–21) for similar statements on the nature of the earliest mother-child interactions in the Mexican family.

acknowledge the more positive, indulgent aspects of Mediterranean patterns of child care, they also emphasize the apparent hostility and aggressiveness of the Mediterranean mother toward her child. Slater (1968:29) writes about the classical Greek family: "Since the direct expression of hostility towards the husband would be inhibited by the wife's dependence upon him, her youth, and her social inferiority [so] destructive unconscious impulses toward male children must have been strong. Both the impulses and the need to deny them would be increased, furthermore, by the greater value assigned to male children."

Mothering styles do not appear to have changed a great deal since classical Greek times. Parsons (1969:30) characterizes contemporary Mediterranean socialization styles as essentially having a "very high aggressive component." This intense, somewhat equivocal, early attachment is further exacerbated by the young boy's relationship to the older males in his family, especially his father. This relationship seems to be dominated by a general paternal aloofness and affective remoteness from the child. Gilmore and Gilmore (1979:288) report their findings in Andalusia, Spain: "Young male children of lower class often have little or no contact with their fathers on a daily basis." When contact does occur with fathers and other older males, aggression toward and ridicule of the boy by these males are not uncommon. This hostility often involves the accusation that the boy is effeminate and a potential homosexual as a result of spending all his time with women.

Eventually the boy is moved from a somewhat privileged existence among women to a submissive position in the world of men. Becoming a man means a drastic break with the female universe and a strict submission to older males (see chapter 3).

The initial period of overidentification with the mother and women in general, combined with the aloofness and emotional remoteness of the father and older males, may account for the adolescent Latin male's excessive concern with being masculine and with denigrating women. These two features constitute the core of what is termed *machismo*.[10]

10. For examples of the extensive literature devoted to machismo, see Adolph (1971:83–92); Aramoni (1972:69–72); Bolton (1979:312–342); Kinzer (1973:300–312); Stevens (1965:848–857; 1973a:90–101; and 1973b:57–63).

Strict submission to and a general emotional remoteness from older males make it difficult for the boy to identify himself with a male figure. This difficulty creates profound doubts in the boy about his sexual and general adequacy. Hypermasculinity, *macho* behavior (see Suárez-Orozco 1981:15–24), and ambivalent emotions toward women may be the central outcome of this dilemma. The hatred and rage of the child toward the mother for expelling him from a more pleasurable existence is, in an egosyntonic fashion, displaced to women generically and coupled with a reaction formation which views the mother, and the ideal woman, as a virginal angel. (Saunders 1981:456 reaches a similar conclusion.)

The following piropos show the form these early experiences take in the expressive life of the Spanish-speaking male. Many piropos are directed at selected parts of a woman's body. This example from Lima illustrates such selective anatomical evaluations. As a woman considered to have large breasts walks by, the man calls out:

> ¡Adios, Primor!...Tienes tú un restaurant para bebés
> Bye, Beauty!...Have you a restaurant for babies
>
> bastante bien instalado.
> pretty well installed.[11]
>
> (Free translation: "Good-bye, beauty! You have a restaurant for babies well installed.")

In symbolic terms the passing female represents the lost nourishing breast. Many piropos articulate this first trauma of the "fallen Don-Juan-to-be." The following piropo from Panama refers to the first irreplaceable loss felt by the Latin "Oedipus":

> Quien fuera bebé.
> Who would be (a) baby.
>
> (Free translation: "How I would love to be a baby.")

The piropeador could have access to the breasts of a woman if he

11. For a Spanish version of this popular piropo, see Beinhauer (1934:120).

were her nursing infant. The following piropo, collected in Mexico City, refers to the same idea:

Mamacita linda...recoge a este huerfanito.
Little Mama pretty...pick up to this little orphan.

(Free translation: "Pretty Mama...pick up this little orphan.")

Other piropos are even more direct. This example from Colombia is to the point:

Nena, eres una dulce invitación al ordeño.
Girl, (you) are a sweet invitation to milking.

The following Peruvian piropo uses soccer (the most popular sport in Latin America) to construct a metaphor referring to the breasts of the addressee:

Quien fuera guarda valla para contener
Who would be keeper goal to stop

esa línea delantera.
that line forward.[12]

(Free translation: "How I would love to be a 'goal keeper'
[in soccer] to stop your forward lines [i.e., breasts].")

Many piropos function with double entendres, most commonly with sexual connotations. This example is directed to a woman considered by the piropeador to be walking sensuously:

Nena, no muevas tanto el "carro" que se me
Girl, no move so much the wagon (i.e., hips) that me

para el "caballo."
stand up the horse (i.e., penis)

(Free translation: "Girl, don't move your 'wagon' so

12. For a Spanish version, see Fribourg (1980:44).

much—you'll make my 'horse' stand up [i.e., 'give me an erection'].")

Another version from Mexico has a similar meaning:

No mueva tanto la "cuna" que me va
No move so much the "crib" (i.e., hips) that me will

a hacer despertar al "nene."
to make wake up the "baby" (i.e., penis).[13]

(Free translation: "Don't shake your hips so much or you'll give me an erection.")

Like the heat of the "Pyr" or fire, the passing female "warms up" the man and causes an erection in fantasy.
  Another double entendre from Argentina is:

¡Qué te tragiste!
What you brought!
(Free translation: "What did you bring?")

This example plays with the phonetic similarity between *te tra* of "te tragiste" and "teta," or breast. The meaning is "What a pair of breasts you have!" A double entendre piropo collected in Buenos Aires states:

¡Quien fuera empresario cinematográfico
Who would be businessman cinematographical

para tenerte siempre en "cinta."
to have you always on film (i.e., pregnant).

(Free translation: "How I would love to be a movie mogul to keep you always on film.")

The piropo is a play on words based on the similarity of "en cinta" (on film) and "encinta" (pregnant).
  Many of these piropos function as outlets of sexual repression.

13. For another version, see Andrews (1977:53).

The following text indicates that a woman elicits an erection in the admiring piropeador:

> ¡Adios ricurita!...Su padre debió ser pirata
> Bye cute one!...Your father must have been a pirate,
>
> porque lleva usted ahí un tesoro escondido, como para
> because you keep there a treasure hidden, as to
>
> tener alerta a mi centinela parado.
> keep alert to my sentry (i.e., penis) standing up (i.e., erect).
>
> (Free translation: "Your father must have been a pirate, because you have there a hidden treasure [sex] which is enough to keep my sentry [penis] alert, standing up [erect].")

The intended allusion here is rather clear: "Your hidden treasure" refers to her sexual attributes which cause an erection, at least in fantasy. This next very popular piropo collected in Mexico City says:

> ¡Quien fuera locomotora para recorrer todas sus curvas!
> Who would be (a) train to go all over your lines!
>
> (Free translation: "How I would love to be a train to go over all your curves.")

The man with his powerful iron horse penis fantasizes penetrating the passing female.

This next Peruvian piropo also has a rather clear sexual double entendre:

> Adios ricura, quien fuera músico para tocarle el órgano
> Bye cute one, who would be (a) musician to play (i.e., touch) you the organ
>
> y enseñarle a tocar la flauta.
> and teach you to play (touch) the flute.
>
> (Free translation: "How I would love to be a musician to

play [touch] your 'organ' [i.e., vagina] and teach you to
play [blow] my flute [penis].")

The next version from Mexico City utilizes the same symbols:

¡Escucha chica!...Yo soy músico...¿No quisieras
Listen chick!...I am (a) musician...No you want that

que te tocara a ti algo?
me play (touch) to you something?

And when there is no response, the man rejoins:

Vamos, no seas malita, ¡déjame que te toque algo!
Come on, no be bad, let me that you touch something!

(Free translation: "Listen chick...I am a musician...
Wouldn't you want me to play you [touch] something?
Come on, don't be bad, let me play you [touch you] a lit-
tle!")

That is, "Let me feel you."

In the following Mexican piropo, the fantasy is about "covering up" the addressee:

¡Como quisiera ser la tela que cubre tu cuerpo!
How (I) would like to be the fabric that covers your body!

Related to the Mediterranean practice of covering up the female,
in this case the piropeador wants to have his virgin and his harlot
at the same time: the woman would be traditionally "covered
up," but by him.

The ideal woman must also be a good cook:

Si como caminas, así cocinas...
If as (you) walk, like (you) cook...

This last Mexican piropo is delivered to a girl who is walking in
what the piropeador considers to be a sensuous way. To him, if
she cooked as well as she walked, she would be a perfect woman.

Many piropos do not disguise these ambivalent attitudes with as much finesse. Piropos such as this one, collected in Buenos Aires, are not uncommon:

¡Como te rompería el culo!
How to you (I would) break the ass!

(Free translation: "How I would like to fuck you in the ass!")

The aggressive nature of this hostile piropo is quite strong. "Rompería el culo" literally means "to tear open the anus." The sadistic fantasy is rather clear, and appears to relieve not just repressed sexuality but to express hostility as well. Texts like this must be kept in mind when considering the flowery definitions of piropos quoted at the beginning of this essay.

Another piropo, also collected in Argentina, is similarly aggressive:

¡Qué ganas de morderte la conchita!
How (I) want to bite the little cunt!")

(Free translation: "I would love to bite your little cunt.")

This fantasy vents sexual hostility with a clearly aggressive tone. Besides expressing a wish, which due to the context and word choice is impossible to realize, these piropos are primarily aimed at degrading the woman.

There is an interesting fact about the delivery of piropos which must be mentioned here. Although there must always be a nominal female addressee, it is quite common for a male to use a piropo to impress his male friends. When a group of young males gathers, piropos are likely to be delivered, at times more for the benefit of the piropeador's male friends than for that of the addressed woman. In this context the male does not necessarily expect to be successful in "picking up" a strange woman. He may be more concerned with enhancing his image of masculinity (often at her expense) vis-á-vis his male companions. By insulting women in the presence of his male peers, a piropeador may seek to publicly demonstrate his independence of the feminine world.

Many aggressive and ironic piropos are at times even addressed to very ugly women and can be best understood purely as a manifestation of male ambivalence toward women. The following piropo collected in Buenos Aires is a good example:

> ¡Nena, que culo!
> Baby, what ass!
>
> (Free translation: "Baby, what a piece of ass you are.")

Culo is a term used to refer not only to the buttocks but also to ugly women.

Many piropos are aimed at simply denigrating the addressee:

> Estás Paco... Pa' cogerte.
> You are Paco... to fuck.
>
> (Free translation: "You are fuckable.")

Other piropos often refer to women as animals:

> Quien fuera toro.
> Who would be (a) bull.
>
> (Free translation: "I would love to be a bull.")

This implies that the passing female is an attractive "cow." This Peruvian version is less subtle:

> Adios corazón de oro, tú eres la vaca y yo soy el toro.
> Good-bye heart of gold, you are the cow and I am the bull.

Hostile piropos with an ironic tone are commonly used by a group of men. For example, this piropo from Uruguay, delivered to two women walking together by one of a pair of male friends, is intended to hurt the feelings of both women:

> A mí me gusta la del medio.
> To me me like the of the middle.
>
> (Free translation: "I like the one in the middle.")

Of course, no one is in the middle, implying that both women are ugly. (Another version from Mexico City, in the same context, is: "I like the one wearing the skirt," to a group of girls in pants.) The piropeador seems to be more concerned with appearing daring, funny, and ingenious to his friends than with making a favorable impression on a woman. A Puerto Rican informant noted this aspect of the piropo syndrome when he described the following typical piropo-delivering context: "Usually men in a cluster either walking or just hanging around will use a piropo when a woman happens to come by. In most cases the man who says the piropo does not do so loud enough for the women to hear. *It is more a joke amongst the men*" (our emphasis).

Piropos are much more than "jokes amongst the men." They are an outlet for men to ventilate the ambivalence of their emotions toward women. (For a curious, brief interpretation of the piropos in the psychological tradition of Jacques Lacan, see Miller 1981:31–50). Dynamically related to this ambivalence are a man's underlying doubts as to his own adequacy and masculinity. We have traced this syndrome through an Oedipal passage from a somewhat privileged period of belonging to the world of women to a submissive entrance to the world of men. It is no wonder that young males, who must constantly prove their worth and masculinity, are the most active bearers of piropos, and most willing to deliver them when in the presence of peers. As Andrews (1977:58) reports from an informant, the piropo "makes a man feel more manly."

Although silence is the usual female response to a piropo today, it would be a mistake to think that women do not participate at all in this cultural phenomenon. A female informant summarized her views on this point: "While the Latin woman's response is apparently aloof, she is nevertheless socialized to expect men to admire her physical attractiveness."

It is clear that the Latin female is caught by the contradictory images she finds in the piropos delivered to her. On the one hand, "socialized to expect to be admired by men," she welcomes poetic and flattering piropos. On the other hand, she is enraged by piropos which are insulting and degrading. Some women resolve this paradox (as did earlier writers on piropos) by dismissing insulting ones as the product of individual sociopaths and not "real piropos." Other female informants indicated that some women deserve aggressive piropos because they dress or walk too suggestively. These defensive rationalizations point to some form of affective dissonance produced by the double binds found in the piropo tradition. Other women expect to have a piropo addressed to them when they walk by a group of men, and failure to elicit such piropos creates anxieties that they are getting old or somehow losing their attractiveness.

Many Latin females are forced to pause and evaluate their attitudes toward piropos while visiting or residing outside the Spanish-speaking world. A Salvadoran informant, after not receiving a single piropo in weeks in Berkeley, California, felt "really unnoticed." Andrews reports: "A number of women mentioned the unpleasant shock of discovering that piropos are not given in the United States. One said, 'this offends the feminine psyche.' Another commented that since she did not get piropos in the United States, she had less motivation to maintain her appearance and, as a result, she was beginning to dress like a peasant" (1977:58). Clearly, most Latin women were puzzled by this change. Some entered depressive states, wondering if they had gained weight, somehow had become uglier, or lost their appeal upon arrival in the United States. Many women, although they despised "dirty" piropos, really missed not receiving any piropos at all in the United States.[14]

Latin American women are also ambivalent about the piropo. They may reject the tradition on the grounds of impropriety or impoliteness but miss the tradition when it is absent. In this sense, the piropo genre of folklore suggests that Latin women may be victimized by the Latin male image of women. They are caught between the idealized demands for sexual repression—virginity—and the urges for sexuality which, if indulged, carry the stigma of harlotry. The piropo provides a microcosmic view of the sexual stresses of both males and females in Latin America.

14. In Latin America, women often feel that visiting North American men are inattentive, cold, or unable to praise a woman's beauty, since U.S. men are unfamiliar with the piropo tradition.

For the student of Latin American cultures, the value of the piropo lies in the contradictory but all-pervasive male cultural image of women it mirrors. This image includes a fantasy about the virginal purity of the ideal woman and its binary opposite, a view of women as harlots. It is the juxtaposition of these opposed views which gives the piropo its paradoxical nature.

5   Couvade in Genesis

In the early second century B.C., Apollonius of Rhodes wrote in *The Argonautica* "Soon after leaving them [the Chalybes] behind, the Argonauts rounded the headland of Genetaean Zeus and sailed in safety past the country of the Tibareni. Here, when a woman is in childbirth, it is the husband who takes to his bed. He lies there groaning with his head wrapped up and his wife feeds him with loving care." Diodorus of Sicily, describing Corsicans in the first century B.C., remarked, "But the most amazing thing which takes place among them is connected with the birth of their children; for when the wife is about to give birth she is the object of no concern as regards her delivery, but it is her husband who takes to his bed, as though sick." In that same time period, Strabo in his *Geography* wrote about the Cantabrians of Iberia. Speaking with admiration of the courage of the women, he stated, "For example, these women till the soil, and when they have given birth to a child, they put their husbands to bed instead of going to bed themselves and minister to them."[1] These

---

1. Apollonius of Rhodes, *The Voyage of Argo* , trans. E. V. Rieu (Harmondsworth: Penguin, 1959), 101; *Diodorus of Sicily*, trans. C. H. Oldfather (Cambridge: Harvard University Press, 1961), vol. 3, 135 [5.14]; *The Geography of Strabo*, trans. Horace Leonard Jones (Cambridge: Harvard University Press, 1960), vol. 2, 113 [3.4.17].

145

independent accounts confirm the presence of couvade in the Mediterranean area two thousand years ago.

Among the dozens of accounts written since Apollonius, Diodorus, and Strabo, we might mention that of Marco Polo, who in the late thirteenth century recounted a singular usage in the province of Yunnan: "As soon as a woman has been delivered of a child, and rising from her bed, has washed and swathed the infant, her husband immediately takes the place she has left, has the child laid beside him, and nurses it for forty days. In the meantime, the friends and relations of the family pay to him their visits of congratulation; whilst the woman attends to the business of the house, carries victuals and drink to the husband in his bed, and suckles the infant at his side."[2] Francis Bacon wrote in his *Sylva Sylvarum* in 1627, "There is an Opinion abroad, (whether Idle or no I cannot say,) that loving and kinde Husbands, have a Sense of their Wives Breeding Childe, by some Accident in their owne Body."[3]

The first appearance of the term *couvade* in print (as opposed to allusions to the custom) was evidently in 1665. In that year Charles de Rochefort wrote about the Caribs as follows: "Mais voicy la brutalité de nos Sauvages, dans leur réjouissance pour l'acroissement de leur famille. C'est qu'au même temps que la femme est delivrée le mary se met au lit, pour s'y plaindre & y faire l'acouchée: coutume, qui bien que Sauvage & ridicule, se trouve néanmoins à ce que l'on dit, parmy les paysans d'une certaine Province de France. Et ils appellent cela *faire la couvade*."[4]

The (anthropological) term *couvade*, derived from the French *couver* (to brood or hatch) was proposed by E. B. Tylor in his *Researches into the Early History of Mankind* in 1865, two hundred years after the de Rochefort account. Tylor used the term to refer to a widespread custom whereby fathers or men about to become

2. *The Travels of Marco Polo the Venetian* (London: J. M. Dent, 1908), 250.

3. See R. Hunter and I. Mac Alpine, *Three Hundred Years of Psychiatry* (London: Oxford University Press, 1963), 207.

4. Charles de Rochefort, *Histoire Naturelle et Morale des les Antilles de l'Amérique*, 2d ed. (Rotterdam: Arnout Leers, 1665), 350–351.

fathers ritually went through the motions of confinement and childbirth. The narrow usage of couvade tends to be restricted to instances of a man's lying in bed. The corresponding term in the German anthropological literature is thus appropriately *Männerkindbett* although as E. S. Hartland pointed out, not all peoples who practice couvade necessarily have Western beds as such and, in fact, women are often delivered on the ground. A broader concept of couvade would include a host of pre or postnatal restrictions—for example, those involving dietary taboos observed by prospective fathers.[5]

Tylor's discussion initiated a voluminous scholarly literature devoted to the couvade. Max Müller, for example, in his review of Tylor's *Researches,* proposed a novel theory to counter Tylor's suggestion that the custom reflected a sympathetic bond between father and child. Rather, argued Müller, a father feels very much out-of-place at the time of his wife's confinement. He gets no attention at such a time and he generally catches hell from mother-in-law, sisters-in-law, and other female relatives.

5. For Hartland's comments, see Edwin Sidney Hartland, *The Legend of Perseus,* vol. 2 (London: David Nutt, 1895), 404–405. Let me indicate a sampling of the early surveys of couvade scholarship: Heinrich Ploss, "Das Männerkindbett (Couvade), seine geographische Verbreitung und ethnographische Bedeutung," *Zehnter Jahresbericht des Vereins von Freunden der Erdkunde zu Leipzig* (1870–1871): 33–48; Karl Friedrichs, "Das männliche Wochenbett, *Das Ausland* 63 (1890): 801–806, 834–839, 856–860, 878–880, 895–898; H. Ling Roth, "On the Signification of Couvade," *Journal of the Anthropological Institute* 22 (1893): 204–243; R.R. Schuller, "A Couvade," *Boletim do Museu Goeldi* (Museu Paraense) 6 (1909): 236–245; Hugo Kunike, "Das sogenannte 'Männerkindbett,'" *Zeitschrift für Ethnologie* 43 (1911): 546–563; J. P. B. de Josselin de Jong, "De Couvade," *Mededeelingen der Koninklijke Academie van Wetenschappen,* Afdeeling Letterkunde, 54, Serie B (1922): 53–84; M. J. Bouwman, "La Couvade," *Revue Anthropologique* 35 (1925): 49–70; Warren Dawson, *The Custom of Couvade* (Manchester: Manchester University Press, 1929), etc. Most of these writers admitted that they were puzzled by the couvade. Dawson, for example, at the conclusion of his book on the subject said, "In the meantime, until fresh facts come to enlighten us, we must. . .humbly admit that the state of our knowledge regarding the original motive of the couvade custom is expressed by a single word —IGNORAMUS." Most folklorists have contented themselves with listing instances of or allusions to couvade, e.g., Wayland D. Hand, "American Analogues of the Couvade," in *Studies in Folklore,* ed. W. Edson Richmond (Bloomington: Indiana University Press, 1957), 212–229; and Enrica Delitala, "La Documentazione sulla 'Covata' e sulla 'Parte del Marito' in Sardegna," *Studi Sardi* 20 (1966–1967): 573–594.

And would it not be best for him to take to his bed at once, and not to get up till all is well over?...It is clear that the poor husband was at first tyrannized over by his female relations, and afterwards frightened into superstition. He then began to make a martyr of himself till he made himself really ill or took to his bed in self-defense. Strange and absurd as the Couvade appears at first sight, there is something in it with which, we believe, most mothers-in-law can sympathize; and if we consider that it has been proved to exist in Spain, Corsica, Pontus, Africa, the Eastern Archipelago, the West Indies, North and South America, we shall be inclined to admit that it arose from some secret spring in human nature, the effects of which may be modified by civilization, but are, perhaps, never entirely obliterated."[6]

(It is true that males feel particularly out of place or useless during childbirth—as "useless as tits on a bull," one might say, and this may not be a bad folk simile to use under the circumstances!)

Tylor was later to change his mind about the significance of couvade. In his classic paper, "On a Method of Investigating the Development of Institutions: Applied to Laws of Marriage and Descent," published in 1889, he indicated his general agreement with the notion previously put forth by Bachofen in the latter's 1861 treatise, *Das Mutterrecht*, in which he argued that couvade represented a sign of the postulated evolutionary shift from a period of mother-right to father-right. Couvade in this view was an attempt by males to replace females in kinship priority. Tylor observed that among certain tribes the couvade provided a legal form by which a father recognized a child as his. "Thus," Tylor concluded, "this apparently absurd custom, which for twenty

6. Max Müller, *Chips from A German Workshop*, vol. 2 (New York: Charles Scribner, 1869), 275, 279.

centuries has been the laughing-stock of mankind, proves to be not merely incidentally an indicator of the tendency of society from maternal to paternal, but the very sign and record of that vast change."[7]

Tylor then became embroiled in a lengthy but fascinating debate with J. A. H. Murray, editor of the *New English Dictionary*, who took issue with Tylor's use of the term. This debate, entitled "Couvade—The Genesis of an anthropological term," which took place in the pages of *The Academy* in a series of sharp exchanges, was mostly concerned with the origin of the term *couvade* itself rather than with the possible meaning or significance of the custom. Tylor eventually tired of trying to prove that his introduction of the word did not constitute an abuse, and on 10 December 1892, he ended his final rebuttal with, "I have only to add that I do not intend to write further on this subject." Part of the discussion turned on whether or not couvade was, in fact, ever practiced among the Basques (since one school of thought insisted the term *couvade* came from a French Basque source). The vexing question of whether or not the Basques practiced couvade in the past or in the present became itself the subject of considerable debate.[8]

The array of theories and explanations advanced to understand the custom of couvade is impressive. The Jesuit Lafitau in his 1724 work, *Moeurs des Sauvages Amériquains, comparées aux moeurs des premiers temps,* discussed the practice whereby husbands among certain peoples went to bed when their wives were

---

7. Edward B. Tylor, "On a Method of Investigating the Development of Institutions: Applied to Laws of Marriage and Descent," *Journal of the Royal Anthropological Institute of Great Britain and Ireland* 18 (1889): 256.

8. For an entry into the Basque couvade question, see M. Lochard, "Notes Relatives à la 'Couvade'" *Bulletin de la Société des Sciences, Lettres et Arts de Pau* 7 (1877-1878): 74-77; J. Brissaud, "La Couvade en Béarn et chez les Basques," *Revue des Pyrénées* 12 (1900): 225-239; Telesforo de Aranzadi, "De la 'Covada' en España," *Anthropos* 5 (1910): 775-778; Rodney Gallop, "Couvade and the Basques," *Folklore* 44 (1936): 310-313; and Justo Gárate, "La Fantástica Historia de la Covada Vizcaína," in *Homenaje a Don Jose Miguel Barandiaran*, vol. 2 (Bilbao: Publicaciones de la Excma. Diputacion de Vizcaya, 1966), 27-54.

about to deliver and were taken care of by these wives in a manner similar to the way women in childbirth are looked after by others elsewhere, remarking that the custom was called *faire couvade* in the French provinces adjacent to Spain. Lafitau suggested that the custom was related to original sin and that it was a form of penitence for parents, instituted for the purpose of expiating that sin. In Genesis 3:16, God says to Eve: "I will greatly multiply thy sorrow and thy conception; in sorrow thou shalt bring forth children." The labor of giving birth, including so-called labor pains, was thus a divine punishment for having eaten of the fruit of the tree of the knowledge of good and evil. Lafitau simply suggested that male participation in couvade was an extension of the original punishment for original sin (although in Genesis Adam is punished by having to labor in the fields to produce food instead of merely eating the food provided in the Garden of Eden).[9] I don't find Lafitau's argument particularly convincing, but I think he may have been quite right in seeing a possible connection between couvade and the events described in Genesis.

Among the other theories proposed is one which claims that couvade uses deception to deceive potential evil spirits. If the father pretends to go through the motions of parturition, then marauding evil spirits may be fooled into directing their maleficent powers towards him. By this means, the mother and/or infant are protected. Or women, anxious to keep their husbands close to them at the time of childbirth, forbade hunting during that period. Moreover, if men hunted, women would then be obliged to prepare the game obtained. Thus, keeping the men at home reduced the workload of women. More recently it has been suggested that couvade is a ritual restriction of a man's productivity, e.g., in hunting, and that this restriction forces a small group of individuals, e.g., in the man's kin group, to help him at this crisis time. Thus, couvade functions to identify those male relatives

9. P. Lafitau, *Moeurs des Sauvages Amériquains, comparées aux moeurs des premiers temps* (Paris: Charles Estienne Hochereau, 1724), 49-50, 256-257.

who have an obligation to help an individual male and to confirm the makeup of this social group.[10]

One reason for the continuing interest in couvade over the centuries has been the reporting of clinical cases of what has been termed the *couvade syndrome* among fathers-to-be in European countries and elsewhere. So alongside the vast ethnographic literature devoted to couvade, one finds a substantial medical discussion of numerous individual case histories. Most of the symptoms of the couvade syndrome "are gastro-intestinal and include loss of appetite, toothache, and vomiting—quite commonly morning sickness—indigestion, and other forms of relatively ill-defined abdominal pain or discomfort, constipation, or diarrhoea."[11] Perhaps the most bizarre medical, or perhaps I should say pseudo-medical, explanation of the couvade yet proposed was one championed by R. Ruggles Gates in the pages of *Man* in 1944. He claimed that the male breathed in or otherwise

10. For useful surveys of couvade explanations, see Paul Hermant, "La Couvade," *Bulletin de la Société Royale Belge de Géographie* 30 (1906): 5–15; Julius Lippert, *The Evolution of Culture* (New York: Macmillan, 1931), pp. 672–673; Georges Smets, "L'Interprétation de la Couvade," *Bulletin de la Classe des Lettres et des Sciences Morales et Politiques*, Académie royale de Belgique, 5th Serie, 35 (1949): 268–288; Raffaele Corso, "La 'couvade' y su interpretación," *Runa* 6 (1953–1954): 133–141; J. Imbelloni, "Desbrozando la 'couvade,'" *Runa* 6 (1953–1954): 175–199; and Wilhelm Schmidt, "Gebrauche des Ehemannes bei Schwangerschaft und Geburt, mit Richtigstellung des Begriffes der Couvade," *Wiener Beiträge zur Kulturgeschichte und Linguistik* 10 (Wien: Herold, 1954). For the suggestion that the couvade functions to solidify a male assistance group, see H. Clyde Wilson and Aram A. Yengoyan, "Couvade: An Example of Adaptation by the Formation of Ritual Groups," *Michigan Discussions in Athropology* 1 (1976): 111–133.

11. M. David Enoch, W. H. Trethowan, and J. C. Barker, *Some Uncommon Psychiatric Syndromes* (Bristol: John Wright, 1967), 61. For representative essays on medical aspects of couvade, see W. H. Trethowan and M. F. Conlon, "The Couvade Syndrome," *British Journal of Psychiatry* 3 (1965): 57–66; André Haynal, "Le Syndrome de Couvade," *Annales médico-psychologiques* 126 (1968): 539–571; and Jesso O. Cavenar, Jr., and William W. Weddington, Jr., "Abdominal Pain in Expectant Fathers," *Psychosomatics* 19 (1978): 761–768. One of the most fascinating studies consists of an attempt to demonstrate a connection between couvade and such eye ailments as styes and tarsal cysts. See W. S. Inman, "The Couvade in Modern England," *British Journal of Medical Psychology* 19 (1941): 37–55.

absorbed the estrins secreted by the female during her pregnancy. These estrins caused the husband to become ill and to manifest "couvade" behavior. Actually, this "theory" had been proposed earlier in 1934 by a West Virginia doctor. In an article, "Estrin Reactions in Husbands of Pregnant Women," which appeared in the *West Virginia Medical Journal*, Dr. Ray I. Frame tried to explain the phenomenon he had often encountered in his country practice whereby married male patients reported they were sick and said they were "breeding." He did not use the term *couvade,* but *breeding* is a standard folk term for couvade, and he did say he was discussing "the very prevalent belief among certain people that the husband shares the discomfort of pregnancy with his wife."[12] Frame contended that "most cases of marked Estrin reaction have been observed in that class of humanity where baths are of infrequent occurrence," that "the negro, whose sweat glands are very active, constitute 75% of the cases seen" and that "in every instance the reaction has only been observed in husbands who sleep with their wives." This is hardly a legitimate scientific study, of course. In fact, there have been many, many reports of couvade symptoms being experienced by men who had been living apart from their wives for months, e.g., in the military, as Lord Raglan pointed out in his rebuttal of Gates's articles in *Man*.[13]

Yet the question of which individual men suffer couvade symptoms is not without interest. In a given culture, some individuals may complain of such symptoms while others may not

12. Ray I. Frame, "Estrin Reactions in Husbands of Pregnant Women," *The West Virginia Medical Journal* 30 (1934): 228–229. A report from England tells of a painter who felt ill. A neighbor explained that he was not really very ill, "but he was carrying—breedin' some folks calls it." See Ethel H. Rudkin, "Couvade," *Folklore* 45 (1934): 158.

13. Gates gives credit to Frame for his hypothesis that "illness of the male results from inhalation of body vapours containing the sex hormone of the pregnant female during sleep." See R. Ruggles Gates, "An Explanation for the Couvade," *Man* 44 (1944): 55. Lord Raglan's rebuttal may be found in "The Custom of Couvade," *Man* 44 (1944): 80. Gates renewed the discussion some years later in "Physiology and Psychology of the the Couvade," *Man* 53 (1953): 89–90. Again, Raglan responded in "Couvade," *Man* 53 (1953): 144. Raglan had earlier proposed a theory of his own to the effect that couvade functioned as a form of ritual marriage for women who had become pregnant prior to formal marriage. See "The Custom of Couvade," *Man* 30 (1930): 112–113.

experience them. It has been suggested that the incidence of couvade may be correlated with cross-sex identification. In other words, in absent-father households, the young male tends to identify with his mother rather than with his father. This supposedly results in his later attempts to imitate female adult behavior, which would include acting out parturition.[14] In a study of couvade in Texas and northeast Mexico, it was reported that individuals who developed the most serious couvade symptoms had "prior to demonstration of those symptoms, and by means of independent criteria, been adjudged by their male peers as 'effeminate,' 'non-masculine,' 'non-macho,' 'hen pecked,' or a 'homebody,' all of which are descriptives which refer to unmanly characteristics."[15]

In the final analysis, it is the connection between paternity and couvade which remains central. Malinowski, for example, claimed that "the couvade and all the customs of its type serve to accentuate the principle of legitimacy, the child's need of a father."[16] But psychologically speaking, it is not the child's need of a father so much as the father's need of a child. It is through childbirth that a man's masculinity is asserted. Freud, in his 1908 paper, "On the Sexual Theories of Children," referred to couvade as "well known among many races as a general practice" and suggested that it "probably has the purpose of contradicting that doubt about paternity that is never quite to be overcome."[17] Freud's intuitive insight about the possible relation-

14. Robert Munroe, Ruth H. Munroe and John W. M. Whiting, "The Couvade: A Psychological Analysis," *Ethos* 1 (1973): 30–74. See also Robert 1. Munroe and Ruth H. Munroe, "Male Pregnancy Symptoms and Cross-Sex Identity in Three Societies," *Journal of Social Psychology* 84 (1971): 11–25; and the same authors, "Psychological Interpretation of Male Initiation Rites: The Case of Male Pregnancy Symptoms," *Ethos* 1 (1973): 490–498.

15. Arthur J. Rubel and Joseph Spielberg, "Aspects of the Couvade in Texas and Northeast Mexico," in *Summa Anthropologica en homenaje a Roberto J. Weitlaner* (Mexico City: Instituto Nacional de Antropologia e Historia, 1966), 299–307.

16. Bronislaw Malinowski, *Sex and Repression in Savage Society* (London: John Routledge, 1927), 216.

17. Sigmund Freud, *Collected Papers*, vol. 2, (London: Hogarth Press, 1924), 72.

ship between couvade and doubts about paternity finds support
in a delightful tale reported from Berat in Albania:

> Once the women of that district felt that it was unfair that,
> while men went scot-free, they should have both the pain of
> bearing children and the trouble of rearing them. At a mass
> meeting they decided to implore the help of the nameless
> Saint of Tomor, the handsome mountain overlooking
> Berat. All together, they prayed to him to divide the bur-
> den, giving the men the pangs of childbirth and leaving the
> women to rear the children. The Saint consented and the
> women left happily for home. Soon afterwards, one's time
> came. Instead of her husband, however, it was a neighbour
> who felt labour pains. When this happened a third time,
> the husbands in general made themselves so unpleasant
> that the women saw things were worse than before. Again
> assembling, they prayed to the Saint to restore the old ways,
> and so women continue to endure the pangs of labor as well
> as the worry of rearing their offspring.[18]

The tale suggests that couvade was a sign that the husband recognized the child as his own (and it also hints that men do not wish
to know they have been cuckolded.)

Theodor Reik in a long essay devoted to couvade suggested an
Oedipal interpretation. According to Reik, a man remembers his
rivalry with his own father and he fears his new child—Reik automatically assumed the child is a son—a common weakness in
male-oriented psychoanalytic theory. Reik also suggested that as
a son grows, the father dies.[19] There is some ethnographic evidence to support this. One example comes from the Ainu. "A curious custom used to exist amongst this people. As soon as a
child was born, the father had to consider himself very ill, and
had, therefore, to stay at home, wrapped by the fire. But the wife,

18. Margaret Hasluck, "Couvade in Albania," *Man* 39 (1939): 20.

19. Theodor Reik, "Couvade and the Psychogenesis of the Fear of Retaliation," in *Ritual: Four Psychoanalytic Studies* (New York: Evergreen, 1962), 73–
74.

poor creature! had to stir about as much and as quickly as possible. The idea seems to have been that life was passing from father into his child."[20] Similarly, in a note entitled "A New Explanation of the Couvade," published in the *Journal of the Bihar and Orissa Research Society* in 1916, C. H. Bompas reported the following: "It is known that among the Hos of the Kolban the father after the birth of a child is isolated and is unclean in exactly the same way as the mother is. I once asked a Ho why this was so; he answered, 'Because the life has gone out of the man.'" Hocart applauded Bompas's asking his informant to explain couvade and felt that the explanation offered "if not right, at least comes nearer to the original reason than anything I have so far come across."[21] These ethnographic reports might help explain why a new father might feel ambivalence towards a newborn son. On the one hand, a son is *prima facie* proof of masculinity, but, on the other hand, the life force required for a son automatically diminishes the longevity of the father. According to Reik, the new father fears retaliation from his own father/own son, but it is not completely clear why the new father should act out parturition because of this supposed fear of retaliation.

Among other various psychiatric explanations proposed is one which argues that men are suffering from sibling rivalry. Recalling his feelings earlier in life when a younger sibling rival was born, the father becomes jealous of his own child. This infant will take the attention of his wife just as the original birth of a sibling rival took the attention of the man's mother years ago.[22] This might very well explain some of the rationale underlying the lying-in-behavior in couvade. The father might simply be identifying with or attempting to supplant the rightful mother by lying in bed. But if the father regarded the newborn baby as a kind of

20. John Batchelor, *The Ainu of Japan* (London: Religious Tract Society, 1892), 44.

21. C. H. Bompas, "A New Explanation of the Couvade," *Journal of the Bihar and Orissa Research Society* 2 (1916): 384–385. For Hocart's praise, see "Couvade," *Man* 31 (1931), no. 281.

22. Jesse O. Cavenar, Jr. and Nancy T. Butts, "Fatherhood and Emotional Illness," *American Journal of Psychiatry* 134 (1977): 429–431.

sibling rival, he might then be indulging in regressive behavior, becoming once again a baby himself in order to receive the attention of his wife (who is substituting for his mother). Thus Lévi-Strauss would be quite right in *The Savage Mind* when, in his brief discussion of the couvade, he observed that "it would be a mistake to suppose that a man is taking the place of the woman in labour." The father does not play the part of the mother, he felt. Rather "he plays the part of the child." However, Lévi-Strauss offered no plausible reason why the father should do this.[23]

Bruno Bettelheim in *Symbolic Wounds* tended to see couvade as an expression of male pregnancy envy. "Men need it to fill the emotional vacuum created by their inability to bear children."[24] Riviere in 1978 suggested, largely on the basis of South American Indian examples and an imagined analogy with the custom of *compadrazgo* (godparenthood), that birth involves both a physical and a spiritual component. Supposedly the woman provides the physical birth of a child, but the man provides the spiritual component—much as *compadrazgo* provides spiritual or god parents in addition to the physical parents of a child.[25] But there is some evidence that men believed that they furnished the physical basis as well. In Western thought, for example, there is a longstanding tradition that it is only the male who is responsible for the nature of his offspring. According to this male chauvinist view, the woman is merely the passive receptacle or container for the male input. Aeschylus articulated this in *The Eumenides*, written in 485 B.C., when he had Apollo say:

The mother is no parent of that which is called her child,
but only nurse of the new-planted seed that grows.
The parent is he who mounts. A stranger she

23. Claude Lévi-Strauss, *The Savage Mind* (London: Weidenfeld and Nicolson, 1966), 195.

24. Bruno Bettelheim, *Symbolic Wounds: Puberty Rites and the Envious Male* (New York: Collier Books, 1962), 111.

25. P. G. Riviere, "The Couvade: A Problem Reborn," *Man* 9 (1978): 423–435.

preserves a stranger's seed, if no god interfere.
I will show you proof of what I have explained.
There can be a father without any mother. There she stands,
the living witness, daughter of Olympian Zeus,
she who was never fostered in the dark of the womb,
yet such a child as no goddess could bring to birth.[26]

Athena, Zeus's literal brainchild, is male creativity (without female assistance) par excellence. Theories of preformation in the
seventeenth century shared a similar premise.[27] According to such
theories, which were popular for centuries before the genetics of
sexual reproduction were discovered, the male contribution was
believed to contain in miniature the entire being to be born. A related idea was that of a homunculus, a tiny man, which was
"planted" in the mother during intercourse and which grew there
until the time of birth. This basic notion can still be found in
contemporary folk speech. A son who is described as "a chip off
the old block" typically implies a physical identity with his father. The folk metaphor is rarely, if ever, used in reference to a
boy's mother. Similarly, if a boy is described as "the spitten image" of his father, the implication is that there is a strong and
marked physical resemblance. (The phrase also suggests that spit
and sperm are symbolic equivalents!) Other idioms or proverbs
could be cited, e.g., "Like father, like son." The point is that we
have analogues to couvade in folk speech which imply that the
father's biological role is critical. The most common metaphor is
"seed" and, by the same token, the most common danger is expressed in the same agricultural tradition—that is, a "barren"
woman. The woman had to be fertile in order to be the carrier of
the male seed. The word *semen*, though referring to thick, whit-

26. Aeschylus, *Oresteia,* trans. Richmond Lattimore (Chicago: University of
Chicago Press, 1953), 158 [lines 658–666]. For a discussion of Aristotle's similar
views in his work *On the Generation of Animals*, see James Hillman, *The Myth
of Analysis* (New York: Harper, 1978), 228–231. See also Luis da Camara Cas-
cudo, "Uma Interpretaçào de Couvade," *Revista do Arquivo Municipal* 29
(1936): 51–62.

27. See Peter J. Bowler, "Preformation and Pre-existence in the Seventeenth
Century: A Brief Analysis," *Journal of the History of Biology,* 4 (1971): 221–244.

ish fluid, derives etymologically from the Latin *semen* meaning, literally, seed. Similarly, the word *sperm* apparently derives from a root meaning seed. Incidentally, this is why in the Old Testament it didn't matter all that much who the mother was. Only the father counted. The children were his, not hers. I submit that the rationale behind the current popular interest in cloning, actual or imagined, may be similarly motivated. A man can, through cloning, reproduce himself with no genetic input from woman! In this context, couvade may represent a ritual playing out of a man's pretense that he, and he alone, is responsible for his progeny.

Having considered various theories of the genesis of couvade, what can we say about couvade in Genesis? I believe we can salvage a great deal from previous studies of couvade. We need not accept Bachofen's rigid evolutionary schema, tracing the supposed development of patriarchy from initial matriarchy, to see a connection between couvade and paternity (and perhaps patrilineality). Bachofen may have attempted to make psychology history. Clearly, couvade is, at least in part, an attempt to rival or replace the female role in parturition (and this is true regardless of whether primitive matriarchy preceded primitive paternity!) We might expect to see couvade in societies where male creation myths are found. The very essence of couvade is that man rests after the birth of his baby—even though it is surely the woman who needs the rest. In Genesis, chapter 1, a male God creates the heaven and the earth. On the sixth day (Gen. 1:27), God creates man: "male and female created He them." What happens after God creates humankind? He rests. "And on the seventh day God ended His work which He had made; and He rested on the seventh day from all His work which He had made" (Gen. 2:2). In theory, an omnipotent God, capable of creating the heaven and earth and all else, would not need to rest. Of course, it is possible that the sanctification of a seventh day may have been merely a device to offer a sacred charter for a religious system which demanded that individuals devote one day a week to that system. Still, in the context of couvade, it makes perfect sense for a male creator to rest after his creative act.

Erich Fromm in *The Forgotten Language*, published in 1951, rightly saw Genesis as a myth of pregnancy envy on the part of males, but he claimed that the male God created by His word.[28] However, creating Eve from Adam's rib is not creating by words alone. When Fromm said, "Quite obviously this establishment of male domination points to a previous situation in which he did not rule" (in speaking of God's ordering Eve to let her husband rule over her), he was echoing Bachofen's views of an evolutionary sequence from matriarchy to patriarchy. Fromm did not mention couvade in his discussion at all, and he made a vain attempt to explain the significance of the sabbath ritual. He was puzzled by God's rest on the seventh day and asked, "What does this 'rest' mean?" He claimed, "The Sabbath is the day of peace between man and nature" and that God is fully God only when He does not work, so man is fully man "only when he does not work."[29] But I would argue that the couvade analogy is much more illuminating in explaining the possible rationale underlying the sabbath ritual.

In the second chapter of Genesis, we have a second account of the creation of man: "And the Lord God formed man of the dust of the ground, and breathed into his nostrils the breath of life; and man became a living soul." Dust and dirt as materials for male creation strongly suggest an anal erotic basis and this theory would also explain why the wind or breath was used by a male creator.[30] But what concerns me here is the curious mode of the creation of woman: "And the Lord God caused a deep sleep

28. Erich Fromm, *The Forgotten Language* (New York: Grove Press, 1951), 223–234.

29. Ibid., 241–249.

30. I have discussed the rationale of anal erotic male creativity in previous publications. See, for example, "Earth-Diver: Creation of the Mythopoeic Male," *American Anthropologist* 64 (1962): 1032–1051; and "A Psychoanalytic Study of the Bullroarer," *Man* 11 (1976): 220–238. Corso cites one Italian proverb which illustrates the male anal equivalent to female parturition, "La gallina fa l'uovo e al gallo gli brucia il c . . ." or "La gallina fa l'uovo e al gallo brucia l'ano." See Raffaele Corso, "Il Rito della Covata in un Racconto Popolare della Corsica," in *Homenaje a Fritz Kruger*, vol. 2 (Mendoza: Universidad Nacional de Cuyo, 1954), 357–367. Corso presented the second form of the proverb in an earlier version of the same paper, "Il Mito della Nascita di Minerva ed un racconto popolare della Corsica," *Folklore* 5 (1950): 3–13.

to fall upon Adam, and he slept; and He took one of his ribs, and closed up the flesh instead thereof. And the rib, which the Lord God had taken from man, made He a woman, and brought her unto the man. And Adam said, 'This is now bone of my bones, and flesh of my flesh; she shall be called Woman, because she was taken out of man'" (Gen. 2:21–23).

The creation of the first woman from man's rib, Motif A 1275.1, is not a very widespread myth. I suspect that a good many of the relatively few versions available in print are definite derivatives of the biblical account. It is a narrative which, if not an embarrassment to theologians over the centuries, has surely tested the credulity, if not the faith, of fundamentalists. William Phipps, in his essay "Adam's Rib: Bone of Contention," published in *Theology Today* in 1976, reviewed some of the interpretations of the narrative including modern feminist perspectives. He began by recalling that Andreas Vesalius, a pioneering figure in the scientific study of anatomy, encountered considerable criticism in 1543 when he wrote, "The ribs are twelve in number on each side in man and woman... The popular belief that man is lacking a rib on one side and that woman has one more rib than man is clearly ridiculous, even though Moses, in the second chapter of Genesis, said that Eve was created by God from one of Adam's ribs."[31] Richard Dorson reported a narrative in which an American Indian examines the skeleton of a man at a museum and discovers that there is no rib missing. The Indian concludes that ministers have deceived him in telling him the story of Adam.[32]

If a literal approach will not work, one may wish to consider a symbolic one instead. In 1902 Eduard Stucken, in his *Beiträge zur orientalischen Mythologie*, suggested that the removal of Adam's rib was castration of a primordial being. Otto Rank later

31. William E. Phipps, "Adam's Rib: Bone of Contention," *Theology Today* 33 (1976–1977): 263–273.

32. This is Motif J 1262.8, "Skeleton has all his ribs." But in Stith Thompson's *Motif-Index of Folk-Literature*, 6 vols. (Bloomington: Indiana University Press, 1955–1958), only one text is cited for the motif and that is found in Richard M. Dorson, "Comic Indian Anecdotes," *Southern Folklore Quarterly* 10 (1946): 113–128. (The text in question is on pp. 120–121.)

offered a similar interpretation.[33] Theodor Reik, in his 1960 book entitled *The Creation of Woman*, accepted the phallic nature of the rib incident, but had a much more ambitious thesis, namely, that the story of Eve's creation is analogous to male puberty initiation rites. He suggested that the rib operation is actually the circumcision of Adam and that the Eve story "in veiled language" tells us of Adam's initiation and circumcision and of his finding a spouse.[34] It is true that in male initiation ritual, men pretend to give birth to other males and that the creation of Eve from Adam's body is a ritual reversal of biological reality, insofar as men are created from women's bodies, but I find the reading of Eve's birth from Adam's rib as a puberty initiation ritual a bit farfetched. While it may be correct to see elements of male envy or imitation of female parturition in both puberty rites and the creation of the Eve story, it would be incorrect to say that the creation story is only a puberty rite in disguise.

Reik also argued that since males in initiation rites know very well that they are not actually giving birth to males, what we have is a culturally sanctioned hoax. Men try to fool women. Similarly, Reik contended that the Bible story is also a kind of hoax, a hoax which has not been recognized as such by overly serious biblical scholars.[35] More insightful, in my opinion, is Reik's observation that since Eve is born from Adam's body, she must in

33. Eduard Stucken, *Beiträge zur orientalischen Mythologie, Mitteilungen der Vorderasiatischen Gesellschaft* 7 (1902): 50; Otto Rank, *Das Inzestmotif in Dichtung und Sage* (Leipzig: F. Deuticke, 1912), 317, and *Psychoanalytische Beiträge zur Mythenforschung* (Leipzig: Internationaler Psychoanalytischer Verlag, 1922), 77.

34. Theodor Reik, *The Creation of Woman* (New York: George Braziller, 1960), 111.

35. Reik, 124–125. This notion finds a parallel in the suggestions of early writers on the couvade that the ritual was in essence a parody of birth. Polish ethnographer Ciszewski proposed this in 1904. See G. Stanislaus Ciszewski, "'Kuwada,' Studyum etnologiczne," *Bulletin International de l'Académie des Sciences de Cracovie* (1904) [1905]: 19–23. For the complete study, see Stanislaw Ciszewski, *"Kuwada, Studyum etnologiczne," Wydzial historico-filozoficzny, Rozprawy*, Ser. 2, 23 (1906): 84–142. Another student of couvade who suggested that it was parody was a Enrique Casas. See his *La Covada y el Origen del Totemismo*. (Toledo: Editorial Católica Toledana, 1924), 5.

some sense be his daughter. Thus the first couple are not only man and wife, but also father and daughter. Incest is a fairly common element in creation myths, though more typically it is a matter of brother-sister incest.[36]

If I am correct in seeing couvade in Genesis, then one can accept the phallic basis of the rib incident without accepting Reik's contention that it masks a male initiation ritual. In medieval Judaism we find the following deliberation attributed to God as He considers which part of man to use to create woman: "I will not create her from the head for she may carry herself haughtily; nor from the eye for she may be too inquisitive; nor from the ear, for she may be an eavesdropper, nor from the mouth for she may be too talkative; nor from the heart for she may be too jealous; nor from the hand for she may be too acquisitive; nor from the foot for she may be a gadabout. I will create her from a hidden part of the body that she may be modest.[37] Another version states, "I will create her from the modest part of man for even when he stands naked, that part is covered."[38] Phipps said that even when man stands naked, his rib is covered, but it could also be that even when a man is naked, he is supposedly required to keep his genitals covered. In the light of the literary construction of the passage in which all the other parts considered are external facets of the anatomy, it would stand to reason that the final one selected would also be an external feature. Richard Rubenstein's comment on this legendary material is, "It is impossible to prove explicitly that in this tradition Eve is created out of Adam's penis. Nevertheless, this seems to be the meaning. The legend sharpens

36. Reik, 131. For a theoretical consideration of sibling incest myths, see Sally Falk Moore, "Descent and Symbolic Filiation," *American Anthropologist* 66 (1964): 1308–1320.

37. Phipps, "Adam's Rib," 264.

38. Richard L. Rubenstein, *The Religious Imagination: A Study in Psychoanalysis and Jewish Theology* (Boston: Beacon Press, 1968), 47–48. Incidentally, an abbreviated version of this formula occurs in Chaucer's "Parson's Tale" (lines 925–929). For further discussion, see Francis Lee Utley, "Abraham Lincoln's *When Adam Was Created*," in *Studies in Folklore*, ed. W. Edson Richmond (Bloomington: Indiana University Press, 1957), 187–212.

the biblical story, in which the normal order of human reproduction is reversed. In the Bible woman comes forth from man."[39]

But I believe there is some evidence to demonstrate conclusively that Eve is created from Adam's penis and I am not referring to arguing from analogy with a Greek myth in which Aphrodite is created from the severed phallus of Uranus. For one thing, the human phallus, unlike the phalluses of his primate relatives, does not have a bone! Man is missing the *os baculum*. This feature of human anatomy could easily have been noticed by early man and certainly by societies that slaughtered game or domestic animals. Rodents, insectivores, and carnivores do have the *os baculum*. Dogs, for example, have it. Consequently, it would be a simple enough empirical observation for men to notice that the human male lacked a bone in this important area of the body.

Of course, it is one thing for us now in the twentieth century to remark upon the absence of the *os baculum* in the human male. It is another to assume that this anatomical feature was necessarily noticed by societies in centuries past. Jane Theodoropoulos, writing a note in the *Psychoanalytic Review* in 1967, suggested that Adam's rib might have been Adam's "boner." This occurred to her in part because, as the mother of three boys, she overheard the use of "boner" as a slang term for erection and, after reading Reik's *The Creation of Woman*, she decided that "the rib" was a displaced "boner."[40] But how can we tell if people in the past really did notice the boneless nature of the human phallus?

Folklore provides evidence to demonstrate that the phallus has been commonly perceived as "the boneless one." Some of this evidence has been conveniently surveyed by linguist Calvert Watkins.[41] He cited, for instance, a text from the *Rigveda*:

39. Rubenstein, *The Religious Imagination*, 52.

40. Jane Theodoropoulos, "Adam's Rib," *Psychoanalytic Review* 54 (1967): 542–544.

41. Calvert Watkins, "ANOSTEOS 'ON PODA TENDEI," *Études et Commentaires* 91 (1978): 231–235.

His stout one appeared in front
hanging down as a boneless shank
his wife *sasvati* noticing said:
"You carry, Lord, a fortunate pleasurer"

Watkins also presented an *Exeter Book* riddle: "I have heard of something which increases in a corner, swelling and rising, lifting the covers. A proud-minded maid seized that boneless thing with her hands; with a garment the prince's daughter covered the swelling thing." Tupper in *The Riddles of the Exeter Book* said that the answer to the riddle is "dough" and that in the riddle one finds a vivid description of the woman's work of kneading, but Watkins doubted that this is the only meaning of this obvious double entendre.[42] From this and other textual evidence, Watkins concluded that "boneless one" is a kenning or riddle for penis.

Since man lacks the *os baculum* and since the folk have evidently recognized this anatomical fact by constructing riddles and metaphors based upon it, we may now return to the text of Genesis. Here we have an account of the creation of woman from a part of man. The part is a bone, for Adam specifically says, "This is now bone of my bones, and flesh of my flesh."

In a male-ordered paradise, the males do the creating. In terms

---

42. Ibid., 233–234. There is additional evidence for the association of bone and phallus. In the mid-nineteenth century, *bone* in Cockney speech referred to the penis erectus. In Shakespeare's day, *bone-ache* referred to venereal disease. See Eric Partridge, *A Dictionary of Historical Slang* (Harmondsworth: Penguin, 1972), 95. The proverb, "The nearer the bone, the sweeter the meat," according to Partridge, was applied by men to a thin woman viewed as a bed-mate. The same sort of bone-phallus metaphorical pattern also exists in contemporary German folk speech. See *knochen* in Ernest Borneman, *Sex im Volksmund* (Reinbek bei Hamburg: Rowohlt, 1971). The irony is that an erect phallus may give the appearance of a bone, but physiologically there is still no *os baculum*. One curious piece of data which links couvade with an erect phallus comes from the Canary Islands. The term used there for couvade is *zorrocloco* but it can reportedly be used to describe a state of sexual excitement which "a menudo le entraba el sorrocloco y no reparaba en lugar u ocasion para satisfacerse." See Elias Serra Rafols, "De la covada en Tenerife. Un caso concreto," in *Homenaje a Don Luis de Hoyos Sainz*, vol. 2 (Madrid: Graficas Valera, 1950), 388–390. For more about the term *zorrocloco*, see José A. Pérez Regalado, "Zorrocloco en España y America," *Archivos Venezolanos de Folklore* 1 (1952): 388–394.

of couvade, they give birth and they rest. Paradise where male creativity is possible is, unfortunately, short-lived. What is of special interest here is the set of conditions imposed by God as the primordial couple leaves Eden. Woman is "punished" by God as follows: Unto the woman He said, "I will greatly multiply thy sorrow and thy conception; in sorrow thou shalt bring forth children..." (Gen. 3:16). The males pretend to assign childbearing and labor pains to females. Here is a myth providing a sociological charter for noncouvade. The very fact that this is the primary punishment imposed by a male God should also serve to underline the concern in Genesis for the childbearing act. It is as if to say that it was only this once that men bore women—a male God producing Eve from Adam's phallus (just as Zeus produced only one brainchild: Athene). Henceforth it would be women who would bear men. And, indeed, just as soon as the couple leaves Eden, Eve conceives and bears Cain and Abel (Gen. 4:1-2).

I believe that the initial act of creation by God (which ends in a day of rest) and the creation of a female from a male body genital—remember that females give birth from their genital parts—and the specific details of God's curse upon women (referring to labor pains) all support the idea that the first two chapters of Genesis consist in part of a form of literary couvade. The critical importance of this psychological constellation is indicated by the widespread distribution of couvade among peoples in many areas of the world, e.g., Asia, Europe, South America, and by its manifestations among individual males in most, if not all, modern urban societies (under the couvade-syndrome label).

While it may well be that the particular individuals who act out couvade behavior may have greater degrees of cross-sex identification than other individuals in the same societies, the occurrence of a form of couvade in Genesis—that is, in perhaps the most basic myth of Western culture—strongly supports the notion that couvade, to a greater or lesser degree, is relevant to most males. To the extent that males feel pregnancy envy but are unwilling to admit this, they may try to protect themselves by projection. Specifically, males will invariably attempt to prove that it is women who envy men. The irrational desire to demean women's childbearing role, plus the insistence upon women's alleged inferiority in so many male chauvinist cultures, no doubt masks a deep-seated feeling of inferiority in men. It is men, after all, who feel constrained to prove their masculinity again and again; in contrast, women do not feel nearly so obliged to prove their femininity. In myths made by men, males do the creating; in theories made by men, e.g., by psychoanalysts, it is females who are said to envy males (think of penis envy, for example, which rarely if ever appears in folklore—except in a few off-color jokes *told by men*!). What we have in Genesis in particular and in the custom of couvade in general is a basic view of male and female roles vis-à-vis one another. I am convinced that many of the pressing psychological problems of both men and women, in societies past and present, are intimately related to the stereotypes and self-images nurtured by Genesis and couvade. As a folklorist, I am trying to bring these stereotypes and self-images from the unconscious level of myth and custom to the level of consciousness. The attempt to make the unconscious conscious is one of my principal goals as a scholar. I am almost tempted to say that it is my baby, but, under the circumstances, that might be an unfortunate choice of words.[43]

43. I wish to thank Ms. Eleanor Walden, for making a valuable preliminary foray into the immense bibliography of couvade, and the members of an undergraduate seminar in anthropology at the University of California, Berkeley, a seminar which in 1979 was devoted to couvade. I would especially like to thank one of the members of the seminar, Scott Morgan, for suggesting the possible relevance of couvade to Genesis. I am also indebted to my colleague, Professor Vincent Sarich, a physical anthropologist, who first mentioned to me the intriguing hypothesis that the absence of the *os baculum* in man might be related to the account of creation in Genesis.

6   The Symbolic Equivalence of Allomotifs in the Rabbit-Herd (AT 570)

One of the perennial difficulties in the study of symbolism concerns the empirical verification of purported symbolic equations. It is one thing to assert that a nose may be a phallic symbol; it is quite another to prove it beyond a reasonable doubt, that is, demonstrate it to the satisfaction of individuals not necessarily favorably disposed towards psychoanalytic theory. Psychoanalysts often appear to offer symbolic readings of events and data without recourse to conventional canons of proof. It is deemed sufficient that a patient volunteered a free association to a symbol occurring in a dream or that an earlier psychoanalyst proclaimed the validity of a particular symbolic equation. How do we know, in short, that A is a symbol of B (or B of A)? Is it only a matter of accepting a proposed symbolic equation on faith, or is there in fact a methodology which would permit a measure of certitude in determining the meaning(s) of symbols?

It is my contention that the folktale (as well as other genres of folklore) can provide a corpus of data which can materially advance our knowledge of symbolism. The only reason why most folklorists have hitherto failed to make proper use of this corpus is because they tend on the whole to be literal, not symbolic, in their overall approach to folktale content. Historic-geographic studies of individual tale types can be and indeed have been undertaken with no thought whatsoever about the possible symbolic implications of any of the constituent motifs or traits of the tale. Yet I am prepared to argue that it is precisely through the comparative study of tales that symbolic equations can be discovered and confirmed. Through a combination of the comparative method *and* structural analysis, I hope to outline a methodology which may prove useful in studying symbols anywhere in the world.

Anyone who has gathered numerous versions of a given folktale knows very well that considerable variation in content may occur within the framework of the basic tale summary plot outline. In historic-geographic studies, this becomes evident when one examines the list of possible subtraits within a selected trait. The problem with using trait variation is that the traits are normally selected *a priori* by the folktale scholar (ordinarily because he believes the particular traits chosen will be useful in determining either the original form or the paths of diffusion of the tale under study). If we adopt a structural view of the folktale—and by that I mean that we consider a folktale as consisting of a sequence of motifemes (Propp's functions), then we stay closer to the tale as it exists when told by a raconteur to an audience. (Traits defined by historic-geographic practitioners are not necessarily structural units. Thus "place where action takes place" or "number of personages" would not be considered as motifemic slots.) If in addition, we examine the various allomotifs which can fill a specific motifemic slot—as determined by empirically reviewing the content of field-collected versions of a tale type—we may gain access to implicit native formulations of symbolic equivalences. If A and B both fulfill the same motifeme, then in some sense is it not reasonable to assume that the folk are equating A and B. In other words, allomotifs are both functionally and symbolically equivalent. Please note that it is the folk themselves who are constructing so-to-speak these symbolic equations, not some biased folklorist wrongly imbued with a particular mindset belonging to one symbolic school or another. I believe that the concept of allomotific equivalence may hold both for intra- and inter-cultural variation. Within a given culture, the range of allomotifs in a particular motifemic slot will show functional equivalence; and comparisons of the same tale in two or more cultures may yield the same or different sets of functional equivalents. In fact, insofar as tale types are cross-

cultural (n.b., this is *not* the same as universal!), e.g., an Indo-
European tale type, an American Indian tale type, an African
tale type, it is precisely at the allomotific level where we may expect to encounter the most striking examples of variation. The
tale type may be the same, but the allomotifs may vary. What I
am really suggesting here is that allomotifs may be symbolically
equivalent. A borrowing culture may accept a tale type from a
donor culture but substitute allomotifs more consonant with its
own symbolic system. Comparative studies of folktales have
been primarily concerned trying to establish which allomotif is
older or logically prior rather than attempting to show how culturally relative allomotifs might signal oicotypes which might in
turn provide significant clues to national character, regional
penchants, or individual idiosyncrasies.

Let me first of all illustrate the principle of symbolic equivalence by citing several versions of a particular text. Consider, for
instance, an anti-Jewish *blason populaire* collected in London in
the spring of 1976:

> Two Jews were walking beside a lake. One of them stuck his
> finger in the water and said, "Wow, the water's cold!" The
> other one stuck his nose in and said, "Yes, and deep, too."

Another version has Texans instead of Jews:

> Two Texans are walking across the Golden Gate Bridge in
> San Francisco. In the middle of the bridge, they decide to
> take a leak [to urinate]. One says, "Boy, this water's cold";
> the other comments, "But not very deep."

The Texas *blason populaire* tradition emphasizes bigness and presumably his organ is so large it touches bottom. (Since phallic
size is presumably positive, the water is judged not deep. In the
anti-Jewish *blason populaire* tradition, nose size is a negative feature and so it is appropriate for the water to be considered deep.[1])
The point here, however, is that these two versions of the same

1. For further discussion of the big-nose portion of the Jewish stereotype, see
Alan Dundes, "A Study of Ethnic Slurs: The Jew and the Polack in the United
States," *Journal of American Folklore* 84 (1971): 195.

joke suggest that in some sense noses and phalluses are equivalent. Isn't this evidence supporting the notion that a nose might be a phallic symbol in some contexts? Of course, one could argue that all the texts show is the functional equivalence of noses and phalluses. In theory, it is just as likely that a phallus is a symbolic nose as it is that a nose is a symbolic phallus. It is perfectly true that examining the allomotific gamut within a particular motifemic slot shows only functional equivalence. We can tell that A and B are functional or symbolic equivalents, but not necessarily that A is a symbol of B or that B is a symbol of A. On the other hand, if we find evidence in a given culture that either A or B is a tabooed subject, then we might well expect that the non-tabooed subject might be substituted for the tabooed subject rather than vice versa.

If we are correct about a nose-phallus equation in Anglo-American folklore, we should not be surprised to find the same paradigm manifested in a variety of genres. Symbols are rarely, if ever, confined to a single genre. Symbolic systems are at least culturewide—not to raise the inevitably tricky question of whether symbolic equations may possibly be cross-cultural. Let us consider a limerick reported in Brunvand's *The Study of American Folklore*:[2]

> There was an old lady from Kent
> Whose nose was most awfully bent
> She followed her nose,
> One day I suppose,
> And nobody knows where she went.

Although there are a number of other limericks using "Kent," surely the most popular of them all concerns a gifted male:[3]

2. Jan Harold Brunvand, *The Study of American Folklore*, 2d ed. (New York: W.W. Norton, 1978), 93.

3. G. Legman, *The Limerick* (New York: Bell, 1969), 65, no. 313. For a representative psychoanalytic discussion of the phallic nature of the nose, see Otto Fenichel, "The 'Longnose'", in *The Collected Papers of Otto Fenichel*, First series (New York: W. W. Norton, 1953), 155-157. A joke circulating in Berkeley in 1979 which strikingly confirms the nose-phallus equation goes as follows: Question. What happened when Snow White (or Cinderella) went out on a date (in Disneyland) with Pinocchio? Answer. She sat on his face and said, "Tell me a lie! Tell me a lie!" (or "Tell me a lie, Tell me the truth, Tell me a lie, Tell me the truth, etc.").

There was a young fellow of Kent
Whose prick was so long that it bent,
So to save himself trouble
He put it in double
And instead of coming he went.

The identical rhyme words of *Kent, bent,* and *went* make it possible to regard the two texts as variants of the same basic limerick. Again in this instance we find that noses and phalluses are equivalent. But we have even better evidence of the hypothetical nose-phallus equation than that cited thus far. In fact, we have the folk's own articulation of the equation. In an old joke, a young woman on her wedding night is sent by her new husband to the pharmacy to buy contraceptives. The druggist asks her what size? She says she is just married and that she has no idea. "Well," said the druggist, "I need to know the size in order to sell you the proper item." "I just don't know," repeated the bride. "All right, how big is his nose?" "Oh, about so big," answered the young woman. "O.K., that means you need a medium." "Wow! That's amazing. To think that you can tell the size of a man's organ by the size of his nose?" "Oh, that's not all. I can also tell the size of a woman's vagina?" "Really, how do you do that?" "By the size of her mouth." "Is that so?" [spoken with tightly pursed lips so as to minimize the mouth].[4]

The important point about these examples is that the symbolic equation is being made by the folk themselves. One may argue that the equation is fallacious or not convincing, but the fact remains that the equation comes from within the culture, not from without. It cannot be dismissed simply as psychoanalytic readings into data. The readings come out of the data.

Please keep in mind that I am not arguing that a nose always stands for a phallus—even just within Western cultures, the provenience of the above-mentioned materials. Sometimes a nose is a nose is a nose! My concern is essentially methodological. Propp's structural work demonstrated the functional equiva-

---

4. For another joke which depends for its effect upon the same linguistic feature, see Alan Dundes, "Jokes and Covert Language Attitudes: The Curious Case of the Wide-Mouth Frog," *Language in Society* 6 (1977): 141–147.

lence of allomotifs; I am now suggesting that allomotifs may in addition be symbolic equivalents.[5]

I should like to further illustrate the nature of allomotific symbolic equivalence by considering briefly Aarne-Thompson tale-type 570, The Rabbit-Herd. This is a widespread European folktale. Kurt Ranke reports 25 versions in his *Schleswig-Holsteinische Volksmärchen* while Paul Delarue and Marie-Louise Tenèze in *Le Conte Populaire Français* synopsize 36 versions.[6] The tale is also contained in Grimm tale 165, "Der Vogel Greif." According to statistics in the tale-type index, there are 79 versions from Finland alone.

The tale plot involves a hero's winning a princess by fulfilling a task. The task typically consists of herding anywhere from one to three hundred rabbits. The hero, often following two unsuccessful attempts by older brothers, is kind to a donor figure who gives him a magic object, e.g., a whistle. Blowing the whistle summons the scattered rabbits. The king, fearful of the hero's success, sends emissaries with instructions to obtain the whistle. The sequence may include a serving girl, the princess, and the queen. Each in turn tries to persuade the hero to relinquish the magic object (or rabbit). He sets a price which may range from a kiss to coitus. After paying the price, the woman takes the rabbit/whistle away, but through magic, it is returned to the hero. Then the king himself tries to get the object. The price for him entails his kissing his horse's ass or committing an act of bestiality with the animal. The tale ends with a final task of filling a sack or tub full of lies. The hero proceeds to recount the tale itself with the serving girl, princess, queen, or king stoutly protesting that the detail about them is not true (with special reference to paying the price for the magic object or rabbit). In many versions, the king manages to interrupt the hero just before his bes-

---

5. Actually when I first proposed the term *allomotif*, I had also thought of the possibility of its relevance to the study of symbolic equivalents. See "From Etic to Emic Units in the Structural Study of Folktales," *Jounal of American Folklore* 75 (1962): 105, n. 26.

6. Kurt Ranke, *Schleswig-Holsteinische Volksmärchen* (Kiel: Ferdinand Hirt, 1958), 264-300; Paul Delarue and Marie-Louise Tenèze, *Le Conte Populaire Français*, vol. 2 (Paris: Maisonneuve, 1964), 454-466.

tial act is about to be revealed and he gives the hero his daughter's hand in marriage.

The tale type is sometimes combined with tale-type 610, The Healing Fruits; tale-type 621, The Louse-Skin; and tale-type 850, The Birthmarks of the Princess. I might note parenthetically that unless one naively believes that young boys actually did herd rabbits with the help of a magic object as a conventional means of winning a bride, one cannot accept an exclusively literal/ historical approach to the tale. Clearly we are in the presence of fantasy and accordingly a symbolic approach is appropriate.

Since the Rabbit-herd has not been the subject of a historic-geographic study, I do not have access to all the versions of the tale, versions which amount to more than 350 texts. Nevertheless, I have seen enough versions to at least illustrate my notion of the symbolic equivalence of allomotifs. For example, in an Irish (or Irish-American) version, the hero and his brothers are threatened by the king. If they do not succeed in the rabbit-herding task, they will be thrown into the snake-pit. In a version from North Carolina, Jack is told that his head will be cut off if he does not succeed. In a version from the Ozarks collected by Vance Randolph, the king threatens to cut the hero's "pecker" off.[7] From a Proppian point of view, it does not matter what motif is used in this slot. The king sets a task for the hero. If he succeeds, he wins

---

7. The Irish or Irish-American version was told by Josephine Gardner. Entitled "That Was Some Whistle," it was recorded on Thos. Tenney Records TG-4." "The White Cat; That Was Some Whistle." The North Carolina version is recorded on "Jack Tales told by Mrs. Maud Long of Hot Springs, N. C.," Long-Playing Record AAFSL47 in the Library of Congress Music Division Recording Laboratory series. The tale is entitled "Jack and the Drill." It is quite similar to "The Enchanted Lady" reported by Isabel Gordon Carter, "Mountain White Folk-Lore: Tales from the Southern Blue Ridge," *Journal of American Folklore* 38 (1925): 350–351, and to "Fill, Bowl! Fill!," in Richard Chase, ed., *The Jack Tales* (Boston: Houghton Mifflin, 1943), 89–95. Vance Randolph's version appeared in *Pissing in the Snow & Other Ozark Folktales* (Urbana: University of Illinois Press, 1976), 47–50. Randolph also reported a nonobscene version from the very same informant who claimed he used it for mixed audiences, that is, ladies and gentlemen. See *Who Blowed Up the Church House?* (New York: Columbia University Press, 1952), 17–19. In this latter version, the king threatens to cut off the hero's head rather than his "pecker." This suggests that allomotific variation at the individual level may sometimes parallel the general allomotific variation within a tale type.

the princess; if he fails, he is punished. The particular punishment is not structurally significant. But once we understand that allomotifs may be symbolic equivalents, we can see that being thrown into a snake pit, being decapitated, and having one's "pecker" cut off are in some sense the same act. Again, please note that these alleged equivalents come from versions of the tale type, not from some armchair Freudian analyst. We may or may not choose to believe a psychoanalyst who tells us that decapitation can be a symbolic substitute for castration, but we simply cannot ignore the relevant evidence from folklore itself. The folk, collectively, are giving us a range of allomotifs which structurally speaking must be considered as functional equivalents.

Let us look at another portion of the tale. An attempt is made to take the magic object or a rabbit away from the hero. Functionally, it apparently makes no difference whether it is the object or the rabbit which the hero must retain. Symbolically then, the magic object and the rabbit are the same. Usually, the object is a whistle which the hero plays or blows to summon the widely dispersed rabbits. But in a North Carolina version, the object is a "seed drill," that is, an object used to facilitate sowing. The symbolism is virtually overt in this instance (although definitely not to the prudish elderly female story teller). The hero must retain control over his sexual organ or he will not be able to marry the princess. Rabbits, in western cultures, are associated with fertility—think of the good luck attached to having a rabbit foot (extremity!) hanging from one's keyring! Numerous idioms and jokes attest to this folk association with rabbits or bunnies. In most versions of the tale type, the rabbits belong to the king and the hero is asked to keep them under control. In sum, the hero is being asked to take charge of the fertility of the king. If he can demonstrate his ability to exercise control over the king's fertility —and not part with his seed drill (or other magic object)—he can triumph over the king and marry the king's daughter. His sexual conquest over all the king's female emissaries: serving wench, daughters, and even wife show the nature of the struggle. The final act of humiliation for the king is to have intercourse with his mare. As shepherds may resort to intercourse with animals in the absence of appropriate female companions, so the

king is reduced to such a situation, signalling his total loss of females. (In other folktales, the king may even be buggered by the
hero suggesting that the king himself becomes feminized, a final
"female" victim for the priapic hero.)[8]

The phallic nature of the task (and magic object) may illuminate an otherwise curious and inexplicable version of the donor
sequence. Typically the donor gives the magic object to the hero
in return for some service rendered, e.g., sharing bread. But in
an Irish (Irish-American) version, the hero finds a woman whose
nose has been caught in a tree for a hundred years. He frees the
woman's nose and in gratitude, she gives him a magic whistle.
Similarly in a Finnish version collected in 1889, the hero removes
a birch club from an old hag's nose, and in another Finnish version collected in 1888, the hero removes the donor's nose from a
pine stump to which it is stuck.[9] In a version collected in 1892 in
Russian Karelia, an old gap-toothed man offers to help the hero
with the rabbit task in return for an act of sexual intercourse.[10] In
essence, it would appear that the hero has to learn how to handle
a magic phallus. Separating a man or woman's nose from a
stump might imply a separation or interruption of a previous
sexual relationship. I believe the hero must end the sexual activity of his parents' generation and begin a new sexual life for himself by seducing and marrying a princess. (The possible symbolic
significance of the nose should be clear from our previous
discussion.)

The magic power of the helpful whistle, seed drill, or rabbit
consists of its being returned to the hero after use. The princess
or the queen "buys" the object through some sexual act—a kiss

8. For an example of such a tale, see Paulo de Carvalho-Neto, *Decameron
Ecuatoriano* (Mexico City: Editorial V. siglos, 1975), 109–119.

9. I must express my thanks to Ms. Linda Koski, who was kind enough to
translate thirty Finnish versions of AT 570 sent to me by the Finnish Folklore Archives. Cited here is a version collected by Maria Österberg in 1889 in Lohja from
Oskar Öhlund from the village Muijala, and a version collected by K. F. Heide-
man and K. W. Palmroch in 1888 in Joutsa from Taavi Urpi, who heard the tale in
Hartola.

10. This version was collected by E. F. Rautell in 1892 in Vuokkiniemi from
Miihkali Mäkeläinen.

or coitus, but her possession of the magic object turns out to be only temporary. One is tempted to suggest that this is a fantastic translation of a child's version of the sexual act insofar as the male appears for the moment to "lose" his magic object when he engages in sexual intercourse. The magic return of the object after each sexual act affirms the male's control over/possession of his sexual organ.

It was not my intention to offer a full-scale interpretation of the Rabbit-herd (AT 570). In order to do so, I would have had to carry out a historic-geographic study of the type and consider all the available versions before attempting to analyze the myriad variations of detail which occur. For example, in German versions, the hero commonly has as preliminary task to mow the grass before breakfast. The hero wins if he cuts the grass farther than the princess can urinate.[11]

My concern in this essay was essentially methodological. I have tried to demonstrate how folklorists interested in symbolism can profitably utilize previous assiduous comparative studies of individual folktales. By placing a structural (motifemic) matrix over a tale type, one can observe the gamut of allomotific variation occurring within a given motifeme. If one assumes that motifs which fill the same structural slot must be equivalent—and further that this equivalence comes from an unreflective, unselfconscious folk process rather than from an *a priori* analytic scheme imposed from without by a Freudian practitioner—then I believe we have a new source or resource for the scientific study of symbols. Recognition of the symbolic equivalence of allomotifs, not just in tale-type 570, Rabbit-herd, but in all folktales (and legends and folksongs, etc.) will permit folklorists to reap an unsuspected harvest of knowledge from the scores and scores of monographic comparative treatments of tale types, monographs which all too commonly stand ignored and unread on

11. Ranke, *Schleswig*, 274–277, 282–283. One is tempted to suggest that grass may be a symbol of pubic hair. The princess wishes to urinate without wetting the "grass" which surrounds her. The hero's symbolic mastery of the princess's pubic hair would be appropriate in light of the general male-female struggle also implicit in the tale type. In the same way, the snake-pit allomotif mentioned earlier might represent a "poison damsel" threat.

dusty library shelves. One could, for example, eventually list a large number of sets of symbolic equivalents coming from a whole group of tales which have been subjected to intensive historic-geographic study. Thus the symbolic equivalents of one tale type might well turn out to be found in another tale type. Propp's morphology, suggesting as it does that Indo-European fairy tales may share a more or less common structure, would certainly argue for the plausibility of seeking to make a cumulative list of symbolic equivalent sets from individual tale types. Such rich comparative data would also serve to indicate whether a given symbolic equation was oicotypical, that is, found exclusively in one particular geographic or cultural area, or whether it was more widespread, e.g., found throughout Indo-European or American Indian cultures. It remains to be seen to what extent this notion of the symbolic equivalence of allomotifs will prove helpful in future investigations of folk symbolism.

7   The American Game of
     "Smear the Queer"
     and the Homosexual
     Component of Male
     Competitive Sport and
     Warfare

One of the principal methodological difficulties in applying psychoanalytic theory to anthropological data concerns validation. How does one know that a prospective insight gained from interpreting an element of a particular culture psychoanalytically is valid? Far too often, readers are simply asked to accept on faith that a given interpretation is sound. Presumably if the reader shares the psychoanalytic bias of the initial interpreter, he will agree with the interpretation; if he does not, he will disagree. This is not a satisfactory state of affairs. Surely if a psychoanalytic perspective does yield new insights in the study of culture, it ought to be possible to demonstrate the authenticity and accuracy of such insights—even to individuals who may be unfamiliar with psychoanalytic theory or who may be downright hostile to it.

The methodological issue in question is a serious one and so long as it is avoided, the reputation of psychoanalytic anthropology among mainstream social scientists will continue to be low. Here is where the materials of folklore offer the psychoanalytic anthropologist an unrivalled opportunity to confront the validation problem. Folklore as a form of autobiographical ethnography provides an emic as opposed to etic set of symbolic equivalences. (See chapter 6.) Freud himself drew attention to the remarkable nature of folkloristic data in the tenth lecture,

"Symbolism in Dreams," in his *A General Introduction to Psychoanalysis:*

> How do we profess to arrive at the meaning of these dream-symbols, about which the dreamer himself can give us little or no information? My answer is that we derive our knowledge from widely different sources: from fairy tales and myths, jokes and witticisms, from folklore, i.e., from what we know of the manners and customs, sayings and songs, of different peoples, and from poetic and colloquial usage of language. (1953:166)

Freud actually demonstrated how to use folkloristic data to illuminate symbolic equivalents in a paper jointly written with Viennese classicist D. E. Oppenheim in 1911. In this important essay, Freud shows how symbolic equations as reported or explicated in dreams which occur in folktales correspond exactly to the "Freudian" interpretations of everyday dreams. In other words, much of Freud's interpretation of dream symbols upon examination turns out to articulate symbolic equations already in some sense "known" by the folk. One apt summary of this view claims "Freud's contribution as far as symbols are concerned is to be regarded as rediscovery laboriously acquired through intellectual analysis, of something which previously was—and in other cultures still is—given knowledge" (Vanggaard 1972:14). One could, of course, argue that both Freudian interpretations and folk symbolic equations are "wrong," but the striking congruence of analytic and folk constructions remains to be explained.

Dozens of explicit or overt symbolic equations in folklore are readily available. One such illustrative instance is the alleged phallic symbolism of snakes. Pioneer psychoanalytic anthropologist Weston La Barre devoted some three chapters of his superb study of snake-handling cults in the United States to serpent symbolism in Africa, the Near East, and elsewhere (1962:53–109). His analytic accounts of the genital and phallic significance of the snake in a variety of cultural contexts are certainly persuasive, but scholars with a strong bias against psychoanalytic theory could try to ignore La Barre's erudite arguments. It might not be so easy to ignore the following versions of a folk cartoon which has been circulated in the United States for many decades. I shall present more than one version of the item to demonstrate that it is indeed traditional inasmuch as it appears in multiple and variant form. (The first version was collected in 1974 in Oakland. The second one comes from the Kinsey Institute for Sexual Research at Indiana University with no date indicated. The third version, as its caption suggests, was collected in Tennessee in 1977. The fourth version comes from the Kinsey Institute and is dated 1964, and the fifth version was collected in San Francisco and bears no date.) Regardless of any effect a flute might really have on a snake's behavior, the occurrence of the flute in the cartoon may itself have symbolic meaning. In American folk speech, "to play the skin flute" refers to male masturbation. Thus playing the flute to arouse a "snake" is not a custom foreign to American culture—despite the apparent foreign setting of the cartoon figure in India. It is hard to imagine that anyone seeing these five variants of a common American folk cartoon could possibly deny that a snake can serve as a phallic image!

Let me give another illustration of how folklore data can "validate" a hypothetical symbolic equation. Psychoanalysts have suggested that the pulling of teeth can represent a symbolic form of castration (Freud 1938:924,n.1; Darlington, 1929; Kanner, 1928). Those unfamiliar with psychoanalysis normally find this symbolic equation farfetched. Yet the following folk cartoon confirms in no uncertain terms the symbolic association of tooth extraction and castration. There seems little doubt that this symbolic equation plays some part in the excessive fear that some males have in visiting their dentist (plus the fear of having their oral cavity "penetrated" by the novocaine needle and the drill). (The first version from the Kinsey Institute was deposited there by the author during his graduate student days in Bloomington, Indiana, in 1960, while the second version was collected in San Francisco in 1971.)

I should like to further illustrate a way in which folkloristic data can be utilized to support or corroborate a hypothetical

An Old Hindoo
Custom!

TENNESSEE ORIENTAL

AN OLD HINDOO CUSTOM

181

symbolic equation derived from psychoanalytic anthropology. In a previous essay (1978), I sought to show how American football represented a form of homosexual ritual combat in which males prove their masculinity at the expense of other males, namely, by feminizing them. The objective of American football could be summarized as trying to get into one's opponent's endzone more times than he gets into one's own endzone. Response to the essay included various sorts of outrage—including written death threats. (As anthropologists work more and more in societies where their informants may read the results of their research, the recording and analysis of informant responses to published research will become increasingly important.) Two different groups who applauded the study each had their own vested interests. Gays liked the implication that supposedly "straight" American males as exemplified by macho football players were acting out a homosexual battle; feminists rightly saw in the analysis a confirmation of their own view that "losers" in American culture were depicted in the role of passive, receiving, put upon, "female" individuals. But the principal objection made by critics of the essay was the question of validation. How did I know that American football was an unconscious homosexual struggle for supremacy? Could I "prove" my allegations?

In my original essay, I presented abundant evidence from folk speech to indicate the sexual nature of the sport. One spoke commonly of the "deepest penetration" yet into an opponent's territory, and there were frequent cheers from fans exhorting their team to "go all the way" and to "score." The term "pass" can also have sexual nuance as confirmed by the folk epigram: Old football players never die, they just keep on making passes. These terms normally applicable to conventional heterosexual relations were in football applied to relations between *males only*. I was not suggesting that football players were homosexuals or that football fans were homosexuals. There is a difference between being a homosexual and engaging in homosexual behavior—just as there is a difference between being an alcoholic and taking a drink at a bar or a cocktail party.

I might have made clearer the fact that I was commenting upon a feature of American culture in which physical contact between males is discouraged. For example, in the United States, men can dance with women; women can dance with women, but men cannot dance with other men (unless a socially sanctioned folk dance, e.g., borrowed from Greece, provides an outlet for such behavior). Again, men can kiss women in public; women can kiss women in public, but few American men are comfortable kissing other men in public. Football, like some other sports, afforded American males the opportunity to touch and embrace one another. I was not arguing that football was unhealthy. If anything is unhealthy, it would be the society which makes it taboo for males to enjoy any kind of physical intimacy. One does not normally pat a male colleague on his buttocks to show approbation or affection except in the context of a football game. I do not intend to rehearse more of my argument here. The interested reader should consult the original essay if he wishes further details. The sole question I am raising now is that of validating my symbolic interpretation of American football. Even those relatively few individuals who indicated they agreed with my interpretation could not offer any additional evidence. They just somehow felt or knew I was right in what I said about American football. But that kind of consensus hardly constitutes scientific data.

Let us consider briefly an American folk game in which a ball (not necessarily a football) is thrown into the air, typically in a schoolyard. In this boys' game, the person who catches the ball would be set upon by all the other players. The person with the ball might try to run evasively so as to avoid the host of would-be tacklers. When the ball carrier is eventually tackled, he had to release the ball by "fumbling" or he might throw it up again into the air which would initiate a new free-for-all. The "rules" for this game are relatively simple and the game is not one taught officially by school authorities. It is nevertheless fairly common—it is played all over the United States, where it is known under a variety of names. These include: "Kill the Guy (man) with the Ball," "Kill the Carrier," "Kill the Quarterback," "Kill the Ham," "Kill the Dill," "Spill the Pill," "Trip the Dip." However, by far the most popular name of the game is "Smear the Queer." The homosexual reference is loud and clear. Even some of the other alternative names reflect this, e.g., "Cream the Queen," "Bag the Fag," "Tag the Fag," and "Smear Butt."

The curious part of the game is that the longer one held on to the ball, the more manly one was. So it was only by assuming the role or slot of the "queer" that one could demonstrate one's masculinity. Anyone demonstrating masculinity was a threat to the other boys—presumably since that individual's masculinity was understood to be at the others' expense. Hence the objective of the game for all except the ball carrier was to chase, grab, wrestle the queer and relieve him of the ball. It is noteworthy that it was at once desirable to be the queer—the queer was the "lucky" person who caught the ball—and dangerous—one had to run for one's life if one were the queer.

The game is played by relatively young boys—elementary school up to junior high school. Boys as young as eight or nine play it. Occasionally, the game might begin during a lull or break in another game. For example, if during a conventional game of handball, an unpopular boy momentarily had possession of the ball, one of the other players might suddenly yell "Smear the queer" and all the others would join in an attempt to gangtackle the "victim." As the boys were aware of the homosexual meaning of the word *queer*, it would appear that the game reflects part of the socialization process from a peer group with respect to attitudes towards homosexuality.

What is the relevance of this game to my analysis of American football? In one of the few references to the game in print, it is referred to as "folk football." According to Knapp and Knapp (1976:43), "In Murder Ball, or Smear the Queer, a player kicks or lobs the ball high into the air and everyone pursues whoever catches it." Other informants agree that "Smear the Queer" seems to be a form of football and such alternative names as "Kill the Quarterback" confirm the connection.

This folk game surely suggests a verbally explicit connection between football and homosexuality. The critical clue is the name of the game: "Smear the Queer." It is absolutely impossible to deny the homosexual connotations of such a name. What we have here is a piece of folkloristic data which reveals a symbolic equation, namely, that jumping on a boy with a ball is labelled by the folk as smearing the queer, that is, attacking a homosexual. It seems to me that this does provide a type of validation of my earlier analysis of football as homosexual combat.

There is other relevant evidence from folklore. Let me cite one version of a popular joke. It was collected in a gay bar in San Francisco in 1979 although other versions were reported in non-homosexual contexts.

> There was this football player. And he wanted to get in one of those fancy frats [fraternities], you know, and he was the typical football player with the typical up-the-butt attitude, and of course the frat accepted him...on the condition that he pass their test. Their test was that he would have to spend an evening in a gay bar. "Well," he thought, "I suppose it won't be so bad, nobody would bother a football player like me anyway." Well, they told him he'd be watched to make sure he was havin' a good time, Ha, Ha, and soon the time came for the big evening. The football player went into the gay bar and sat down at the bar where there was no-one else sittin' 'cause he was nervous an' everything, and after a while he calmed down 'cause nobody was accosting him. But sure enough, in comes this queer like the

cement out of a dump truck and sits himself right next to the football player, who is obviously disturbed. But, as football players are, this one became rude after realizing the queer wasn't gonna do anything to him, so he began bumpin' the queer's arm every time he tried to sip his drink. Eventually, the queer got mad, and turned to the football player and said, "I bet you play football, huh?"

The player answered, "Yeah, what about it, faggot?"

"I bet I can play football better than you can."

This made the football player mad, 'cause this queer was challenging him on a weak point.

Then the queer said, "Come on, baby, dontcha got any balls?" He then called over the bartender, and the bartender brought him a huge pitcher of beer. The queer took the beer and downed it with one slug. Then he turned to the football player and said, "Queers six, football players, nothing." Then the queer got off his barstool, bent over, took down his pants, and let out a fart that musta killed all the old ladies within a block of the bar. And he said, "Queers seven, football players, nothing."

The football player was a bit surprised 'cause this wasn't exactly what he'd had in mind, but he knew he was being watched, so he had no choice but to defend his honor. So he called over the bartender, who brought the beer and he downed the beer just as the queer did. He turned to the queer and said, "Queers seven, football player, six." Then he got off his chair, pulled down his pants, bent over, and just as he was about to blow gas, the queer whipped out his cock, shoved it into the football player's asshole, and shouted, "BLOCK THAT KICK, BLOCK THAT KICK!!"

In other versions of this standard joke, the touchdown is scored by belching rather than by drinking beer, but the extra point is invariably a farting contest which allows for the same punchline in all the versions. Many important themes are contained in this text: the desire of the football player to join an all-male fraternity, the peer group's observation of the initiate in a blatant homosexual context, and the final submission to sodomy. It is reminiscent of initiation rites in aboriginal Australia, New

Guinea, and elsewhere, in which younger men are subjected to active homosexual anal intercourse by older members of the male group (Dundes 1976). In any event, there is a parallel to the game of "Smear the Queer" insofar as a football player attempting to prove his masculinity is subjected to attack. It thus offers additional "folk" support for my analysis of American football.

The allusion to blocking a kick also suggests a possible clarification of the curious custom of football fans beginning a postgame victory celebration by tearing down their own team's goalposts (or in basketball the basketball hoop and net). If we assume that the goalposts represent a kind of entrance to the endzone—and it is certainly true that so-called "extra points" following a touchdown as well as three-point field goals must be kicked between the uprights—then removing the goalposts may symbolize the end of possible penetrations by the enemy team. Without the goalposts in place, the enemy would be rendered impotent, unable to kick the ball into one's "endzone."

Having found further confirmation from folklore of the homosexual component of American football, we may briefly examine some other male sports. American football is but one manifestation of an underlying paradigm which affords males in many cultures an opportunity to indulge in homosexual combat. Soccer, perhaps the most popular male sport in Europe and Latin America has been successfully analyzed in this light (Suárez-Orozco 1982:15–24) with the help of quotations from traditional chants and song texts with explicit homosexual content. Again, the folklore associated with sport makes overt references to homosexuality. In a study of rugby, we find that one of the bawdy songs traditional in rugby circles has as its chorus (Sheard and Dunning 1973:15):

> For we're all queers together
> Excuse us while we go upstairs
> For we're all queers together,
> That's why we go round in pairs.

This verse, typically sung to the tune of the Eton Boating Song, is an apparent celebration of homosexuality. It has been suggested (Sheard and Dunning 1973:14) that the obscene songs which are traditionally enjoyed by rugby clubs serve "to mock homosexuals and homosexuality" but this ignores the possible pleasure in acting out homosexual behavior which would make the songs much more than simply a matter of ridiculing homosexuality. The same false argument could be made with "Smear the Queer" that it is only a means of poking fun at homosexuals, but that would not explain why one took pleasure in being "it" in such a game and in proving one's masculinity by withstanding the attacks from one's peers.

Once the underlying homosexual paradigm has been identified, it becomes considerably easier to understand much of the behavior associated with male sports. For example, in an extended discussion of the rowdy actions of British soccer fans, it is observed that the chants directed by them at the opposing team imply "that the enemy is unmanly, effeminate, or actually female. Goalkeepers have to suffer the accusation that they are homosexuals" (Marsh and Harre 1978:65). To the extent that it is the goalkeepers who, so to speak, are the ones scored upon, who are penetrated, it makes sense to consider them (passive) homosexuals.

In the light of the paradigm, one can profitably examine almost any male competitive sport. In basketball, for instance, the objective is to shoot the ball through the enemy's hoop (which normally has a net "skirt" attached). The hoop is attached to the "backboard." The sexual content of basketball is signaled by a piece of folklore, a joking question dating at least back to the 1940s: "Why couldn't the basketball player's wife have children? Because he always dribbles before he shoots." Dribble is, of course, a technical term in basketball referring to bouncing and controlling the ball with one hand while walking or running with the ball at the same time (Frommer 1979:49). The joke implies some sort of heterosexual inadequacy, perhaps premature ejaculation. The sexual equation of "shooting" and ejaculation is overt. But in basketball—as in other male competitive ball games—the opponent is male, not female.

One wonders about such folk speech terms as *back door* (referring to a situation in which a player on offense takes a position behind the defense under his own basket to receive a pass—*back door* is also homosexual slang for anus) or a *rim shot* referring to a ball which strikes the basket's circular metal frame—*rim* is a standard item of homosexual slang for anilingus (Rodgers, 1972:172) or *swish* (referring to a ball's passing through the hoop without touching the rim—*swish* is a standard term for a passive homosexual (Rodgers 1972:192). Perhaps the occurrence of terms like *back door*, *rim*, and *swish* in both basketball and homosexual slang is merely coincidence. But the paradigm suggests otherwise. One of the most devastating and spectacular shots in basketball is the so-called *slam dunk*—also termed a *stuff* in which the ball is literally forced or crammed through the hoop. One gets no extra points or credit for stuffing or slam dunking the ball. However, the opposing team and its fans no doubt feel it to be especially humiliating. It is precisely analogous to the symbolic function of the *spike* in American football which similarly serves to prolong or accentuate the moment of penetration by the team on offense. The defensive team and all that team's supporters must endure the disgrace of taking the offensive thrust without offering any resistance. A more conventional desirable shot is the *lay-up* or *lay-in* in which a player drives towards the hoop and if not impeded can simply *lay* the ball in the hoop. *Lay* is a standard term for intercourse (usually heterosexual). The question is why should a standard term for heterosexual intercourse be used in basketball, a game initially played by males only? The answer is that the game is a (homo)sexual battle with the male loser forced to occupy a "female" position.

One element in male sports which is as obvious as the sexual component is war imagery. Most male competitive sports make little or no effort to conceal the frequent allusions to violence and aggression. In American football, one refers to a line—the seven men who make it possible for the other four to move the ball forward. In warfare, one speaks of battle lines. When an offensive line and a defensive line in a football game are pretty evenly matched, a radio play-by-play commentator may refer to a *war* down in the *trenches*. A *blitz* refers to a sudden, furious mass attack on the enemy quarterback while a *bomb* is a long forward pass made by a quarterback (Frommer 1979:89). So it would not be unfair to characterize games such as American football as resembling warfare. Football terminology may even be consciously aping military usage as in the term *platoon* for a unit trained especially for offense or defense (Frommer 1979:100). In professional football, if the game ends in a tie, there is a *sudden death* extra period of play. The first team to score wins. If a football game can end with sudden death, it would seemingly be analogous to war!

But if games are like war, so is war like games. One even refers to "war games" when military maneuvers are engaged in during peace time. There is striking evidence confirming the metaphorical equivalence of games and warfare. Fussell speaks (1975:25) of the "classic equation between war and sport," remarking that "One way of showing the sporting spirit was to kick a football toward the enemy lines while attacking" (1975:25,27). He cites several documented instances of this practice during World War I engagements against the Germans in July 1916, and the Turks in November 1917.

If games and war are structural or functional equivalents, and if the homosexual battle paradigm applies to the latent content of competitive games, then it may well apply as well to war. This would explain why governments (dominated by males) are so reluctant to allow women in the armed forces. If women are inducted into the armed services, it is more or less understood that they will not be permitted to participate in actual combat. (They are rather expected to serve in auxiliary capacities behind the lines.) If warfare, like male competitive sports, is a thinly disguised homosexual struggle for supremacy, then it is easy to understand why there is so much resistance (by males) to the idea of women fighting on the front lines. An exclusively male homosexual ritual has no place for women. Moreover, in male chauvinist terms, it would constitute a risk of losing one's honor if one's women were on the front line inasmuch as the women could be exposed to direct assaults and possible penetration by the "weapons" of one's enemies. Women are just as unwelcome on battle lines as they are on men's teams playing professional football or basketball.

The inordinate fear of homosexuality in the armed services—for years it has constituted grounds for immediate dismissal from a service—with an undesirable discharge—may now be more comprehensible. I can still remember a "canned" lecture delivered to me and a host of other Naval Reserve Officer Training Corps midshipmen on the deck of the U.S.S. *Juneau* in the summer of 1954. A crusty old Lieutenant tried to warn us about the dangers of what he termed *dabbling*. One must be careful, he said, in the shower not to engage in any activity which might be construed as dabbling and so forth. Such an accusation could well put an end to a promising career. At the end of some thirty minutes on the subject, the speaker paused and said he would be glad to answer any questions we might have, although he was admittedly no expert. One wiseacre voice from our midst remarked, "Yeah, he just dabbles," evoking a ripple of tension-reducing laughter.

The Navy has always been worried about homosexuality—maybe even more than the other branches of the military, in view of the sometimes long period at sea which guaranteed total isolation from contact with members of the opposite sex. (Sexual segregation in prison almost invariably produces homosexual relationships.) A variant of a classic joke, reported by Legman (1975:144-145) distinguishes the Army and the Navy in this regard:

> Saint Peter gave wings to a soldier and a sailor entering Paradise, with the proviso that they would drop off if the wearer had a dirty thought. Proud of their wings, the two men started walking smartly down the golden streets naked. A naked female angel passed coyly by, glancing at them, and the soldier's wings fell off. He looked and saw the sailor's still secure, so he shamefacedly bent over to pick up his wings. As he stooped, the sailor's wings fell off.

The overt and covert homosexual impulses found among single-sex military groups has long been known. Fussell's illuminating chapter "Soldier Boys" describes in detail what he calls homo-eroticism among World War I English soldiers, with much supporting evidence from their biographical and literary reminiscences (1975:270-309). Yet despite Fussell's perceptive insight that the language of warfare—"assault, impact, thrust, penetration"—has sexual nuances, he seems to limit his consideration of homosexual tendencies to the English, failing to see that if (1) the language of warfare is sexual, and (2) the participants in warfare are essentially exclusively male, then warfare, like football, presumably represents in part a ritualized form of homosexual combat.

It is dangerous to speculate about the underlying psychology of so complex a phenomenon as war which clearly has economic and political causal factors. Yet it is tempting to see a kind of continuum from struggles for dominance among primates (in which weaker males may show subordinate status by presenting their rumps to higher ranking males) through competitive sports (in which the weaker team is feminized by being scored upon by the stronger team) ending with warfare. It should be noted incidentally that many zoologists and primatologists emphatically deny the blatant sexuality of male animals mounting other males (or female animals mounting other females). In a chapter entitled "Apparent Homosexual Behavior," ethologist Wolfgang Wickler, while admitting that it is sometimes difficult to decide whether a given act among animals can be construed as homosexual behavior, suggests that such activities are very probably a struggle to assert dominance. "From what we have already said it becomes clear that when male baboons mount each other, this need not be homosexual behavior but could also be a demonstration of rank. When a subordinate male assumes the role of the female in face of the victor, because this role is also a sign of submission, we are dealing once again with a demonstration of rank and not with homosexuality" (1973:46–48). The question is obviously begged as to why overt sexual positions are assumed to demonstrate rank. Rank can be achieved through other means, e.g., threatening gestures, growling sounds, etc. One could argue that zoologists' unwillingness to label male baboons mounting other male baboons who "assume the role of female" as homosexual behavior is a form of denial. The denial is part of the same cultural pattern which compels men to express their homosexual tendencies in such "safe" symbolic forms as football and warfare. If one empirically observes baboons, it is the sexual act which is explicit in contrast to the labelling of such behavior as signs of "rank" or "dominance" which appear to depend upon the subjective interpretative judgment of the human observer.

Leaving aside the question of whether primate same-sex mounting constitutes bona fide homosexuality, what can we say about the possible homosexual underpinnings of human warfare? If there is any sort of isomorphism between conceptions of the body and of one's home state or nation, one could argue that the invasion of one's homeland by an enemy constituted a kind of penetration of one's perimeter. Enduring the establishment of an enemy beachhead on one's shores or being attacked by paratroopers jumping down from airplanes above are symbolic violations of what may be perceived of as extensions of one's personal space. "If you attack my country, you attack me." The obvious penetration of individual bodies by arrows, spears, bayonet, and bullets shot or thrust by male adversaries only confirms the symbolic import. (Machismo requires that victories be won by proper penetration rather than by unfair [unsporting] techniques such as bacteriological or chemical warfare—cf. Fussell [1975:26–27] on the German use of chlorine gas in World War I as reflecting the Prussians' inadequate concept of "playing the game.")

In a few isolated instances victors in warfare did apparently submit prisoners to anal intercourse. So Lawrence of Arabia was evidently forced to endure sodomy by his Turkish captors at Deraa in 1917 (Knightley and Simpson 1969:214). But whether actual sodomy occurs or not is hardly the issue. It is a traditional image invoked to signify humiliating defeat. Once again, we find there is unequivocal folkloristic data which elucidates the latent content of warfare. A song popular among British soldiers in World War II (and possibly World War I as well) which begins: "I don't want to be a soldier, I don't want to go to war..." has the following second stanza (Page 1975:21):

> Don't want a bullet up me arsehole,
> Don't want me bollocks shot away,
> I'd rather live in England,
> In merry, merry England,
> And fornicate me fucking life away.

Folklore is a vehicle for making the unconscious conscious. The fear of warfare is unquestionably manifested in (homo)sexual terms. The singer doesn't want to be anally attacked—why does he fear a bullet in his "arsehole" rather than some other part of the anatomy? And he doesn't want to be emasculated by having his testicles shot off. Rather he wants to remain home in England as an active heterosexual fornicator. One stanza from one folksong is scarcely conclusive, but it is certainly suggestive— especially when we remember the lesson taught by "Smear the Queer." That lesson is that the folk may have more insight into the nature of human behavior than do the most learned scholars of the academy. From folklore, we may find data essential for the necessary validation of psychoanalytic anthropological hypotheses.

Bibliography

Index

Bibliography

Aarlow, J. 1961. "Ego Psychology and the Study of Mythology." *Journal of the American Psychoanalytic Association* 9:371–393.

Aarne, A., and S. Thompson. 1961. *The Types of the Folktale*. Helsinki: Academia Scientiarum Fennica.

Abraham, K. 1913 *Dreams and Myths: A Study in Race Psychology*. Nervous and Mental Disease Monograph Series, no. 15. New York: The Journal of Nervous and Mental Health Publishing Company.

Abraham, K. 1953. "Contributions to the Theory of the Anal Character." *Selected Papers on Psychoanalysis*. New York: Basic Books, pp. 370–392.

Adam, L. 1922. "Potlatch, Eine Ethnologische Rechtwissenschaftliche Betrachtung." *Festchrift Eduard Seler*. ed. Walter Lehmann, pp. 27–45. Stuttgart: Verlag von Strecker und Schroder.

Adams, J. W. 1973. *The Gitksan Potlatch*. Toronto: Holt, Rinehart and Winston.

Adolph, J. 1971. "The South American Macho: Mythos and Mystique." *Impact of Science on Society* (UNESCO) 21:83–92.

Allen, R. A. 1956. "The Potlatch and Social Equilibrium." *Davidson Journal of Anthropology* 2:43–54.

Andrews, D. 1977. "Flirtation Walk: Piropos in Latin America." *Journal of Popular Culture* 11:49–61.

Anonymous. 1957. *Piropos seleccionados: Requiebros de todos estilos*. Mexico, D.F.: Editores Mexicanos Unidos.

Anonymous. 1958. *Piropos criollos: Método práctico para conquistar mujeres en cinco minutos*. Mexico, D.F.: Editores Mexicanos Unidos.

197

Anonymous. 1975a. *Piropos seleccionados: Requiebros de todos estilos.* Mexico, D.F.: Offset Alfado Hnos, S.A.

Anonymous. 1975b. *Piropos y requiebros.* Mexico, D.F.: Editorial y Distribuidora Mexicana.

Aramoni, A. 1972. "Machismo." *Psychology Today* 5 (no. 8): 69–72.

Barbeau, C. M. 1911–12. "Du 'potlatch,' en Colombie Britannique." *Bulletin de la Societe de Geographie de Québec.* 5:275–279; 325–334; 6:177–188.

Barnett, H. G. 1938. "The Nature of the Potlatch." *American Anthropologist.* 40:349–358.

Barnouw, V. 1955. "A Psychoanalytic Interpretation of a Chippewa Origin Legend." *Journal of American Folklore* 68:73–85, 211–223, 341–355.

Barnouw, V. 1977. *Wisconsin Chippewa Myths & Tales.* Madison: University of Wisconsin Press.

Bataille, G. 1967. "Le don de rivalité: Le potlatch." *La Part maudite,* Paris: Les Editions de Minuit, pp. 107–124.

Beinhauer, W. 1934. "Über Piropos (Eine Studie über spanische Liebessprache)." *Volkstum und Kultur der Romanen* 7 (no. 2/3):111–163.

Beit, H. v. 1952, 1956, 1957. *Symbolik des Märchens. Versuch einer Deutung.* 3 Bde. Bern: Francke.

Benedict, R. 1946. *Patterns of Culture.* New York: Mentor.

Bergmann, M. S. 1966. "The Impact of Ego Psychology on the Study of Myth." *American Imago* 23:257–264.

Bettelheim, B. 1962. *Symbolic Wounds: Puberty Rites and the Envious Male.* New York: Collier.

Bettelheim, B. 1977. *The Uses of Enchantment: The Meaning and Importance of Fairy Tales.* New York: Vintage Books.

Birket-Smith, K. 1964. "An Analysis of the Potlatch Institution of North America." *Folk* 6, (no. 2):5–13.

Bishop, J. 1971. "A Preliminary Inquiry into the Piropo. Manuscript.

Boas, F. 1893. "Vocabulary of the Kwakiutl Language." *Proceedings of the American Philosophical Society,* 31:34–82.

Boas, F. 1897. "The Social Organization and the Secret Societies of the Kwakiutl Indians." *Report of the U.S. National Museum for 1895.* Washington, D.C.: Government Printing Office, pp. 311–738.

Boas, F. 1909. "The Kwakiutl of Vancouver Island." *Publications of the Jesup North Pacific Expedition* 5, part 2:301–522.

Boas, F. 1916. *Tsimshian Mythology.* Annual Report of the Bureau of American Ethnology 31. Washington, D.C.: Government Printing Office.

Boas, F. 1921. *Ethnology of the Kwakiutl.* Annual Report of the Bureau of American Ethnology 35. Washington, D.C.: Government Printing Office.

Boas, F. 1925. *Contributions to the Ethnology of the Kwakiutl.* Columbia University Contributions to Anthropology 3. New York: Columbia University Press.

Boas, F. 1930. *The Religion of the Kwakiutl Indians.* Part 2. New York: Columbia University Press.

Boas, F. 1932. "Current Beliefs of the Kwakiutl Indians." *Journal of American Folklore* 45:177-260.

Boas, F. 1934. *Geographical Names of the Kwakiutl Indians.* New York: Columbia University Press.

Boas, F. 1935a. *Kwakiutl Culture as Reflected in Mythology.* Memoirs of the American Folklore Society 28. New York: G. E. Stechert.

Boas, F. 1935b. *Kwakiutl Tales.* New Series, part 1. New York: Columbia University Press.

Boas, F. 1966. *Kwakiutl Ethnography.* Helen Codere, ed. Chicago: University of Chicago Press.

Boas, F. and G. Hunt. 1908. *Kwakiutl Texts.* Second Series. Memoirs of the American Museum of Natural History, part 1. New York: G. E. Stechert.

Bohannan, P. 1963. *Social Anthropology.* New York: Holt, Rinehart, and Winston.

Bolton, R. 1979. "Machismo in Motion: The Ethos of Peruvian Truckers." *Ethos* 7:312-342.

Boyer, L. B. 1979. *Childhood and Folklore: A Psychoanalytic Study of Apache Personality.* New York: Library of Psychological Anthropology.

Brandes, S. 1974. "Crianza infantil y comportamiento relativo a roles familiares." *Ethnica: Revista de Antropologia* 8:35-47.

Brandes, S. 1980. *Metaphors of Masculinity: Sex and Status in Andalusian Folklore.* Philadelphia: University of Pennsylvania Press.

Brill, A. A. 1914. "Fairy Tales as a Determinant of Dreams and Neurotic Symptoms." *New York Medical Journal* 99:561-567.

Brill, A.A. 1921. *Fundamental Conceptions of Psychoanalysis.* New York: Harcourt, Brace, and Company.

Carvalho-Neto, P. d. 1972. *Folklore and Psychoanalysis.* Coral Gables: University of Miami Press.

Chamberlain, V. 1968. "Symbolic Green: A Time-Honored Characterizing Device in Spanish Literature." *Hispania* 51:29-37.

Cheney, C. O. 1927. "The Psychology of Mythology." *Psychiatric Quarterly* 1:190-209.

Clutesi, G. 1969. *Potlatch.* Sidney, British Columbia: Gray's Publishing.

Codere, H. 1950. *"Fighting with Property:* A Study of Kwakiutl Potlatching and Warfare 1792-1930." Monographs of the American Ethnological Society 18. New York: J. J. Augustin.

Codere, H. 1956. "The Amiable Side of Kwakiut Life: The Potlatch and the Play Potlatch." *American Anthropologist* 58:334-351.

Codere, H. 1957. "Kwakiutl Society: Rank without Class." *American Anthropologist* 59:473-486.

Corominas, J. 1954. *Diccionario crítico etimológico de la lengua castellana.* Vol. 3. Madrid: Editorial Gredos.

Couture, A., and J. O. Edwards. 1964. "Origin of Copper Used by Canadian West Coast Indians in the Manufacture of Ornamental Plaques." *Contributions to Anthropology 1961-1962*, part 2. National Museum of Canada Bulletin no. 194, Anthropological Series no. 62. Ottawa: Department of the Secretary of State, pp. 199-220.

Curtis, E. S. 1915. *The North American Indian.* Vol. 10, Norwood, Mass.: Plimpton Press.

Darlington, H. S. 1929. "Tooth Evulsion and Circumcision." *Psychoanalytic Review* 16:272-290.

Davy, G. 1922. *La foi jurée.* Paris: F. Alcan.

Deans, J. 1896. "When Potlatches are Observed," *American Antiquarian* 18:329-331.

Desmonde, W. H. 1951. "Jack and the Beanstalk." *American Imago* 8:287-288.

Devereux, G. 1951. "Cultural and Characterological Traits of the Mohave Related to the Anal Stage of Psychosexual Development." *Psychoanalytic Quarterly* 20:398-422.

Dieckmann, H. 1977. *Märchen und Symbole: Tiefenpsychologische Deutung orientalischer Märchen.* Stuttgart: Verlag Adolf Bonz.

Drucker, P. 1951. *The Northern and Central Nootkan Tribes.* Bulletin of the Bureau of American Ethnology 144. Washington, D.C.: Government Printing Office.

Drucker, P., and R. F. Heizer. 1967 *To Make My Name Good.* Berkeley and Los Angeles: University of California Press.

Dundes, 1962. "Earth-Diver: Creation of the Mythopoeic Male." *American Anthropologist* 64:1032-1051.

Dundes, A. 1963. "Summoning Deity through Ritual Fasting." *American Imago* 20:213-220.

Dundes, A. 1967. "Comment on Beryl Sandford's 'Cinderella.' " *The Psychoanalytic Forum* 2:139-141.

Dundes, A. 1976a. "A Psychoanalytic Study of the Bullroarer." *Man* 11:220-238.

Dundes, A. 1976b. "Projection in Folklore: A Plea for Psychoanalytic Semiotics." *Modern Language Notes* 91:1500-1533.

Dundes, A. 1976c. " 'To Love My Father All': A Psychoanalytic Study of the Folktale Source of *King Lear*." *Southern Folklore Quarterly* 40:353-366.

Dundes, A. 1978. "Into the Endzone for a Touchdown: A Psychoanalytic Consideration of American Football." *Western Folklore* 37:75-88.

Dundes, A. 1981. "The Hero Pattern and the Life of Jesus." In *The Psychoanalytic Study of Society*, vol. 9, edited by W. Muensterberger, L. B. Boyer, and S. A. Grolnick. New York: Psychohistory Press.

Dundes, A. 1983. *Cinderella: A Casebook*. New York: Wildman Press.

Dundes, A. 1984. *Life is Like a Chicken Coop Ladder: A Portrait of German Culture through Folklore*. New York: Columbia University Press.

Edmunds, L., and R. Ingber. 1977. "Psychoanalytic Writings on the Oedipus Legend: A Bibliography." *American Imago* 34:374-386.

Edmunds, L., and A. Dundes. 1983. *Oedipus: A Folklore Casebook*. New York: Garland.

Eells, M. 1883. "The Potlatches of Puget Sound." *American Antiquarian and Oriental Journal* 5:135-147.

Ehrlich, A. S. 1961. "A Navaho Myth: The Hero Twins: A Psychoanalytic Evaluation." *Proceedings of the Minnesota Academy of Science* 29:24-32.

Erikson, E. H. 1943. "Observations on the Yurok: Childhood and World Image." *University of California Publications in American Archaeology and Ethnology* 35:257-301.

Fenichel, O. 1954. "The Drive to Amass Wealth." *The Collected Papers of Otto Fenichel*, pp. 89-108. Second Series. New York: W. W. Norton.

Ferenczi, S. 1956. "The Ontogenesis of the Interest in Money." *Sex in Psycho-Analysis*, pp. 269-279. New York: Dover.

Ford, C. S. 1941. *Smoke from Their Fires: The Life of a Kwakiutl Chief*. New Haven: Yale University Press.

Freud, S. 1901. *The Psychopathology of Everyday Life*. Vol. 6 of *The Complete Psychological Works of Sigmund Freud: Standard Edition*. London: Hogarth Press.

Freud, S. 1905. *Jokes and Their Relation to the Unconscious*. Vol. 8 of *The Standard Edition*.

Freud, S. 1908. "Creative Writers and Day-Dreaming." Vol. 9 of *The Standard Edition*.

Freud, S. 1910. Letter to Dr. Friedrich S. Krauss on *Anthropophyteia*. Vol. 11 of *The Standard Edition*.

Freud, S. 1913a. Preface to Bourke's *Scatalogic Rites of All Nations*. Vol. 12 of *The Standard Edition*.

Freud, S. 1913b. "The Occurrence in Dreams of Material from Fairy Tales." Vol. 12 of *The Standard Edition*.

Freud, S. 1913c. "The Theme of the 'Three Caskets.' " Vol. 12 of *The Standard Edition*.

Freud, S. 1913d. *Totem and Taboo*. Vol. 13 of *The Standard Edition*.

Freud, S. 1916. *Introductory Lectures on Psycho-Analysis*. Vols. 15 and 16 of *The Standard Edition*.

Freud, S. 1938. *The Basic Writings of Sigmund Freud*. New York: Modern Library.

Freud, S. 1953. *A General Introduction to Psychoanalysis*. Garden City: Permabooks.

Freud, S. 1959. "Character and Anal Erotism." *Collected Papers*. Vol. 2, pp. 45-50. New York: Basic Books.

Freud, S., and D. E. Oppenheim. 1958. *Dreams in Folklore*. New York: International Universities Press.

Fribourg, J. 1980. "Les piropos." *Cahiers de Littérature Orale* 7:15-51.

Fromm, E. 1951. *The Forgotten Language: An Introduction to the Understanding of Dreams, Fairy Tales and Myths*. New York: Grove Press.

Frommer, H. 1979. *Sports Lingo: A Dictionary of the Language of Sports*. New York: Atheneum.

Fussell, P. 1975. *The Great War and Modern Memory*. London: Oxford University Press.

Giehrl, H. E. 1970. *Volksmärchen und Tiefenpsychologie*. München: Ehrenwirth Verlag.

Gilmore, M., and D. Gilmore. 1979. "Machismo: A Psychodynamic Approach (Spain)." *Journal of Psychological Anthropology* 2:281-299.

Glenn, J. 1976. "Psychoanalytic Writings on Classical Mythology and Religion, 1909-1960." *Classical World* 70:225-247.

Goldman, I. 1975. *The Mouth of Heaven: An Introduction to Kwakiutl Religious Thought*. New York: John Wiley & Sons.

Gómez Tabanera, J. M. 1968. *El folklore español*. Madrid: Instituto Español de Antropologia Aplicada.

Gould, S. J. 1977. *Ontogeny and Phylogeny*. Cambridge: Belknap Press of Harvard University Press.

Hägglund, T-B, and V. Hägglund. 1981. "The Boy Who Killed His Father and Wed His Mother: The Oedipus Theme in Finnish Folklore." *International Review of Psycho-Analysis* 8:53–62.

Harris, M. 1968. *The Rise of Anthropological Theory*. New York: Thomas Y. Crowell.

Harris, M. 1975. *Potlatch. Cows, Pigs, Wars, and Witches: The Riddles of Culture*. New York: Vintage Books, pp. 111–130.

Herskovits, M. J., and F. S. Herskovits. 1958. *Dahomean Narrative: A Cross-Cultural Analysis*. Evanston: Northwestern University Press.

Heuscher, J. E. 1963. *A Psychiatric Study of Fairy Tales: Their Origin, Meaning and Usefulness*. Springfield, Ill.: Charles C. Thomas.

Heyman, S. R. 1977. "Freud and the Concept of the Inherited Racial Memories." *Psychoanalytic Review* 65:461–464.

Hippler, A. E., L. B. Boyer, and R. M. Boyer. 1975. "The Psycho-cultural Significance of the Alaska Athabascan Potlatch Ceremony." *The Psychoanalytic Study of Society* 6:204–234.

Irvin, T. T. 1977. "The Northwest Coast Potlatch Since Boas. 1897–1972." *Anthropology* 1:65–77.

Jacobs, M. 1952. "Psychological Inferences from a Chinook Myth." *Journal of American Folklore* 65:121–137.

Jacobs, M. 1959. *The Content and Style of an Oral Literature*. Chicago: University of Chicago Press.

Jones, E. 1930. "Psycho-Analysis and Folklore." *Jubilee Congress of the Folk-Lore Society: Papers and Transactions*. London: William Glaisher, pp. 220–237.

Jones, E. 1951. *Essays in Applied Psycho-Analysis*. Vol. 2 London: Hogarth.

Jones, E. 1961. "Anal-Erotic Character Traits." *Papers on Psycho-analysis*, pp. 413–437. Boston: Beacon Press.

Jones, E. 1971. *On the Nightmare*. New York: Liveright.

Jung, C. G. 1958. "The Phenomenology of the Spirit in Fairy Tales." In *Psyche and Symbol*, ed. Violet S. de Laszlo, pp. 61–112. Garden City: Doubleday Anchor.

Jung, C. G. 1963. "The Psychology of the Child Archetype." In *Essays on a Science of Mythology*, ed. C. G. Jung and C. Kereny, pp. 70–100. New York: Harper Torchbook.

Kanner, L. 1928. "The Tooth as a Folkloristic Symbol." *Psychoanalytic Review* 15:27–52.

Kaplan, B. 1962. "Psychological Themes in Zuni Mythology and Zuni TAT's." *The Psychoanalytic Study of Society*. Vol. 2. New York: International Universities Press.

Kardiner, A. 1939. *The Individual and His Society.* New York: Columbia University Press.

Kardiner, A. 1945. *The Psychological Frontiers of Society.* New York: Columbia University Press.

Kardiner, A. 1977. *My Analysis with Freud: Reminiscences.* New York: Norton.

Karlson, K. J. 1914. "Psychoanalysis and Mythology." *Journal of Religious Psychology* 7:137–213.

Keithahn, E. L. 1964. "Origin of the 'Chief's Copper' or 'Tinneh.' " *Anthropological Papers of the University of Alaska* 12:59–78.

Kiell, N., ed. 1982. *Psychoanalysis, Psychology, and Literature: A Bibliography.* 2d ed., 2 vols. Metuchen, N. J.: Scarecrow Press.

Kinzer, N. 1973. "Priests, Machos and Babies: Or, Latin American Women and the Manichaean Heresy." *Journal of Marriage and the Family* 35:300–312.

Kline, P. 1977. "Cross-cultural Studies and Freudian Theory." *Studies in Cross-Cultural Psychology.* Vol. I, Neil Warren, pp. 51–90. London: Academic Press.

Knapp, M., and H. Knapp. 1976. *One Potato, Two Potato... The Secret Education of American Children.* New York: Norton.

Knightley, P., and C. Simpson. 1969. *The Secret Lives of Lawrence of Arabia.* London: Thomas Nelson.

Krause, A. 1956. *The Tlingit Indians.* Seattle: University of Washington Press.

Krauss, F. S. 1910. "Nachwort des Herausgebers." *Anthropophyteia* 7:471–477.

Krauss, F. S. 1935. "Die Ödipussage in Sudslawischer Volksüberlieferung." *Imago* 22:358–367.

Kroeber, A. L. 1948. *Anthropology.* New York: Harcourt, Brace.

La Barre, W. 1948. "Folklore and Psychology." *Journal of American Folklore* 60:382–390.

La Barre, W. 1962. *They Shall Take Up Serpents: Psychology of the Southern Snake-Handling Cult.* Minneapolis: University of Minnesota Press.

Laguna, F. de. 1972. *Under Mount Saint Elias: The History and Culture of the Yakutat Tlingit.* Smithsonian Contributions to Anthropology 7. Washington, D.C.: Smithsonian Institution Press.

Lambert, J. N. 1974. "Potlatch et féodalité du bétail: Essai de synthèse d'ethnologie et d'histoire juridiques." *Nomos* 1:87–173.

Legman, G. 1952. "Rationale of the Dirty Joke." *Neurotica* 9:49–64.

Legman, G. 1968. *Rationale of the Dirty Joke: An Analysis of Sexual Humor.* New York: Grove Press.

Legman, G. 1975. *No Laughing Matter: Rationale of the Dirty Joke,* *Second Series*, New York: Breaking Point.

Lenoir, R. 1924. "Sur l'Institution du potlatch." *Revue Philosophique* 97:233–267.

Lévy-Bruhl, L. 1975. *The Notebooks on Primitive Mentality.* New York: Harper and Row.

Lewis, O. 1951. *Life in a Mexican Village: Tepoztlan Restudied.* Urbana: University of Illinois Press.

Locher, G. W. 1932. *The Serpent in Kwakiutl Religion.* Leiden: E. J. Brill.

Lorand, S. 1935. "Fairy Tales and Neurosis." *Psychoanalytic Quarterly* 4:234–243.

Loudon, J. B. 1975. "Stools, Mansions & Syndromes." *Royal Anthropological Institute News*, no. 10:1–5.

McClellan, C. 1954. "The Interrelations of Social Structure with Northern Tlingit Ceremonialism." *Southwestern Journal of Anthropology* 10:75–96.

McClellan, C. 1963. "Wealth Woman and Frogs among the Tagish Indians." *Anthropos* 58:121–128.

McClellan, C. 1970. *The Girl Who Married the Bear:* A Masterpiece of Indian Oral Tradition. National Museum of Man Publications in Ethnology, no. 2 Ottawa: National Museums of Canada.

Machado y Alvarez, A. 1883. *El folk-lore andaluz.* Madrid: Editorial Trescatorcediecisiete.

McIlwraith, T. F. 1948. *The Bella Coola Indians.* 2 Vols. Toronto: University of Toronto Press.

McKennan, R. A. 1959. *The Upper Tanana Indians.* Yale University Publications in Anthropology 55. New Haven: Yale University Press.

McLaren, C. S. 1978. "Moment of Death: Gift of Life, A Reinterpretation of the Northwest Coast Image 'Hawk.' " *Anthropologica* 20:65–90.

Maeder, A. E. 1908. "Die Symbolik in den Legenden, Märchen, Gebräuchen und Träumen." *Psychiatrisch-Neurologisch Wochenschrift* 6:45–49.

Maeder, A. E. 1909. "Die Symbolik in den Legenden, Märchen, Gebräuchen und Träumen. *Psychiatrisch-Neurologisch Wochenschrift* 10:55–57.

Mafud, J. 1965. *Psicología de la viveza criolla.* Buenos Aires: Editorial Américalee.

Makarius, L. 1970. "Ritual Clowns and Symbolical Behaviour." *Diogenes* 69:44–73.

Marañón, G. 1940. *Don Juan.* Buenos Aires: Espasa.

Marsh, P., and R. Harre. 1978. "The World of Football Hooligans." *Human Nature* 1 (no. 10): 62–69.

Mauss, Marcel. 1967. *The Gift*. New York: Norton.

Menninger, W. C. 1943. "Characterologic and Symptomatic Expressions Related to the Anal Phase of Psychosexual Development." *Psychoanalytic Quarterly* 12:161–193.

Miller, J-A. 1981. *Cinco conferencias caraqueñias sobre Lacan*. Caracas: Editoria Ateneo de Caracas.

Murdock, G. P. 1936. *Rank and Potlatch among the Haida*. Yale University Publications in Anthropology 13. New Haven: Yale University Press.

Nunberg, H., and E. Federn. 1967. *Minutes of the Vienna Psychoanalytic Society*. Vol. 2, *1908–1910*. New York: International Universities Press.

Nunberg, H., and E. Federn. 1974. *Minutes of the Vienna Psychoanalytic Society*. Vol. 3, *1910–1911*. New York: International Universities Press.

Olson, R. L. 1954. "Social Life of the Owikeno Kwakiutl." *Anthropological Records* 14:213-259.

Olson, R. L. 1967. "Social Structure and Social Life of the Tlingit in Alaska." *Anthropological Records* 26:1-123.

Orans, M. 1975. "Domesticating the Functional Dragon: An Analysis of Piddocke's Potlatch." *American Anthropologist* 77:312–328.

Oring, E. 1984. *The Jokes of Sigmund Freud: A Study in Humor and Jewish Identity*. Philadelphia: University of Pennsylvania Press.

Page, M., ed. 1975. *Kiss Me Goodnight, Sergeant Major: The Songs and Ballads of World War II*. Frogmore, St. Albans: Panther Books.

Parker, S. 1964. "The Kwakiutl Indians: 'Amiable' and 'Atrocious.'" *Anthropologica* 6:131–158.

Parsons, A. 1969. *Belief, Magic and Anomie*. New York: The Free Press.

Piddocke, S. 1965. "The Potlatch System of the Southern Kwakiutl: A New Perspective." *Southwestern Journal of Anthropology* 21:244-264.

Pitt-Rivers, J. A. 1954. *The People of the Sierra*. New York: Criterion Books.

Posinsky, S. H. 1956. "Yurok Shell Money and 'Pains': A Freudian Interpretation." *Psychiatric Quarterly* 30:598–632.

Posinsky, S. H. 1957. "The Problem of Yurok Anality." *American Imago* 14:3–31.

Postal, S. K. 1965. "Body-Image and Identity: A Comparison of Kwakiutl and Hopi." *American Anthropologist* 67:455–462.

Pratt, D. 1960. "The Don Juan Myth." *American Imago* 17:321–335.
Propp, V. 1968. *The Morphology of the Folktale.* Austin: University of Texas Press.
Ralske, N. N. 1966. "Derivatives of Coprophagia." *Psychoanalytic Quarterly* 35:169–171.
Ramírez, S., and R. Parres. 1957. "Some Dynamic Patterns in the Organization of the Mexican Family." *International Journal of Social Psychiatry* 3:18–21.
Ramos, A. 1958. *Estudos de Folk-lore.* 2d ed. Rio de Janeiro: Livraria-Editoria da Casa do Estudante do Brasil.
Randolph, V. 1976. *Pissing in the Snow and Other Ozark Folktales.* Urbana: University of Illinois Press.
Rank, O. 1922. *Psychoanalytische Beiträge zur Mythenforschung.* Leipzig: Internationaler Psychoanalytischer Verlag.
Rank, O. 1959. *The Myth of the Birth of the Hero.* New York: Vintage.
Rank, O. 1975. *The Don Juan Legend.* Princeton: Princeton University Press.
Rank, O., and H. Sachs. 1916. *The Significance of Psychoanalysis for the Mental Sciences.* Nervous and Mental Disease Monograph Series, no. 23. New York: The Nervous and Mental Disease Publishing Company.
Ray, V. F. 1945. "The Contrary Behavior Pattern in American Indian Ceremonialism." *Southwestern Journal of Anthropology* 1:75–113.
Richard, T. A. 1939. "The Use of Iron and Copper by the Indians of British Columbia." *British Columbia Historical Quarterly* 3:25–50.
Ricklin, F. 1915. *Wishfulfillment and Symbolism in Fairy Tales.* Nervous and Mental Disease Monograph Series, no. 21. New York: The Nervous and Mental Disease Publishing Company.
Ritvo, L. B. 1965. "Darwin as the Source of Freud's Neo-Lamarckianism." *Journal of the American Psychoanalytic Association* 13:499–517.
Rodgers, B. 1972. *The Queens' Vernacular: A Gay Lexicon.* San Francisco: Straight Arrow Books.
Róheim, G. 1922. "Psycho-analysis and the Folk-Tale." *International Journal of Psycho-Analysis* 3:180–186.
Róheim, G. 1930. "Mother Earth and the Children of the Sun." *Jubilee Congress of the Folk-Lore Society: Papers and Transactions* pp. 238–264. London: William Glaisher.
Róheim, G. 1940. "Magic and Theft in European Folk-Lore." *Journal of Criminal Psychopathology* 2:54–61.
Róheim, G. 1941. "Myth and Folk-Tale." *American Imago* 2:266–279.

Róheim, G. 1952a. *The Gates of the Dream*. New York: International Universities Press.

Róheim G. 1952b. "Review of Helen Codere, *Fighting with Property*." *Psychoanalytic Quarterly* 21:120–121.

Róheim, G. 1953a. "Fairy Tale and Dream." *The Psychoanalytic Study of the Child* 8:394–403.

Róheim, G. 1953b. "Dame Holle: Dream and Folk Tale." In *Explorations in Psychoanalysis*, ed. Robert Lindner, pp. 84–94. New York: Julian Press.

Róheim, G. 1955. *Magic and Schizophrenia*. New York: International Universities Press.

Rommey, K., and R. Rommey. 1966. *The Mixtecans of Juxtlahuaca, Mexico*. New York: John Wiley.

Roppolo, J. 1953. "Blue: Indecent, Obscene." *American Speech* 28:12–21.

Rosman, A., and P. G. Rubel. 1972. "The Potlatch: A Structural Analysis." *American Anthropologist* 74:658–671.

Sapir, E., and M. Swadesh. 1955. *Native Accounts of Nootka Ethnography*. Indiana University Research Center in Anthropology, Folklore, and Linguistics, Publication 1. Bloomington: Indiana University Research Center in Anthropology, Folklore, and Linguistics.

Saunders, G. 1981. "Men and Women in Southern Europe: A Review of Some Aspects of Cultural Complexity." *Journal of Psychoanalytic Anthropology* 4:435–466.

Sequin, C. A. 1972. "Ethno-Psychiatry and Folklore Psychiatry." *Interamerican Journal of Psychology* 6:75–80.

Sheard, K. G., and E. G. Dunning. 1973. "The Rugby Football Club as a Type of 'Male Preserve': Some Sociological Notes." *International Review of Sport Sociology* 3-4:5–24.

Silberer, H. 1910. "Phantasie und Mythos." *Jahrbuch für Psychoanalytische und Psychopathologische Forschungen* 2:541–652.

Silberer, H. 1912. "Märchensymbolik." *Imago* 1:176–187.

Silberer, H. 1914. "Das Zerstückelungsmotif in Mythos." *Imago* 3:502–503.

Slater, P. 1968. *The Glory of Hera: Greek Mythology and the Greek Family*. Boston: Beacon Press.

Snyder, S. 1964. "Skagit Socity and Its Existential Basis: An Ethnofolklorist Reconstruction." Ph.D. diss., Department of Anthropology, University of Washington.

Snyder, S. 1975. "Quest for the Sacred in Northern Puget Sound: An Interpretation of Potlatch." *Ethnology* 14:149–161.

Spradley, J. P. 1969. *Guests Never Leave Hungry: The Autobiography of James Sewid, a Kwakiutl Indian*. New Haven: Yale University Press.

Steiner, R. 1929. *The Interpretation of Fairy Tales*. New York: Anthroposophic Press.

Stern, B. J. 1934. *The Lummi Indians of Northwest Washington*. New York: Columbia University Press.

Stevens, E. 1965. "Mexican Machismo: Politics and Value Orientations." *Western Political Quarterly* 28:848–857.

Stevens, E. 1973a. "Marianismo: The Other Face of Machismo in Latin America." In *Female and Male in Latin America*, ed. Ann Pescatello. Pittsburgh: University of Pittsburgh Press.

Stevens, E. 1973b. "Machismo and Marianismo." *Society* 10:57–63.

Storfer, A. J. 1912. "Zwei Typen der Märchenerotic." *Sexualprobleme* 8:257–262.

Strathern, A. 1975. "Why is Shame on the Skin?" *Ethnology* 14:347–356.

Súarez-Orozco, M. 1982. "A Study of Argentine Soccer: The Dynamics of Its Fans and Their Folklore." *Journal of Psychoanalytic Anthropology* 5:7–28.

Sulloway, F. J. 1983. *Freud: Biologist of the Mind*. New York: Basic Books.

Suttles, W. 1960. "Affinal Ties, Subsistence, and Prestige Among the Coast Salish." *American Anthropologist* 62:296–305.

Swanton, J. R. 1908. "Social Condition, Beliefs, and Linguistic Relationship of the Tlingit Indians." Annual Report of the Bureau of American Ethnology 26. Washington, D.C.: Government Printing Office.

Swanton, J. R. 1909. *Tlingit Myths and Texts. Bulletin of the Bureau of American Ethnology* 39. Washington, D.C.: Government Printing Office.

Tanzi, E., 1890. 'Il Folk-lore nella patologia mentale." *Revista di Filosofia Scientifica* 9:385–419.

Tanzi, E. 1891. "The Germs of Delerium." *The Alienist and Neurologist* 12:51–85.

Thompson, S. (1955–1958). *Motif-Index of Folk-Literature*. 2d ed., 6 vols. Bloomington: Indiana University Press.

Torrey, E. F. 1973. *The Mind Game: Witchdoctors and Psychiatrists*. New York: Bantam.

Tybjerg, 1977. "Potlatch and Trade among the Tlingit Indians of the American Northwest Coast." *Temenos* 13:189–204.

Vanggaard, Thorkil. 1972. *Phallos: A Symbol and Its History in the*

Male World. New York: International Universities Press.

Vayda, A. P. 1961. "A Re-Examination of Northwest Coast Economic Systems." *Transactions of the New York Academy of Sciences,* Series 2, 23:618–624.

Von Franz, M–L. 1970. *An Introduction to the Psychology of Fairy Tales*. New York: Spring Publications.

Von Franz, M–L. 1972a. *Patterns of Creativity Mirrored in Creation Myths*. Zurich: Spring Publications.

Von Franz, M–L. 1972b. *Problems of the Feminine in Fairytales*. Zurich: Spring Publications.

Von Franz, M–L. 1974. *Shadow and Evil in Fairy Tales*. Zurich: Spring Publications:

Von Franz, M–L. 1977. *Individuation in Fairytales*. Zurich: Spring Publications.

Von Franz, M–L. 1980. *The Psychological Meaning of Redemption Motifs in Fairytales*. Toronto: Inner City Books.

Wallace, E. R. 1983. *Freud and Anthropology: A History and Reappraisal*. New York: International Universities Press.

Wells, H. T., S. H. Whiteley, and C.E. Karegeannes. 1976. *Origins of NASA Names*. NASA SP-4402. Washington, D.C.: National Aeronautics and Space Administration.

Wickler, W. 1973. *The Sexual Code: The Social Behavior of Animals and Men*. Garden City: Anchor Books.

Wolfenstein, M. 1978. *Children's Humor: A Psychological Analysis*. Bloomington: Indiana University Press.

Index

211